Quotations

Project Team

Managing Editor   Elizabeth Knowles

Senior Editor   Susan Ratcliffe

Reading Programme   Jean Harker
                         Verity Mason
                         Penelope Newsome
                         Helen Rappaport

Library Research   Ralph Bates
                         Marie G. Diaz

Proof-reading   Fabia Claris
                         Penny Trumble

Oxford
Irish Quotations

Edited by
Bernard O'Donoghue

OXFORD
UNIVERSITY PRESS

OXFORD
UNIVERSITY PRESS

Great Clarendon Street, Oxford OX2 6DP

Oxford University Press is a department of the University of Oxford.
It furthers the University's objective of excellence in research, scholarship,
and education by publishing worldwide in

Oxford New York

Athens Auckland Bangkok Bogotá Buenos Aires Calcutta
Cape Town Chennai Dar es Salaam Delhi Florence Hong Kong Istanbul
Karachi Kuala Lumpur Madrid Melbourne Mexico City Mumbai
Nairobi Paris São Paulo Singapore Taipei Tokyo Toronto Warsaw

with associated companies in Berlin Ibadan

Oxford is a registered trade mark of Oxford University Press
in the UK and in certain other countries

Published in the United States
by Oxford University Press Inc., New York

British Library Cataloguing in Publication Data

Data available

Library of Congress Cataloging in Publication Data

Data available
ISBN 0-19-860239-1

10 9 8 7 6 5 4 3 2 1

Typeset in Photina and Meta
by Interactive Sciences Ltd
Printed in Great Britain by
Mackays of Chatham plc
Chatham, Kent

Introduction

A dictionary of Irish quotations—even a relatively modest one like this—has to cover a soberingly (if that's the right adverb) wide range of topics and times. It seems to involve several peoples: in her inaugural presidential speech in 1990, Mary Robinson said 'there are 70 million people living on this globe who claim Irish descent'. As the world gets smaller, Irishness gets bigger: there are more 'varieties of Irishness', in Roy Foster's phrase. Frank McCourt's modern masterpiece *Angela's Ashes* (what is 'North of Ireland bitter Presbyterian hair'?) is culturally very dense.

It seems, in the words of Joyce's Haines in *Ulysses*, that history is to blame. Irishness has 1500 years of variety behind it, in at least two languages and three countries. Take two categories under 'A': *animals* have to trawl from the medieval monk's cat in Irish ('Pangur Bán'), to Joyce's Citizen's mangy dog Garryowen, to the Celtic tiger of the modern economic miracle. Attitudes to *alcohol* have shifted: the great nineteenth-century temperance reformer Father Theobald Mathew is far removed from St Brigid of Kildare who expressed her love of God in the sixth century by wishing for 'a great lake of ale for the King of Kings'.

In more conceptual fields, there is a dizzying change of political perception over the ages. Mary Robinson's presidential successor Mary McAleese says 'the day of the dinosaurs is over. The future belongs to the bridge-builders, not the wreckers.' *Are* ancient quarrels healing? Are things getting better? There is plenty of quoted evidence here, both for and against, both nostalgic and modernising. Maeve Binchy says firmly 'On balance Right Now is a lot better than the Good Old Days.' Emigration, it has been pointed out, has gone into reverse. The Irish economy, to use the standard cheerful term for it, is flying.

Beyond this variety, there is another introductory dilemma: at what stage does a usage become a quotation? How often does something need to have been said to be a quotation rather than a remark? Happily for the present purpose, in Ireland things are said a lot; Oscar Wilde said we are the greatest talkers since the Greeks. In 1997 the Kerry publican-politician Jackie Healy-Rae, challenged at the hustings to say what he meant by 'the real people of Ireland', replied: 'I mean the people who have their dinner in the middle of the day.' A veritable quotation! It is brief, simple and unexpected. It is ridiculous but also true.

Despite the difficulty—and maybe undesirability—of such pronouncements on the essence of Irishness, there has been a long history of taking Irishness and the epigrammatic together which attracts the anthologist. Not that the epigram, like the Irish bull, is peculiar to Ireland; but it is remarkably resilient there, in both English and Irish. Recent attempts to reclaim Oscar Wilde as an Irishman ('as good an Irishman as ever wore a hat' would be the terms in Flann O'Brien's 'Catechism of Cliché') find him squarely in this tradition. Wilde's 'Duty is what one expects from others; it is not what one does oneself' means the same as the traditional Irish saying *Do bhata féin is each do chomharsan* ('your own stick and your neighbour's horse': that is, rights without responsibility).

Dangerous terrain, of course: one person's aphorism is the next person's cliché. And there is the trap of stereotypical 'stage Irish': of Victorian imaginative Celticism and Hugh Kenner's astringent 'Irish fact' (which tells you not what is the case but what you want to hear). A dictionary of Irish quotations needs to be more than a compendium of 'Irishisms'. It must also include great truths such as Edmund Burke's 'the age of chivalry is gone' and John Philpot Curran's 'the condition upon which God hath given liberty to man is eternal vigilance.' And the great literary moments must be there too: Austin Clarke's

And O! she was the Sunday
in every week,

Yeat's 'terrible beauty' and Heaney's 'neighbourly murder'; 'the cracked lookingglass of a servant' from Joyce's snobbish Stephen Dedalus; Maria Edgeworth's 'Our Irish blunders

are never blunders of the heart'; Flann O'Brien's teeth and
bicycles. Neither must a comprehensive Dictionary draw only
on quotations from Irish speakers and writers; it must concern
itself with what the medieval romance-anthologist would have
called 'the matter of Ireland'. 'Irish for the Irish', perhaps; but
you don't have to be Irish to have experience of and views on
Ireland. Lord Randolph Churchill's 'Ulster will fight and Ulster
will be right' is indispensable, on rhetorical grounds but also
for the context it provides for the more
recent 'Ulster says no'.

So what does it all amount to? What *is* the matter of
Ireland—or the matter with Ireland? Conor Cruise O'Brien
says 'it is the condition of being involved in the Irish situation,
and usually of being mauled by it.' At the opposite, lyrical
extreme, Heinrich Böll in his luminous *Irish Journal*, with its
'Thoughts on Irish Rain' and 'Mayo—God help us!', finds the
essence in the serene acceptance of paradox: the ability to live
with contradiction in 'an overwhelmingly Catholic country,
then, in which strikes flourish as obedience does elsewhere.'

Maybe the epigrammatic essence is not in language,
after all, but in a way of thinking: a take on the world. One
of the things that is nostalgic in Böll's 1950's perspective is
his unapologetic fondness for the way things then were in the
Irish Republic: 'the dogs of Dukinella', chasing the running-
boards of motor-cars; the 'lovely children, the Irish tinkers,
the fuchsia hedges'. It is the Golden Age that Binchy's Here
and Now is better than.

But—to quote one of the most repeated Irish comfort-
phrases in use among Flann O'Brien's Plain People of
Ireland—what harm! The beauty of the anthologist's position
is that they do not have to vote: for Ireland or England or
Anglo-Ireland; for North or South; for common sense or
whimsy; for humour or elegy; whether to laugh or cry. Such
indefiniteness has the approval of the most respected of Irish
aphorists and political theorists: Burke said 'it is the nature of
all greatness not to be exact.' This Dictionary is an attempt to
embrace in brief a wide range of what has repeatedly been

thought and said by and about Ireland and the Irish. And the reader can choose and add to their heart's content. To give the last word to the voice of Flann O'Brien's public house: 'whatever you are having yourself!'

I am grateful to the very many people with whom I have discussed Irish wit and wisdom over the years. More particular thanks are due to James Bracegirdle, Eileen Carney, Tadhg Foley, Roy Foster, Seamus Heaney, John Kelly, Jim McMahon, Andrew McNeillie, Seamus Ó Cróinin, Heather O'Donoghue, Margaret MacCarron, Tom Paulin, Susan Ratcliffe, John Redmond, and Norman Vance. I owe a huge debt to the extraordinary resources and deployment of the Oxford University Press Bank of Quotations. But my primary indebtedness is to two people: to Elizabeth Knowles of Oxford University Press who provided a great deal more of the expertise and knowledge for this enterprise than she is willing to claim, and to Michael Henry who let me draw repeatedly on his unrivalled knowledge of Irish verbal culture, both literary and oral.

Bernard O'Donoghue

List of themes

A

Advice
Age
Alcohol
America *see*
   Ireland and America
Anger
The Anglo-Irish
Animals
Appearance
Architecture
Armagh
The Armed Forces
Art

B

Beauty
Belfast
Biography
Birds
The Body
Books
Britain
Business

C

Celebrations
Censorship
Change
Chaos *see Order and Chaos*
Children
Christmas
Clare
Class
The Clergy
Clonmacnoise
Coleraine
Conversation

Cork
Courage
Criticism
Curses

D

Danger
Death
Debt
Democracy
Determination
De Valera
Diaries
Dictionaries
Donegal
Dress
Drink *see Food and Drink*
Dublin

E

Easter 1916
Education
Elegy
Emigration
Endurance
Enemies
England and the English
England *see also*
   Ireland and England
Envy
Epitaphs
Evil *see Good and Evil*
Excess and Moderation
Execution
Exile
Experience

Advice

1 Advice has been pouring in:
   'One look and I told you—
   he's a no-goodnik, but you said you
   liked his shoes, so there's no point
   talking to you is there?'
   Julie O'Callaghan 1954– : 'Yuppie Considering Life in her Loft Apartment'

2 I have given my advice to my countrymen, and whenever I
   feel it necessary I shall continue to do so, careless whether
   it pleases or displeases this house or any mad person out of
   it.
   Daniel O'Connell 1775–1847: in *Dictionary of National Biography* (1917–)

3 Get the advice of everybody whose advice is worth
   having—they are very few—and then do what you think
   best yourself.
   Charles Stewart Parnell 1846–91: Conor Cruise O'Brien *Parnell* (1957)

4 I'm not a teacher: only a fellow-traveller of whom you
   asked the way. I pointed ahead—ahead of myself as well as
   you.
   George Bernard Shaw 1856–1950: *Getting Married* (1911)

5 I always pass on good advice. It is the only thing to do with
   it. It is never of any use to oneself.
   Oscar Wilde 1854–1900: *An Ideal Husband* (1895)

Age see also Youth

1 Perhaps my best years are gone . . . but I wouldn't want
   them back. Not with the fire that's in me now.
   Samuel Beckett 1906–89: *Krapp's Last Tape* (1959)

2 Fiftieth birthdays should be times of huge goodwill . . . Only people who put on fake tan and pretend to be younger than they are don't get to join the party.
Maeve Binchy 1940– : in *Irish Times* 25 April 1998

3 It is better to die young than to outlive all one loved, and all that rendered one lovable.
Lady Blessington 1789–1849: *The Confessions of an Elderly Lady* (1838)

4 As a white candle
In a holy place,
So is the beauty
Of an aged face.
Joseph Campbell 1879–1944: 'The Old Woman' (1913)

5 How happy he who crowns in shades like these,
A youth of labour with an age of ease.
Oliver Goldsmith 1728–74: *The Deserted Village* (1770)

6 Me waiting until I was nearly fifty
To credit marvels.
Seamus Heaney 1939– : 'Fosterling' (1991)

7 PRISONER: Ah! my Lord, I'm a very old man, and I'll never do that sentence.
JUDGE HOLMES: Well, try to do as much of it as you can.
Hugh Holmes 1840–1916: Maurice Healy *The Old Munster Circuit* (1939)

8 My biological clock is ticking so loud I'm nearly deafened by it. They search me going into planes.
Marian Keyes: 'Late Opening at the Last Chance Saloon' (1997)

9 In those days people confused old age with valour; they called her a great old warrior. This had the effect of inspiring her to gasp even more distressingly by way of proving them right and herself indomitable.
Hugh Leonard 1926– : *Home Before Night* (1979)

10 I woke up this morning and I was still alive, so I am pretty cheerful.
on being 79
Spike Milligan 1918– : in *Irish Times* 8 November 1997

11 I'm having difficulty getting the doctors around here to sign the appropriate form.
on seeking permission to celebrate his 80th birthday with a 12,000 ft skydive
Spike Milligan 1918– : in *Irish Times* 18 April 1998 'This Week They Said'

12 Like dolmens round my childhood, the old people.
John Montague 1929– : 'Like Dolmens Round my Childhood' (1972)

13 The older I get, the happier I get.
Kate Cruise O'Brien 1948–98: in *Times* 2 April 1998, obituary

14 Are you a woman
between the ages of 49 and 51?
I bet you feel like
elbowing the person
beside you at the cucumber display.
Julie O'Callaghan 1954– : 'Change'

15 Some of the greatest battles ever fought were fought by leaders much older than me.
launching his campaign against the peace agreement
Ian Paisley 1926– : in *Times* 16 April 1998

16 *Seanbhean is ea mise anois, a bhfuil cos léi san uaigh is an cos eile ar a bruach.*
I am an old woman now, with one leg in the grave and the other leg on its edge.
Peig Sayers 1873–1958: *Peig* (1936)

17 Every man over forty is a scoundrel.
George Bernard Shaw 1856–1950: *Man and Superman* (1903) 'Maxims: Stray Sayings'

18 Every man desires to live long; but no man would be old.
Jonathan Swift 1667–1745: *Thoughts on Various Subjects* (1727 ed.)

19 Old men and comets have been reverenced for the same
reason; their long beards, and pretences to foretell events.
Jonathan Swift 1667–1745: *Thoughts on Various Subjects* (1727 ed.)

20 Thirty-five is a very attractive age. London society is full of
women of the very highest birth who have, of their own
free choice, remained thirty-five for years.
Oscar Wilde 1854–1900: *The Importance of Being Earnest* (1895)

21 An aged man is but a paltry thing,
A tattered coat upon a stick, unless
Soul clap its hands and sing, and louder sing
For every tatter in its mortal dress.
W. B. Yeats 1865–1939: 'Sailing to Byzantium' (1928)

22 When you are old and grey and full of sleep,
And nodding by the fire, take down this book
And slowly read and dream of the soft look
Your eyes had once, and of their shadows deep.
W. B. Yeats 1865–1939: 'When You Are Old' (1893)

23 What shall I do with this absurdity—
O heart, O troubled heart—this caricature,
Decrepit age that has been tied to me
As to a dog's tail?
W. B. Yeats 1865–1939: 'The Tower' (1928)

Alcohol see also Food and Drink

1 If we keep on having price increases like this, we'll end up
drinking water.
Bertie Ahern 1951– : comment, 1993

2 Guinness is good for you.
*reply universally given to researchers asking people why they
drank Guinness*
Anonymous: advertising slogan from *c.*1929

3 Like the Murphy's, I'm not bitter.
Anonymous: advertising slogan, 1990s

4 So fill to me the parting glass.
Good night, and joy be with you all!
Anonymous: 'The Parting Glass' (19th century song)

5 I only take a drink on two occasions—when I'm thirsty
and when I'm not.
Brendan Behan 1923–64: attributed

6 I should like a great lake of ale
For the King of Kings.
Brigid of Kildare d. *c.*525: attributed

7 When I die I want to decompose in a barrel of porter and
have it served in all the pubs in Dublin. I wonder would
they all know it was me?
J. P. Donleavy 1926– : *The Ginger Man* (1955)

8 There is wan thing, an' on'y wan thing, to be said in
favour iv dhrink, an' that is that it has caused manny a
lady to be loved that otherwise might've died single.
Finley Peter Dunne 1867–1936: *Mr. Dooley Says* (1910)

9 He is said also to be the inventor of raspberry whiskey,
which is very likely, as nobody has ever appeared to dispute
it with him.
Maria Edgeworth 1767–1849: *Castle Rackrent* (1800)

10 I have fed purely upon ale; I have eat my ale, drank my
ale, and I always sleep upon ale.
George Farquhar 1678–1707: *The Beaux' Stratagem* (1707)

11 Let schoolmasters puzzle their brain,
With grammar, and nonsense, and learning,
Good liquor, I stoutly maintain,
Gives genius a better discerning.
Oliver Goldsmith 1728–74: *She Stoops to Conquer* (1773)

12 I was blue mouldy for the want of that pint. Declare to God
I could hear it hit the pit of my stomach with a click.
James Joyce 1882–1941: *Ulysses* (1922)

13 One knows where one is with a drunk, but teetotalism in an Irishman is unnatural; if it is not checked, he becomes unpredictable and repays watching.
Hugh Leonard 1926– : *Rover and Other Cats* (1992)

14 Drink! Drink!
cry of Father Jack
Graham Linehan and **Arthur Mathews**: 'New Jack City' (1996), episode from *Father Ted* (Channel 4 TV, 1994–8)

15 In New York, with Prohibition in full swing, he thought he had died and gone to hell for his sins. Then he discovered speakeasies and he rejoiced.
Frank McCourt 1930– : *Angela's Ashes* (1996)

16 A pint of Guinness, or a large whiskey, or maybe two.
when asked how he proposed to celebrate the agreement on Northern Ireland
Seamus Mallon 1936– : in *Times* 11 April 1998

17 Here goes—in the name of the Lord.
signing the pledge of total abstinence, 10 April 1838
Theobald Mathew 1790–1856: in *Dictionary of National Biography* (1917–)

18 A pint of plain is your only man.
Flann O'Brien 1911–66: *At Swim-Two-Birds* (1939)

19 'I wouldn't mind *that* at all [indicates glass]. I *know* what I have there. There's eatin' and' drinkin' in that. Damn the harm *that* done annywan, bar been taken to excess.'
the pub bore
Flann O'Brien 1911–66: *The Best of Myles* (1968)

20 What did 'moppy' mean? Well, here are a few synonyms: Moppy; drunk; jarred; fluthered; canned; rotten; plasthered; elephants; fluthery-eyed; spiflicated; screwed;

Alcohol

tight; mouldy; maggoty; full to the brim; footless; blind; spaychless; blotto; scattered; merry; well on; shook; inebriated; tanked up; oiled; well-oiled; cock-eyed; cross-eyed; crooked; boozed; muzzy; sozzled; bat-eyed; pie-eyed; having quantum sufficio; and under the influence of intoxicating liquor.
Flann O'Brien 1911–66: *The Best of Myles* (1968)

21 I blame the Anglo-Irish agreement for Sunday drinking.
Ian Paisley 1926– : comment, 1987

22 I would be quite happy to see the Devil's buttermilk banned from society.
of draught Guinness
Ian Paisley 1926– : in *Irish Times* 14 March 1998 'This Week They Said'

23 I'm only a beer teetotaller, not a champagne teetotaller.
George Bernard Shaw 1856–1950: *Candida* (1898)

24 I seem to have spent the first half of my life seeking after-hours drink, and the second half trying to avoid it.
Dick Spring 1950– : in 1992, attributed

25 I am, dear Prue, a little in drink, but at all times your faithful husband.
Richard Steele 1672–1729: letter to his wife, 20 September 1708

26 I drink little, miss my glass often, put water in my wine, and go away before the rest, which I take to be a good receipt for sobriety.
Jonathan Swift 1667–1745: *Journal to Stella* 21 April 1711

27 I have made an important discovery . . . that alcohol, taken in sufficient quantities, produces all the effects of intoxication.
Oscar Wilde 1854–1900: *In Conversation*

America see Ireland and America

Anger

1 No one, Dora thought, could get through the violent
tedium of young, daily married life, without becoming
angry, so that the very way a husband ate a meal could
become a matter for thought-murder.
Polly Devlin 1944– : *Dora* (1990)

2 I have no mettle for the angry role.
Seamus Heaney 1939– : 'Station Island'

3 It's my rule never to lose me temper till it would be
dethrimental to keep it.
Sean O'Casey 1880–1964: *The Plough and the Stars* (1926)

4 Angry young man.
Leslie Paul 1905–85: title of book (1951); the phrase subsequently
associated with John Osborne's play *Look Back in Anger* (1956)

The Anglo-Irish

1 PAT: He was an Anglo-Irishman.
MEG: In the blessed name of God what's that?
PAT: A Protestant with a horse.
Brendan Behan 1923–64: *The Hostage* (1958)

2 The Anglo-Irish might consider themselves Irish . . . but of
course they were nothing of the sort. They were as English
as the people who lived across the sea. Their only problem
was that they didn't realise it.
Maeve Binchy 1940– : *Circle of Friends* (1990)

3 My family got their position and drew their power from a
situation that shows an inherent wrong. In the grip of that
situation, England and Ireland each turned to the other a

closed, harsh, distorted face—a face that, in each case,
their lovers would hardly know.
Elizabeth Bowen 1899–1973: *Bowen's Court* (afterword, ed. 2, 1964)

4 For the house of the planter
Is known by the trees.
Austin Clarke 1896–1974: 'The Planter's Daughter' (1929)

5 The Anglo-Irish were a superior people. Better born, but
less snobbish; cleverer than the English and fonder of
horses; they were poorer no doubt but with a poverty that
brought into relief their natural aristocracy.
Cyril Connolly 1903–74: *Enemies of Promise* (1938)

6 [Like] some tall tree of noxious growth, lifting its head to
Heaven and poisoning the atmosphere of the land so far as
its shadow can extend . . . now at last the day has come
when, as we hope, the axe has been laid to the root.
of Ascendancy domination
W. E. Gladstone 1809–98: speech, 1867

7 All the Protestants were poor and had big houses. We
entertained a lot but we had poor food, bad wine and no
heat. It was an absolute duty to be amusing.
Molly Keane 1904–96: in *Independent* 1 June 1996

8 The Anglo-Irish were the best Irish but I can see very little
future for them as the present belongs to that crazy
Gaeldom which is growing dominant about us.
George William Russell (Æ) 1867–1935: letter to W. B. Yeats, 23 May
1932

9 The owners of the land are not much pitied at the present
day, or much deserving of pity; and yet one cannot quite
forget that they are the descendants of what was, at one
time, in the eighteenth century, a high-spirited and highly
cultivated aristocracy. The broken greenhouses and mouse-
eaten libraries, that were designed and collected by men
who voted with Grattan, are perhaps as mournful in the

end as the four mud walls that are so often left in Wicklow
as the only remnants of a farmhouse.

John Millington Synge 1871–1909: *In Wicklow and West Kerry* (1912)

10 We . . . are no petty people. We are one of the great stocks
of Europe. We are the people of Burke; we are the people of
Swift, the people of Emmet, the people of Parnell. We have
created most of the modern literature of this country. We
have created the best of its political intelligence.

W. B. Yeats 1865–1939: speech in the Irish Senate, 11 June 1925, in the
debate on divorce

Animals

1 Surely this son of a mare is not dearer to you than that son
of God?
*to Oswin of Deira, who had protested against Aidan's giving to
a beggar a horse that had been Oswin's gift to him*
St Aidan d. 651: Bede *Ecclesiastical History of the English People*

2 As multitudinous as the sands of the sea or as sparks of fire
or as dew-drops on a May-day morning or as the stars of
heaven were the lice and fleas biting his feet.
Anonymous: *Aislinge meic Conglinne* ('Vision of Mac Conglinne',
12th-century satire translated by Kuno Meyer)

3 But who is going to feed them?
on the proposal to put gondolas on the Blessington lakes
Anonymous: an unidentified Wicklow County Councillor

4 I and Pangur Bán, my cat,
'Tis a like task we are at;
Hunting mice is his delight,
Hunting words I sit all night.

    . . . So in peace our tasks we ply,
Pangur Bán, my cat, and I;

In our arts we find our bliss,
I have mine and he has his.
Anonymous: 'Pangur Bán', Latin poem found in the margins of an
8th-century *Epistles of St Paul* belonging to an Austrian monastery founded
by Irish monks; translated 1931 by Robin Flower

5 Like Lanna Macree's dog—a piece of the road with
everybody.
William Boyle 1853–1922: *The Eloquent Dempsey* (1906); cf. **Political
Parties 1**

6 Bede says that there are only two kinds of harmful beasts in
Ireland, namely, wolves and foxes. I would add the mouse
as a third, and say that it was very harmful indeed.
Giraldus Cambrensis *c.*1146–1223: *The History and Topography of Ireland*

7 Of all kinds of reptiles only those that are not harmful are
found in Ireland. It has no poisonous reptiles. It has no
serpents or snakes, toads or frogs, tortoises or scorpions. It
has no dragons. It has, however, spiders, leeches and
lizards—but they are entirely harmless.
Giraldus Cambrensis *c.*1146–1223: *The History and Topography of Ireland*

8 The really marvellous exhibition of cynanthropy given by
the famous old Irish red wolfdog setter formerly known by
the *sobriquet* of Garryowen and recently rechristened by his
large circle of friends and acquaintances as Owen Garry.
James Joyce 1882–1941: *Ulysses* (1922)

9 I think everyone has their favourite animal that they hate.
of a ferret
Molly Keane 1904–96: *Two Days in Aragon* (1941)

10 What the horse is to the Arab, or the dog is to the
Greenlander, the pig is to the Irishman.
J. G. Kohl 1808–78: *Ireland, Scotland and England* (1844)

11 Its tail was a plume of such magnificence that it almost
wore the cat.
Hugh Leonard 1926– : *Rover and Other Cats* (1992)

12 Where are you going
With your fetlocks blowing in the . . . wind

I want to shower you with sugar lumps
And ride you over . . . fences
I want to polish your hooves every single day
And bring you to the horse . . . dentist.
'*My Lovely Horse*' *as sung by Fathers Ted and Dougal*
Graham Linehan and **Arthur Mathews**: 'A Song for Europe' (1996), episode
from *Father Ted* (Channel 4 TV, 1994–)

13 People ask me what does the Celtic Tiger look like; it looks
like this place.
visiting Clonaslee in Co. Laois
Mary McAleese 1951– : in *Irish Times* 13 April 1998

14 'Tis like the howling of Irish wolves against the moon.
William Shakespeare 1564–1616: *As You Like It* (1599)

15 Maria did pretty well as a lion: she hunted all dogs
unmistakably smaller than herself, and whenever it was
reasonably possible to do so she devoured the spoils of the
chase . . . It was as a lamb that she failed; objectionable as I
have no doubt a lamb would be as a domestic pet, it at least
would not snatch the cold beef from the luncheon-table,
nor yet, if banished for its crimes, would it spend the night
in scratching the paint off the hall door.
Edith Œ. Somerville 1858–1949 and **Martin Ross** 1862–1915: *Some
Experiences of an Irish R.M.* (1899)

16 So, naturalists observe, a flea
Hath smaller fleas that on him prey;
And these have smaller fleas to bite 'em,
And so proceed *ad infinitum*.
Jonathan Swift 1667–1745: 'On Poetry' (1733)

Animals

17 We don't have the land to build houses, let alone cater for
horses. Next week the pet of the month could be elephants
or crocodiles. Do we have to provide facilities for them?
*spokesman for the Dublin Corporation on the implementation of
the Control of Horses Act, 1996*
Declan Wallace: in *Irish Times* 16 August 1997 'This Week They Said'

Appearance

1 If you're a woman on television they're only interested in
how you look—your hair, eyes, nails. All that is
commented on and the message is lost.
Máire Geoghegan-Quinn 1950– : in 1996, attributed

2 Her skin had that lightly olive, Protestant quality to it, that
you get in Ireland.
Katy Hayes: *Curtains* (1997)

3 You have a very odd manner . . . 'Tis that sneaky little
Presbyterian smile.
Frank McCourt 1930– : *Angela's Ashes* (1996)

4 Her ugliness was destined to bloom late, hidden first by the
unformed gawkiness of youth, budding to plainness in
young womanhood and now flowering to slow maturity in
her early forties.
Brian Moore 1921– : *The Lonely Passion of Judith Hearne* (1955)

5 My general appearance, and especially my face, have
always been a source of depression to me.
William Orpen 1878–1931: *Stories of Old Ireland and Myself* (1924)

6 Whenever most people of my generation look at our
parents' photograph albums, we always see Sinatra. He's
present in the way our fathers and uncles slicked their hair,

in the cut of their best suits, in the angle at which they held
their cigarettes.
Fintan O'Toole 1958– : in *Irish Times* 23 May 1998 'This Week They Said'

7   There is no trusting appearance.
Richard Brinsley Sheridan 1751–1816: *The School for Scandal* (1777)

8   An unforgiving eye, and a damned disinheriting
countenance!
Richard Brinsley Sheridan 1751–1816: *The School for Scandal* (1777)

9   A ragbag held together by diamond brooches.
of 'Mrs Knox'
Edith Œ. Somerville 1858–1949 and **Martin Ross** 1862–1915: *Further
Experiences of an Irish R.M.* (1908)

10 He [the emperor] is taller by almost the breadth of my nail
than any of his court, which alone is enough to strike an
awe into the beholders.
Jonathan Swift 1667–1745: *Gulliver's Travels* (1726) 'A Voyage to Lilliput'

11 Last week I saw a woman flayed, and you will hardly
believe, how much it altered her person for the worse.
Jonathan Swift 1667–1745: *A Tale of a Tub* (1704)

12 It is only shallow people who do not judge by appearances.
Oscar Wilde 1854–1900: *The Picture of Dorian Gray* (1891)

Architecture see also Houses

1   The floozie in the jacuzzi.
*popular description of the monument in O'Connell Street,
Dublin*
Anonymous: comment, *c.*1988

2   A man must be stronger than God to build to the west of
his house.
Anonymous: traditional saying; Frank O'Connor *Irish Miles* (1947)

3   Here is the very spirit
    Of hard-drinking, sea-mouldering Galway:
    A building ugly as sin.
    Austin Clarke 1896–1974: 'The New Cathedral in Galway' (1968)

4   I live like many other Irish gentlemen, who never are, but
    always to be, blest with a good house. I began on too large
    a scale, and can never hope to live to finish it.
    Maria Edgeworth 1767–1849: *The Absentee* (1812)

5   When offered a commission in Ireland, refuse it.
    of working as an architect in Ireland
    Edward William Godwin 1833–86: in *British Architect* (1878) vol. 10

6   Whatever these ancient buildings may have been, the Irish
    have now for them the greatest possible veneration.
    of round towers
    Chevalier de Latocnaye: in 1796; *A Frenchman's Walk Through Ireland,
    1796–7* (tr. John Stevenson, 1917)

7   A lady in the morning without her make-up on.
    on Dublin inner-city architecture
    Jim Tunney: comment, 1987

Armagh

1   Armagh: where two cathedrals sit upon opposing hills like
    the horns of a dilemma.
    Sam Hanna Bell 1909–90: 'In Praise of Ulster' (radio broadcast, *c.*1960)

2   There is a through-otherness about Armagh
    Of tower and steeple,
    Up on the hills are the arguing graves of the kings,
    And below are the people.
    W. R. Rodgers 1909–69: 'Armagh'

The Armed Forces see also War

1 The wild geese—the wild geese,—'tis long since they flew,
O'er the billowy ocean's bright bosom of blue.
Michael Joseph Barry 1817–89: in *Spirit of the Nation* (Dublin, 1845)

2 I can always guarantee that the Irish Citizen Army will
fight, but I cannot guarantee that it will be on time.
James Connolly 1868–1916: Diana Norman *Terrible Beauty* (1987)

3 Our colonel comes from Brian's race,
His wounds are in his breast and face.
Thomas Davis 1814–45: 'Clare's Dragoons' (1845)

4 The Wild Geese fly where others walk;
The Wild Geese do what others talk.
Thomas Davis 1814–45: 'When South Winds Blow' (1845)

5 The general who heroically risks his men's lives is seldom
cheated of victory.
Lynn C. Doyle 1873–1961: *A Bowl of Broth* (1945)

6 Soldiers are we, whose lives are pledged to Ireland,
Some have come from a land beyond the wave.
Peadair Kearney 1883–1942: 'The Soldier's Song' (1911)

7 Old days! the wild geese are flighting,
Head to the storm as they faced it before.
Rudyard Kipling 1865–1936: 'The Irish Guards'

8 I joined the British Army because she stood between
Ireland and an enemy common to our civilization and I
would not have her say she defended us while we did
nothing but pass resolutions.
Francis Ledwidge 1891–1917: Alice Curtayne *Francis Ledwidge* (1972)

9 For the boys march at morn from the South to the North,
Led by Kelly, the boy from Killann!
Patrick Joseph McCall 1861–1918: 'Kelly the Boy from Killann'

Ⓐ

10   'Tis Ireland gives England her soldiers, her generals too.
   George Meredith 1828–1909: *Diana of the Crossways* (1885)

11   The Minstrel Boy to the war is gone,
   In the ranks of death you'll find him;
   His father's sword he has girded on,
   And his wild harp slung behind him.
   Thomas Moore 1779–1852: *Irish Melodies* (1807) 'The Minstrel Boy'

12   The confession meant the end of the IRA for me . . . it
   meant either that Hayes was a traitor, in which case the
   IRA was a lousy organization for having such a man at the
   top, or else he was innocent, in which case the IRA was a
   doubly lousy organization to extract such a document from
   him.
   in 1941 the former IRA Chief of Staff, Stephen Hayes, was
   accused of being an informer and made to write a confession
   Tarlach O'hUid: Tim Pat Coogan *The IRA* (1995)

13   Ere long there shall be an Irish army on the Irish hillsides
   ready to do battle for Irish independence and drive back
   from the green and sacred Isle of Erin those ruthless tyrants
   who have desolated our homes and driven us wandering
   exiles over the whole earth.
   John O'Mahony 1819–77: in *Irish People* 13 February 1864

14   I am glad that the Orangemen have armed, for it is a
   goodly thing to see arms in Irish hands . . . I should like to
   see any and every body of Irish citizens armed.
   Patrick Pearse 1879–1916: speech, 1916

15   Oh, you are a very poor soldier—a chocolate cream soldier!
   George Bernard Shaw 1856–1950: *Arms and the Man* (1898)

16   When the military man approaches, the world locks up its
   spoons and packs off its womankind.
   George Bernard Shaw 1856–1950: *Man and Superman* (1903)

Armed Forces

17 I had walked the paths of Kerry and dared not say the
       word;
    I had trod the paths of Leinster all broken by the sword,
    O Ulster, Munster, Connacht, He gave Who can restore,
    The Wild Geese, the Wild Geese, they have come home
       once more.
    Dora Sigerson 1866–1918: *Sixteen Dead Men* (1919) 'The Wild Geese'

18 Does anyone suppose that any of us enjoy the prospect of
    playing a part for which so many of us are not obviously
    suited? I myself am a middle-aged lawyer, more at home,
    and I may perhaps add more highly remunerated, in the
    law courts than I am likely to be on the parade ground.
    of his role in the Ulster Volunteer Force
    F. E. Smith 1872–1930: speech to the House of Commons, 1913

19   When we're worn,
    Hacked hewn with constant service, thrown aside
    To rust in peace, or rot in hospitals.
    Thomas Southerne 1660–1746: *The Loyal Brother* (1682)

20 'Our armies swore terribly in Flanders,' cried my uncle
    Toby,—'but nothing to this.'
    Laurence Sterne 1713–68: *Tristram Shandy* (1759–67)

21 The General was essentially a man of peace, except in his
    domestic life.
    Oscar Wilde 1854–1900: *The Importance of Being Earnest* (1895)

Art

1 I think of what great art removes:
   Hazard and death, the future and the past.
   Eavan Boland 1944– : 'From the painting *Back from Market* by Chardin'

2 Painting became everything to me . . . Through it I made articulate all that I saw and felt, all that went on inside the mind that was housed within my useless body like a prisoner in a cell.
Christy Brown 1932–81: *My Left Foot* (1954)

3 The artist, like the God of the creation, remains within or behind or beyond or above his handiwork, invisible, refined out of existence, indifferent, paring his fingernails.
James Joyce 1882–1941: *A Portrait of the Artist as a Young Man* (1916)

4 It is a symbol of Irish art. The cracked lookingglass of a servant.
James Joyce 1882–1941: *Ulysses* (1922)

5 I have felt ashamed of having spent my life trying to please sitters and make friends instead of telling the truth and making enemies.
John Lavery 1856–1941: *The Life of a Painter* (1940)

6 The perfect aesthete logically feels that the artist is strictly a turkish bath attendant.
Flann O'Brien 1911–66: *The Best of Myles* (1968)

7 I remember an officer saying to me, 'Paint the Somme? I could do it from memory—just a flat horizon-line and mud-holes and water, with the stumps of a few battered trees,' but one could not paint the smell.
as an official war artist in the First World War
William Orpen 1878–1931: *An Onlooker in France* (1921)

8 All that I desire to point out is the general principle that Life imitates Art far more than Art imitates Life.
Oscar Wilde 1854–1900: *Intentions* (1891)

9 The intellect of man is forced to choose
Perfection of the life, or of the work.
W. B. Yeats 1865–1939: 'Coole Park and Ballylee, 1931' (1933)

Beauty

1 Beauty in distress is much the most affecting beauty.
Edmund Burke 1729–97: *On the Sublime and Beautiful* (1757)

2 Brightness of brightness lonely met me where I wandered,
Crystal of crystal only by her eyes were splendid.
Aodhagán Ó Rathaille *c.*1670–1729: 'Brightness of Brightness' (translated by Frank O'Connor)

3 The beauty of the world hath made me sad,
This beauty that will pass.
Patrick Pearse 1879–1916: 'The Wayfarer'

4 Beauty is all very well at first sight; but who ever looks at it when it has been in the house three days?
George Bernard Shaw 1856–1950: *Man and Superman* (1903)

5 It is better to be beautiful than to be good. But . . . it is better to be good than to be ugly.
Oscar Wilde 1854–1900: *The Picture of Dorian Gray* (1891)

6 A woman of so shining loveliness
That men threshed corn at midnight by a tress,
A little stolen tress.
W. B. Yeats 1865–1939: 'The Secret Rose' (1899)

Belfast see also The North

1 Buy now while shops last.
Anonymous: graffito, 1970s

2 May God in His mercy look down on Belfast.
Anonymous: traditional refrain

3 O the bricks they will bleed and the rain it will weep
And the damp Lagan fog lull the city to sleep;
It's to hell with the future and live on the past:
May the Lord in His mercy be kind to Belfast.
based on the traditional refrain; cf. **Belfast 2** *above*
Maurice James Craig 1919– : 'Ballad to a Traditional Refrain' (1974)

4 With the possible exceptions of Jerusalem and Mecca,
Belfast must be the most religion-conscious city in the
world.
Tyrone Guthrie 1900–71: *A Life in the Theatre* (1959)

5 Born in Belfast, which drew the landless in,
that river-straddling, hill-rimmed town.
John Hewitt 1907–87: 'An Ulsterman'

6 Belfast is a village. Strangers meeting always have mutual
friends or acquaintances.
Robert Johnstone 1951– : *Images of Belfast* (1983)

7 One thing to be said in favour of Belfast—you can get out
of it quickly.
Sean O'Faolain 1900–91: *An Irish Journey* (1940)

8   Ah, those brick canyons
Where Brookeborough unsheathes a sabre,
Shouting 'No Surrender' from the back of a lorry.
Tom Paulin 1949– : 'In the Lost Province' (1980)

Biography

1 No quailing, Mrs Gaskell! no drawing back!
apropos her undertaking to write the life of Charlotte Brontë
Patrick Brontë 1777–1861: letter from Mrs Gaskell to Ellen Nussey, 24 July
1855

2 I can take some credit for having achieved the opposite of what biographers usually do. I wrote about someone famous and succeeded in plunging him into public obscurity.

her assessment of the effect of her biography of Patrick Pearse
Ruth Dudley Edwards 1944– : 'Confessions of an Irish Revisionist' (1988)

3 Every great man nowadays has his disciples, and it is always Judas who writes the biography.
Oscar Wilde 1854–1900: *Intentions* (1891) 'The Critic as Artist' pt. 1

Birds

1 What little throat
Has framed that note?
What gold beak shot
It far away?
A blackbird on
His leafy throne
Tossed it alone
Across the bay?
Anonymous: 'The Blackbird by Belfast Lough', *c.*8th century poem,
translated by Frank O'Connor *Kings, Lords and Commons* (1959)

2 As I heard the sweet lark sing
In the clear air of the day.
Samuel Ferguson 1810–86: 'The Lark in the Clear Air'

3 He shall not hear the bittern cry
In the wild sky where he is lain,
Nor voices of the sweeter birds
Above the wailing of the rain.
Francis Ledwidge 1891–1917: 'Lament for Thomas MacDonagh' (1917)

4 Oh the yellow bittern that never broke out
On a drinking bout might as well have drunk.
Cathal Buí Mac Giolla Ghunna ?1680–1756: 'An Bonnán Buí' (lament for a bittern found dead of thirst), translated by Thomas MacDonagh

5 Old miners at Coalisland
   Going into the ground.
   Swinging, for fear of the gas,
   The soft flame of a canary.
   Paul Muldoon 1951– : 'Ma'

6 She remembered a big bird in the likeness of a swan being
   seen on the gable of the church and that people were
   saying that it was St Kathleen herself in the likeness of a
   swan.
   Peig Sayers 1873–1958: *An Old Woman's Reflections* (translated by Séamus
   Ennis, 1962)

7 A robin that isn't a robin redbreast, looks like a bank
   messenger in mufti.
   Jack B. Yeats 1871–1957: *The Charmed Life* (1938)

8 A sudden blow: the great wings beating still
   Above the staggering girl, her thighs caressed
   By the dark webs, her nape caught in his bill,
   He holds her helpless breast upon his breast.
   W. B. Yeats 1865–1939: 'Leda and the Swan' (1928)

The Body

1 An evil eye had Balor the Fomorian. The eye was never
   opened save on the battle-field. Four men used to lift up the
   eye with a polished handle which passed through it. If any
   army looked at that eye, though they were many
   thousands in number, they could not resist a few warriors.
   Anonymous: Celtic mythological cycle; Sean O'Faolain *The Irish* (1947)

2 If I had the use of my body I would throw it out of the
   window.
   Samuel Beckett 1906–89: *Malone Dies* (1988)

3 People don't come in my size until they're old . . . I used to
   think people were born with big bones and large frames,
   but apparently these grow when you're about sixty-eight.
   Maeve Binchy 1940– : *Circle of Friends* (1990)

4 I've got difficult feet. They're almost round, like an
   elephant's. Lengthways they're size ten and sideways size
   twelve.
   Patrick Campbell 1913–80: *Gullible Travels* (1969)

5 He . . . saw the dark tangled curls of his bush floating,
   floating hair of the stream around the limp father of
   thousands, a languid floating flower.
   James Joyce 1882–1941: *Ulysses* (1922)

6 Genetics had the final say . . . If my father had married a
   dainty little woman, I might have had a very different life.
   Very different thighs, certainly.
   Marian Keyes: *Rachel's Holiday* (1997)

7 If your mother had married a proper decent Limerickman
   you wouldn't have this standing up, North of Ireland,
   Presbyterian hair.
   Frank McCourt 1930– : *Angela's Ashes* (1996)

8 Glory be, it's not my jaw, I can still talk.
   on breaking her arm just before the general election, June 1927
   Constance Markievicz 1868–1927: Diana Norman *Terrible Beauty* (1987)

9 'Twas from Kathleen's eyes he flew,
   Eyes of most unholy blue!
   Thomas Moore 1779–1852: *Irish Melodies* (1807) 'By that Lake'

10 *Oileán is ea do chorp*
   i lár na mara móire.
   Tá do ghéaga spréite ar bhraillín
   gléigeal os farraige faoileán.

   Your body is an island
   Amid the great ocean.
   Your limbs are spread on a sheet,

Body

White as pelagic gull.
Nuala Ní Dhomhnaill 1952- : 'Oileán'

11 Each of his thighs was as thick as a horse's belly,
narrowing to a calf as thick as the belly of a foal. Three
fifties of fosterlings could engage with handball against the
wideness of his backside, which was wide enough to halt
the march of men through a mountain-pass.
Flann O'Brien 1911–66: *At-Swim-Two-Birds* (1939)

12 It's heartbreakin' to see a young fella thinkin' of anything,
or admirin' anything, but silk thransparent stockin's
showin' off the shape of a little lassie's legs!
Sean O'Casey 1880–1964: *The Plough and the Stars* (1926)

13 Ringlet on ringlet flowed tress on tress of yellow flaming
hair.
Aodhagán Ó Rathaille *c.*1670–1729: 'Brightness of Brightness' (translated
by Frank O'Connor)

14 Mrs Bennett . . . had but two back teeth in her head, but,
thank God, they still met.
Edith Œ. Somerville 1858–1949 and **Martin Ross** 1862–1915: *Some
Experiences of an Irish R.M.* (1899)

Books

1 Books, in Mallow, were heard of and even owned; they
were the proper fittings of a gentleman's house.
Elizabeth Bowen 1899–1973: *Bowen's Court* (1942)

2 Charlotte has been writing a book, and it is much better
than likely.
to his daughters Anne and Emily, on first reading Jane Eyre
Patrick Brontë 1777–1861: Elizabeth Gaskell *The Life of Charlotte Brontë*
(1857)

3 To every cow her calf, to every book its copy.
St Columcille ?521–97: attributed

4 The demand that I make of my reader is that he should
   devote his whole LIFE to reading my works.
   James Joyce 1882–1941: Richard Ellmann *James Joyce* (1982)

5 I have just got a letter asking me why I don't give Bloom a
   rest. The writer of it wants more Stephen. But Stephen no
   longer interests me to the same extent. He has a shape that
   can't be changed.
   James Joyce 1882–1941: Frank Budgen *James Joyce and the Making of
   Ulysses* (1934)

6 'That's what has put yourself wrong,' said Maura the
   Rosses, with an air of finality. 'It was the readin' and the
   books. I did my best to keep ye from the readin' but ye
   wouldn't take heed what I said.'
   Patrick MacGill 1891–1963: *The Children of the Dead End* (1914)

7 Some savage faculty for observation told him that most
   respectable and estimable people usually had a lot of books
   in their houses.
   Flann O'Brien 1911–66: *The Best of Myles* (1968)

8 I opened it at page 96—the secret page on which I write
   my name to catch out borrowers and book-sharks.
   Flann O'Brien 1911–66: *Myles Away from Dublin* (1990)

9 Peig Sayers was the droning voice of Irish failure, the kind
   of literary character that only a truly colonised society
   could produce.
   Joseph O'Connor 1963– : *The Irish Male at Home and Abroad* (1996)

10 Books, like men their authors, have no more than one way
    of coming into the world, but there are ten thousand to go
    out of it, and return no more.
    Jonathan Swift 1667–1745: *A Tale of a Tub* (1704) 'Epistle Dedicatory'

11 There is no such thing as a moral or an immoral book.
    Books are well written, or badly written.
    Oscar Wilde 1854–1900: *The Picture of Dorian Gray* (1891)

Britain see also **England and the English, Ireland and England**

1 Forget Cool Britannia—the action is in Cool Hibernia.
   Anonymous: in *Financial Times* June 1996

2 The Isle of Man . . . is equidistant from the north of Ireland
   and Britain. There was a great controversy in antiquity
   concerning the question, to which of the two countries
   should the island properly belong? . . . All agreed that since
   it allowed poisonous reptiles to live in it, it should belong to
   Britain.
   Giraldus Cambrensis *c.*1146–1223: *The History and Topography of Ireland*

3 Can it be that we only get a fit of neutrality when we have
   a chance of being neutral against the British?
   John M. Kelly 1931– : comment, April 1986

4 He [the Briton] is a barbarian, and thinks that the customs
   of his tribe and island are the laws of nature.
   George Bernard Shaw 1856–1950: *Caesar and Cleopatra* (1901)

5 To many, no doubt, he will seem blatant and bumptious,
   but we prefer to regard him as being simply British.
   Oscar Wilde 1854–1900: in *Pall Mall Gazette* 18 November 1886

Business

1 Ireland is not at peace. It is smothered war. England has
   sown her laws as dragon's teeth, and they have sprung up
   as armed men.
   in 1779, arguing for the repeal of restrictive acts on Irish trade
   Walter Hussey Burgh 1742–83: in *Dictionary of National Biography*
   (1917–)

2 It is the interest of the commercial world that wealth should be found everywhere.
Edmund Burke 1729–97: letter, 23 April 1778

3 At the risk of a horrible mixed metaphor, we can say that the Celtic Tiger needs a human face and a human heart.
Cahal Daly 1917– : in *Irish Times* 10 January 1998 'This Week They Said'

4 Honour sinks where commerce long prevails.
Oliver Goldsmith 1728–74: *The Traveller* (1764)

5 Could Henry Ford produce the Book of Kells? Certainly not. He would quarrel initially with the advisability of such a project and then prove it was impossible.
Flann O'Brien 1911–66: *Myles Away from Dublin* (1990)

6 Oh, is it that filly? . . . I swapped her and £6 for a three-year-old Ironmonger colt, and after that I swapped the colt and £19 for that Bandon horse I rode last week at your place, and after that again I sold the Bandon horse for £75 to old Welply, and I had to give him a couple of sovereigns luck-money. You see I did pretty well with the filly after all.
Edith Œ. Somerville 1858–1949 and **Martin Ross** 1862–1915: *Some Experiences of an Irish R.M.* (1899)

7 I have heard of a man who had a mind to sell his house, and therefore carried a piece of brick in his pocket, which he showed as a pattern to encourage purchasers.
Jonathan Swift 1667–1745: *The Drapier's Letters* (1724)

8 It is very vulgar to talk about one's business. Only people like stockbrokers do that, and then merely at dinner parties.
Oscar Wilde 1854–1900: *The Importance of Being Earnest* (1895)

Celebrations

1 I dread the year now upon us and all the fuss in store for me . . . I'll make myself scarce while it lasts, where I don't know. Perhaps the Great Wall of China, crouch behind it till the coast is clear.
on the celebrations expected for his 75th birthday
Samuel Beckett 1906–89: letter to Jocelyn Herbert, 11 January 1981

2 Never ask the children to tell the class what they did for Easter or Christmas or Confirmation or St Patrick's Day . . . Nothing points up the inequality of people's lives more starkly than asking innocent children to tell you how they spent what was meant to be a festival.
Maeve Binchy 1940– : in *Irish Times* 14 March 1998

3 It was a city of bonfires. The Protestants had more than we had. They had the twelfth of July, when they celebrated the triumph of Protestant armies at the Battle of the Boyne in 1690; then they had the twelfth of August when they celebrated the liberation of the city from a besieging Catholic army in 1689; then they had the burning of Lundy's effigy on the eighteenth of December . . . We had only the fifteenth of August bonfires; it was a church festival but we made it into a political one as well.
Seamus Deane 1940– : *Reading in the Dark* (1996)

4 What were we celebrating? At this rate the Angelus doesn't have a chance of remaining on RTÉ if we've managed to get St Patrick out of his own parade.
on not seeing a single figure of the saint in the Dublin parade
Stephen Harris: in *Irish Times* 28 March 1998 'This Week They Said'

5 What's that? A garden festival? Something to do with flowers?
a visitor from Montreal on Bloomsday
Margo Hubbard: in *Irish Times* 20 June 1998 'This Week They Said'

6 Bloomsday threatens to become the Mardi Gras of Ireland.
David Norris 1944– : in June 1992, attributed

7 In the whole dismal cornucopia of abject anniversaries, foul festive frolics and rancid rejoicings is there anything really worse than Saint Valentine's Day?
Joseph O'Connor 1963– : *The Secret World of the Irish Male* (1994)

8 I've seen Patrick's Day parades and Corpus Christi parades and Macnas parades and every other kind of parade the South has to offer. I've seen Irish parades in America. But I never saw such a genuine people's festival as the Twelfth parade in Belfast. It is a wonderful thing to have happening on our island, and the only pity is that the South knows nothing about it, and the North has no plans to share it with the South.
Nuala O'Faolain: in *Irish Times* 20 July 1998

9 Dear Lord, the day of eggs is here.
Amanda McKitterick Ros 1861–1939: 'Ode to Easter'

Censorship

1 We are changing the function of the editor of the *Irish Times* and the other papers to myself and my staff. It is now we who have the final say on what to cut out, not the editors.
as official Censor, c.1940
Frank Aiken 1898–1983: Tony Gray *The Lost Years: the Emergency in Ireland 1939–45* (1997)

2 There are no alternatives to 'bastard' agreeable to me.
Nevertheless I have offered them 'swine' in its place.
on changes to the text of Endgame *required by the Lord
Chamberlain for the London production, summer 1958*
Samuel Beckett 1906–89: James Knowlson *Damned to Fame* (1996)

3 An undue hostility to foreign influences (mainly to things
English) and a concentration on the pastoral aspects of
Irish culture have tended to create an uneasy vision in the
public mind of what the country would be like if the Gaels
controlled it.
Tim Pat Coogan 1935– : *Ireland Since the Rising* (1966)

4 It's because it's in English, you can get away with much
more in French. Think what you could get away with in
Japanese!
*on the refusal of the Lord Chamberlain to grant a licence to
Samuel Beckett's* Endgame, *February 1958*
George Devine 1910–66: Irving Wardle *The Theatres of George Devine*
(1978)

5 I'll stitch up my mouth with tightened string,
and say nothing about their nasty little legalities.
*having heard that brothers and friars were forbidden to compose
    verses or songs in Irish monasteries*
Pádraigin Haicéad d. 1654: translation in P. J. Kavanagh *Voices in Ireland*
(1994)

6 No less than twenty-two publishers and printers read the
manuscript of *Dubliners* and when at last it was printed
some very kind person bought out the entire edition and
had it burnt in Dublin.
James Joyce 1882–1941: letter, 2 April 1932

7 Careful now!
placard alerting Craggy Island to a banned film
Graham Linehan and **Arthur Mathews**: 'The Passion of St Tibulus' (1994),
episode from *Father Ted* (Channel 4 TV, 1994–8)

8   *Pompadour* is banned in Ireland. This always happens
    because one or 2 sentences are objected to, and sometimes
    one cuts them out in another edition. So I eagerly asked
    what were the operative paragraphs and was told it was
    banned because of the title.
    of her biography of Madame de Pompadour
    Nancy Mitford 1904–73: letter, June/July 1954

9   I am between the devil and the Holy See . . . [My task is to
    prevent] the Californication of Ireland.
    on being appointed Irish film censor
    James Montgomery: Ulick O'Connor *Oliver St John Gogarty* (1964)

10 'You know perfectly well, Dotey,' said Martin, 'that your
    solicitous Dev doesn't let an immoral rag within three
    hundred miles of you. This country is Heaven's ante-
    room . . . whether we like it or not.'
    Kate O'Brien 1897–1974: *The Last of Summer* (1943)

11 Here we have bishops, priests, and deacons, a Censorship
    Board, vigilant librarians, confraternities and sodalities,
    Duce Maria, Legions of Mary, Knights of this Christian
    order and Knights of that one, all surrounding the sinner's
    free will in an embattled circle.
    Sean O'Casey 1880–1964: letter to the *Irish Times*, 8 June 1957

12 Mr de Valera, like Mr Cosgrave, regarded literary
    censorship as part of our freedom to achieve fuller freedom.
    Brendan Ó hEithir 1930– : *The Begrudger's Guide to Irish Politics*

13 The censors strive with a certain sadness in their hearts, for
    they feel that whatever they do the trouble cannot really be
    removed, only 'regulated'.
    William Ryan 1867–1942: *Ecclesiastics, Eve and Literature*

14 Assassination is the extreme form of censorship.
    George Bernard Shaw 1856–1950: *The Showing-Up of Blanco Posnet* (1911)

15 'This country . . . has already got a State Censorship of
Films which is said to be the strictest in Europe.'
'It's not strict enough.'
Mervyn Wall 1908– : *Leaves for the Burning* (1952)

16 I think you can leave the arts, superior or inferior, to the
conscience of mankind.
W. B. Yeats 1865–1939: speech in the Irish Senate, 7 June 1923

Change

1 It's a change of muck. And if all muck is the same muck
that doesn't matter, it's good to have a change of muck, to
move from one heap to another a little further on, from
time to time.
Samuel Beckett 1906–89: *Molloy* (1951)

2 In these past few days, the irresistible force, the political
will, has met the immovable object, the legacy of the past,
and we have moved it.
*speech from the steps of Stormont, after Senator Mitchell's
announcement that an agreement had been reached*
Tony Blair 1953– : in *Times* 11 April 1998

3 Yeats' *Terrible Beauty* truly has become a sick and
sectarian, angry and repressive old crone.
Noel Browne 1915–97: in *Irish Times* 23 December 1972

4 A state without the means of some change is without the
means of its conservation.
Edmund Burke 1729–97: *Reflections on the Revolution in France* (1790)

5 If revolution is the kicking down of a rotten door, evolution
is more like pushing the stone from the mouth of the tomb.
There is an Easter energy about it, a sense of arrival rather
than wreckage.
Seamus Heaney 1939– : in *Observer* 12 April 1998

6 That's the first time I have seen that man that I didn't want
to take a swing at him.
watching David Trimble campaigning for a Yes vote in the
referendum on Northern Ireland
Traolaoch Mac Gabain: in *Irish Times* 16 May 1998 'This Week They Said'

7 You gave me the key of your heart, my love;
Then why did you make me knock?
Oh that was yesterday, saints above!
And last night—I changed the lock!
John Boyle O'Reilly 1844–90: 'Constancy'

8 All changed, changed utterly.
W. B. Yeats 1865–1939: 'Easter, 1916' (1921)

Chaos see Order and Chaos

Children

1 What is it our mammas bewitches
To plague us little boys with breeches?
Mary Barber *c.*1690–1757: 'Written for My Son, and Spoken by Him at His
First Putting on Breeches' (1731)

2 Those lighting devils that go by the wrong name of
innocent children.
Maeve Binchy 1940– : *The Copper Beech* (1992)

3 Our children were your poems of which I was the Father
sowing the unrest and storm which made them possible
and you the mother who brought them forth in suffering
and in the highest beauty and our children had wings.
Maud Gonne 1867–1953: letter to W. B. Yeats, 15 September 1911

4 When I look back on my childhood I wonder how I
managed to survive at all. It was, of course, a miserable
childhood: the happy childhood is hardly worth your while.
Worse than the ordinary miserable childhood is the

miserable Irish childhood, and worse yet is the miserable
Irish Catholic childhood.
Frank McCourt 1930– : *Angela's Ashes* (1996)

5 Do engine-drivers, I wonder, eternally wish they were small
boys?
Flann O'Brien 1911–66: *The Best of Myles* (1968)

Christmas

1 Once in royal David's city
Stood a lowly cattle-shed,
Where a mother laid her baby
In a manger for his bed:
Mary was that mother mild,
Jesus Christ her little child.
Cecil Frances Alexander 1818–95: 'Once in royal David's city' (1848)

2 Christmas Eve can be hell on earth . . . Everyone running
round doing their last-minute shopping. It's as if Christmas
comes on people by surprise, as it they hadn't known for
weeks it was on its way.
Maeve Binchy 1940– : *The Glass Lake* (1994)

3 If the Three Wise Men arrived here tonight, the likelihood
is that they would be deported.
advocating an amnesty for asylum-seekers
Proinsias de Rossa: in *Irish Times* 20 December 1997 'This Week They Said'

4 Do they know it's Christmas?
Bob Geldof 1954– and **Midge Ure** 1953– : title of song (1984)

5 Cassiopeia was over
Cassidy's hanging hill,
I looked and three whin bushes rode across
The horizon — the Three Wise Kings.
Patrick Kavanagh 1904–67: 'A Christmas Childhood' (1947)

6 Astrologers or three wise men
Who may shortly be setting out
For a small house up the Shankill
Or the Falls, should pause on their way
To buy gifts at Jim Gibson's shop,
Dates and chestnuts and tangerines.
Michael Longley 1939– : 'The Greengrocer' (1979)

7 There are some people who want to throw their arms
round you simply because it is Christmas; there are other
people who want to strangle you simply because it is
Christmas.
Robert Lynd 1879–1949: *The Book of This and That* (1915)

8 The Christmas songs. Cliff Richard warbling about puppies
and yule logs and international peace . . . John Lennon's
unspeakably turgid *So This Is Christmas and What Have You
Done?* The answer being, in his case, half a pound of
cocaine and a couple of tabs of acid.
Joseph O'Connor 1963– : *The Secret World of the Irish Male* (1994)

9 Long-winded schismatics shall rule the roast,
And Father Christmas mourn his revels lost.
Jonathan Swift 1667–1745: 'The Swan Club Tribe in Dublin'

Clare

1 God help you there, poor County Clare,
Between Kerry and Kiltimagh.
Anonymous: traditional jingle

2 Stony seaboard, far and foreign,
Stony hills poured over space,
Stony outcrop of the Burren,
Stones in every fertile place,
Little fields with boulders dotted,
Grey-stone shoulders saffron-spotted,
Stone-walled cabins thatched with reeds,

Where a Stone Age people breeds
The last of Europe's stone age race.
John Betjeman 1906–84: 'Ireland with Emily' (1945)

3 Home is heaven, tho' it were
A burrow in the rock of Clare:
And Clare is seventh heaven to me,
Hanging on the hungry sea.
Joseph Campbell 1879–1944: 'The Exile' (1913)

Class

1 The rich man in his castle,
The poor man at his gate,
God made them, high or lowly,
And ordered their estate.
Cecil Frances Alexander 1818–95: 'All Things Bright and Beautiful' (1848)

2 Only the Irish working class remain as the incorruptible
inheritors of the fight for freedom in Ireland.
James Connolly 1868–1916: Nicholas Mansergh *The Irish Question* (ed. 3,
1975)

3 The English working class will *never accomplish anything*
before it has got rid of Ireland. The lever must be applied in
Ireland. That is why the Irish question is so important for
the social movement in general.
Karl Marx 1818–83: letter to Friedrich Engels, 1869

4 When I want a peerage, I shall buy it like an honest man.
Lord Northcliffe 1865–1922: Tom Driberg *Swaff* (1974)

5 The ancient native order [of Irish society] was patriarchal
and aristocratic, the people knew their place (i.e. the
scullery).
Flann O'Brien 1911–66: *The Hair of the Dogma* (1977)

6 The landlords gave us some few leaders, and I like them for
that, and the artisans have given us great numbers of good
patriots, and so I like them best; but you I do not like at all,
for you have never given us anyone.
to a gathering of Tipperary farmers, on his return from prison
John O'Leary 1830–1907: W. B. Yeats *Essays* (1924)

7 I think the noble young man has no business to make any
apology. He is a gentleman, and none such should be asked
to make an apology, because no gentleman could mean to
give offence.
*on the motion to expel Lord Edward Fitzgerald from the Irish
Parliament, c.1796*
Boyle Roche 1743–1807: Jonah Barrington *Personal Sketches and
Recollections of his own Time* (1827)

8 Mr Knox . . . was a fair, spare young man, who looked like
a stableboy among gentlemen, and a gentleman among
stableboys.
Edith Œ. Somerville 1858–1949 and **Martin Ross** 1862–1915: *Some
Experiences of an Irish R.M.* (1899)

9 [In Ireland] there is an upper and a lower class. The middle
class evidently does not exist, or else is confined to the
towns as in the Middle Ages.
Alexis de Tocqueville 1805–59: *Voyage en Angleterre et en Irlande de 1835*
(ed. J. P. Mayer, 1958)

The Clergy

1 *Ná bí mór nó beag leis an chléir.*
Don't be friendly or distant with the clergy.
Anonymous: traditional saying

2 Of priests we can offer a charming variety,
Far renowned for larnin' and piety;
Still I'd advance ye widout impropriety,

Father O'Flynn is the flower of them all.
Arthur Percival Graves 1846–1931: 'Father O'Flynn'

3 The clergy of this country are on the whole to be
commended for their observance.
Giraldus Cambrensis *c.*1146–1223: *The History and Topography of Ireland*

4 We, the Christian Brothers in Ireland, wish to express our
deep regret to anyone who suffered ill-treatment while in
our care.
Irish Christian Brothers: advertisement in national newspapers, April
1998

5 'There are two kinds of priests,' he declared. 'There are the
priests who made themselves and the kind who are made
by their mothers.'
John B. Keane 1928– : *Letters of an Irish Parish Priest*

6 It's great being a priest, isn't it, Ted?
Graham Linehan and **Arthur Mathews:** 'Good Luck, Father Ted' (1994),
episode from *Father Ted* (Channel 4 TV, 1994–8)

7 They were good and bad. Those who were good were very
good. Those who were bad were mental, to tell you the
truth.
a former pupil's view of the Christian Brothers
Martin McGuinness: in *Irish Times* 4 April 1998 'This Week They Said'

8 Anyone that got money out of a priest ought to have a
statue put up to them.
Frank O'Connor 1903–66: *Crab Apple Jelly* (1944)

9 'She has always had a gift for the Church,' I said.
'Not curates?' said Lady Knox, in her deep voice.
I made haste to reply that it was the elders of the Church
who were venerated by my wife.
Edith Œ. Somerville 1858–1949 and **Martin Ross** 1862–1915: *Some
Experiences of an Irish R.M.* (1899)

10   I never saw, heard, nor read, that the clergy were beloved
in any nation where Christianity was the religion of the
country. Nothing can render them popular, but some
degree of persecution.
Jonathan Swift 1667–1745: *Thoughts on Religion* (1765)

11   I never quite forgave Mahaffy for getting himself suspended
from preaching in the College Chapel. Ever since his
sermons were discontinued, I suffer from insomnia in
church.
George Tyrrell 1861–1909: Oliver St John Gogarty *As I Was Going Down
Sackville Street* (1937)

12   I became a wandering friar . . . I have become expert in
demonology and in detecting the darker acts of sorcery. On
my way to town to town I clear the lovers from the ditches
and the doorways, but that's in the nature of a sideline.
Mervyn Wall 1908– : *The Unfortunate Fursey* (1946)

Clonmacnoise

1   The annals say: when the monks of Clonmacnoise
Were all at prayers inside the oratory
A ship appeared above them in the air.
Seamus Heaney 1939– : 'Lightenings viii' (1991)

2   In a smelly, weedy place, a place of mourning,
Stand some heaps of ruined stones
Where the Irish middle classes under massive heaps of
    granite
Rest their bones.
Frank O'Connor 1903–66: *Leinster, Munster and Connaught* (1950)

3   In a quiet watered land, a land of roses,
Stands Saint Kieran's city fair:
And the warriors of Erin in their famous generations

Slumber there.
T. W. Rolleston 1857–1920: 'The Dead at Clonmacnois' (1909)

Coleraine

1 As beautiful Kitty one morning was tripping
With a pitcher of milk from the fair of Coleraine.
Anonymous: 'Kitty of Coleraine' (traditional ballad)

2 That is what this really is—a British market town, in a fine
farming centre, with a lovely setting of wood and river. I
felt myself at a great distance from home in Coleraine.
Sean O'Faolain 1900–91: *An Irish Journey* (1991)

Conversation

1 It wasn't every day that you overheard a conversation that
covered lies and virginity and knickers and God-all-bloody-
mighty.
Dublin was changing.
Maeve Binchy 1940– : *The Glass Lake* (1994)

2 I see people in terms of dialogue and I believe that people
are their talk.
Roddy Doyle 1958– : John Ardagh *Ireland and the Irish* (1994)

3 We cannot judge either of the feelings or of the character of
men with perfect accuracy, from their actions or their
appearance in public; it is from their careless conversation,
their half-finished sentences, that we may hope with the
greatest probability of success to discover their real
character.
Maria Edgeworth 1767–1849: *Castle Rackrent* (1800)

4 It was a typical 'Ulster' conversation, with gaps and deliberate omissions reaching right back to the Boyne and the Penal Laws. Better keep your mouth shut and no harm done.
Denis Ireland 1894–1980: *From the Jungle of Belfast* (1973)

5 Margaret was the only one of us who spoke to our neighbours, happy to discuss hip replacements, grandchildren's First Communions, the unusually wet weather and the availability of Tayto in Chicago.
Marian Keyes: *Rachel's Holiday* (1997)

6 She . . . couldn't take a phone call without getting into a seminar on the meaning of life with the caller.
Mary Maher: 'Lucy's Story' (1997)

7 Question and answer is not a civilized form of conversation.
Patrick O'Brian 1914– : *Clarissa Oakes* (1992)

8 Talk to him about yourself: then he will love you—to your great alarm.
George Bernard Shaw 1856–1950: 'Aphorism'

9 It has been said by an excellent authority that children and dogs spoil conversation. I can confidently say that had Madame de Sévigné and Dr Johnson joined me and my family on our wonted Sunday afternoon walk to the kennels they would have known what it was to be ignored.
Edith Œ. Somerville 1858–1949 and **Martin Ross** 1862–1915: *Further Experiences of an Irish R.M.* (1908)

10 Good conversation is not to be expected in much company, because few listen, and there is continual interruption.
Jonathan Swift 1667–1745: *Hints on Good Manners*

11 Faith, that's as well said, as if I had said it myself.
Jonathan Swift 1667–1745: *Polite Conversation* (1738)

12 If one could only teach the English how to talk, and the Irish how to listen, society here would be quite civilized.
Oscar Wilde 1854–1900: *An Ideal Husband* (1895)

Conversation

13 We Irish will never achieve anything; but we are the
greatest talkers since the Greeks.
Oscar Wilde 1854–1900: Mícheál Mac Liammóir *The Importance of Being
Oscar* (1961)

Cork

1 Fine girl you are!
You're the girl I do adore.
And still I live in hope to see
The Holy Ground once more.
'*The Holy Ground' perhaps the name of a brothel in Cork*
Anonymous: 'The Holy Ground' (song, 19th century)

2 From the courthouse to the college
They have every sort of knowledge
But still the half of Cork they haven't seen.
Anonymous: 'Dear old city by the Lee' (song, 20th century)

3 'Here's up 'em all!' says the boys of Fair Hill.
Anonymous: 'The Boys of Fair Hill' (song, 20th century)

4 That is a confusing city, of which Irishmen everywhere
who do not come from Cork profess to be afraid. And it is a
fact that while it reclines there between the arms of the
River Lee, looking beautiful and a little raffish and a little
tired, as though it had too many things to remember, it is
also a volcano of energy spouting out people who go out
and take over great tracts of government and industry in
Dublin, Pittsburgh and Sydney.
Claud Cockburn 1917– : *I, Claud* (1967)

5 I felt at times as if I was among a people as mysterious as
the Chinese, a people who have taken hold of the English
language and moulded it to their cross-purposes.
Conor Cruise O'Brien 1917– : in Cork, 1974

6 A Corkman can be homesick even when he is at home.
Niall Tóibín 1929– : attributed

Courage

1 I believe today that courage has triumphed.
speech from the steps of Stormont, after Senator Mitchell's announcement that an agreement had been reached
Tony Blair 1953– : in *Guardian* 11 April 1998

2 Courage is not simply *one* of the virtues but the form of every virtue at the testing point.
C. S. Lewis 1898–1963: Cyril Connolly *The Unquiet Grave* (1944)

3 It takes courage to push things forward.
on her decision to visit Loyalist prisoners in The Maze
Mo Mowlam: in *Guardian* 8 January 1998

4 What's the advantage of your passing through Oxford if you can't face a bull with a gun in your hand?
Sean O'Casey 1880–1964: *Purple Dust* (1940)

5 The best way to avoid danger is to meet it plump.
Boyle Roche 1743–1807: Jonah Barrington *Personal Sketches and Recollections of his own Times* (1827)

6 And may God save Ireland from her heroes
For what we need is not heroism,
But normal courage.
W. R. Rodgers 1909–69: epilogue to 'The Character of Ireland' (*Poems*, 1993)

7 As an old soldier I admit the cowardice: it's as universal as sea sickness, and matters just as little.
George Bernard Shaw 1856–1950: *Man and Superman* (1903)

8 My valour is certainly going!—it is sneaking off!—I feel it oozing out as it were at the palms of my hands!
Richard Brinsley Sheridan 1751–1816: *The Rivals* (1775)

Criticism

1 The carping malice of the vulgar world; who think it a
   proof of sense to dislike every thing that is writ by Women.
   Susannah Centlivre c.1669–1723: *The Platonic Lady* (1707) dedication

2 Like all good dramatic critics, we retired to the pub across
   the road.
   Eric Cross 1905–80: *The Tailor and Ansty* (1942)

3 They are now disfigured by all manner of crooked marks of
   Papa's critical indignation, besides various abusive margin
   notes.
   of the draft pages of her first book, Letters for Literary Ladies
   Maria Edgeworth 1767–1849: letter to Sophy Ruxton, February 1794

4 If there's 10,000 people of all ages and races screaming
   and dancing and going wild out there, and one person in
   the audience decides to do a hatchet job, how could that be
   right?
   Michael Flatley: in *Irish Times* 1 November 1997

5 If I make a good movie they say I'm a British director and if
   I make what they think is a bad one, they say I'm Irish!
   Neil Jordan 1951– : in *Independent* 3 February 1993

6 There's only one kind of critic I do resent . . . The kind that
   affects to believe that I am writing with my tongue in my
   cheek.
   James Joyce 1882–1941: Frank Budgen *James Joyce and the Making of
   Ulysses* (1934)

7 You don't expect me to know what to say about a play
   when I don't know who the author is, do you?
   George Bernard Shaw 1856–1950: *Fanny's First Play* (1914)

8 If it is abuse,—why one is always sure to hear of it from
   one damned goodnatured friend or another!
   Richard Brinsley Sheridan 1751–1816: *The Critic* (1779)

9 Of all the cants which are canted in this canting world,—
  though the cant of hypocrites may be the worst,—the cant
  of criticism is the most tormenting!
  Laurence Sterne 1713–68: *Tristram Shandy* (1759–67)

10 Yet malice never was his aim;
   He lashed the vice, but spared the name;
   No individual could resent,
   Where thousands equally were meant.
   Jonathan Swift 1667–1745: 'Verses on the Death of Dr Swift' (1731)

Curses

1 Bredin's mother stood outside the door and cursed all
  within it, long and bitter, for having ruined her son's life.
  That they might never have luck in this life, nor peace in
  the next. That they be blackened with misery, seed, breed
  and generation from this day forward. That they might
  never have a house where they could live that was not
  cursed. That they might see his face every day and night
  until the end of their days.
  Seamus Deane 1940– : *Reading in the Dark* (1996)

2 May the mange consume his head, may the fleas devour
    his bed,
  May the Divil sweep the hairy creature soon.
  He's as greedy as a sow, as the crow behind the plough,
  That black man from the mountain, Seáneen Rua.
  John B. Keane 1928– : *Sive* (1959)

3 If curses came from the heart, it would be a sin. But it is
  from the lips they come, and we use them only to give force
  to our speech, and they are a great relief of the heart.
  Peig Sayers 1873–1958: Robin Flower *The Western Island* (1944)

4 Mrs Cadogan greeted me with the prayer that the divil
   might roast Julia McCarthy, that legged it away to the
   races like a wild goose, and left the cream afther her.
   Edith Œ. Somerville 1858–1949 and **Martin Ross** 1862–1915: *Some
   Experiences of an Irish R.M.* (1899)

5 Lord, confound this surly sister,
   Blight her brow with blotch and blister,
   Cramp her larynx, lung and liver,
   In her guts a galling give her.
   on a friend's sister who had criticized The Playboy of the
      Western World
   John Millington Synge 1871–1909: 'A Curse'

Dance

1 Come ant daunce wyt me,
   in irlaunde.
   Anonymous: fourteenth century; cf. **Ireland 1**

2 During the intervals the devil is busy; yes, very busy, as sad
   experience proves, and on the way home in the small hours
   of the morning, he is busier still.
   Bishops' Pastoral Letter: in *Irish Catholic* 1933

3 Do you want the whole countryside to be laughing at
   us?—women of our years?—mature women, *dancing*?
   Brian Friel 1929– : *Dancing at Lughnasa* (1990)

4 We were about twenty boys and only one girl. She was well
   danced.
   Patrick Kavanagh 1904–67: *The Green Fool* (1938)

5 Two of the men nearly came to blows over the number of times you meet and go back before you cross over. Apparently one of them was confusing the Walls of Limerick with the Siege of Ennis, the way you do.
Marian Keyes: *Rachel's Holiday* (1997)

6 If my pals see my mother dragging me through the streets to an Irish dancing class I'll be disgraced entirely.
Frank McCourt 1930– : *Angela's Ashes* (1996)

7 A new parish priest . . . told the people to cease dancing, but they would not listen to him. 'When we get a new parish priest we don't want a new God,' they said. 'The old God who allowed dancing is good enough for us.'
Patrick MacGill 1891–1963: *The Children of the Dead End* (1914)

8 He waltzes like a Protestant curate.
Kate O'Brien 1897–1974: *The Last of Summer* (1943)

9 They say that jig was twenty pounds in Mrs Knox's pocket at the next rent day; but though this statement is open to doubt, I believe that if she and Flurry had taken the hat round there and then she would have got in the best part of her arrears.
Edith Œ. Somerville 1858–1949 and **Martin Ross** 1862–1915: *Some Experiences of an Irish R.M.* (1899)

10 [Dancing is] a perpendicular expression of a horizontal desire.
George Bernard Shaw 1856–1950: quoted in *New Statesman* 23 March 1962

11 On the church gate a hand-painted notice with two spelling mistakes announced that owing to the welcome presence of the Redemptorist Fathers in the town there would be no dance on Sunday.
Honor Tracy 1915– : *Mind You, I've Said Nothing* (1953)

12 O body swayed to music, O brightening glance
How can we know the dancer from the dance?
W. B. Yeats 1865–1939: 'Among School Children' (1928)

Dance

Danger

1 I always carry gelignite; dynamite isn't safe.
   Brendan Behan 1923–64: attributed

2 Dangers by being despised grow great.
   Edmund Burke 1729–97: speech on the Petition of the Unitarians, 11 May
   1792

3 My own fellow-countrymen won't kill me.
   before leaving for Cork, where he was shot from ambush
   Michael Collins 1890–1922: James Mackay *Michael Collins* (1996)

4 All that I crave for my own part is, that if I am to have my
   throat cut, it may not be by a man with his face blackened
   by charcoal.
   Maria Edgeworth 1767–1849: letter to Mrs Ruxton, January 1796

5 He is sending you, my dear friend, to Ireland, as he sent
   Gordon to Khartoum. I advise you to look out for yourself.
   *to John Morley, appointed by Gladstone as Chief Secretary for
   Ireland*
   Thomas Henry Huxley 1825–95: John Morley *Recollections* (1917)

6 We are all mariners on the deep, bound for a port still seen
   only through storm and spray, sailing on a sea full of
   dangers and hardships and bitter toil.
   Richard Mulcahy 1886–1971: at the grave of Michael Collins, 1922

7 The Volkswagen parked in the gap,
   But gently ticking over.
   You wonder if it's lovers
   And not men hurrying back
   Across two fields and a river.
   Paul Muldoon 1951– : 'Ireland' (1980)

8 Mr Speaker, I smell a rat; I see him forming in the air and
   darkening the sky; but I'll nip him in the bud.
   Boyle Roche 1743–1807: attributed

Death see also Execution

1 Even death is unreliable: instead of zero it may be some
ghastly hallucination, such as the square root of minus
one.
Samuel Beckett 1906–89: attributed

2   Some of us made it
To the forest edge, but many of us did not

Make it, although their unborn children did—
Such as you whom the camp commandant branded
Sid Vicious of the Sex Pistols. Jesus, break his fall:

There—but for the clutch of luck—go we all.
Paul Durcan 1944– : 'The Death by Heroin of Sid Vicious' (1980)

3 And found myself thinking: if it were nowadays,
This is how Death would summon Everyman.
Seamus Heaney 1939– : 'A Call' (1996)

4 University students are rarely able to cope with universals
and death is the most embarrassing universal.
Kate Cruise O'Brien 1948–98: *A Gift Horse* (1978)

5 Now I shall cease, death comes, and I must not delay
By Laune and Laine and Lee, diminished of their pride,
I shall go after the heroes, ay, into the clay—
My fathers followed theirs before Christ was crucified.
Aodhagán Ó Rathaille *c.*1670–1729: 'Last Lines' (translated by Frank
O'Connor)

6 Life levels all men: death reveals the eminent.
George Bernard Shaw 1856–1950: *Man and Superman* (1903) 'Maxims:
Fame'

7 I wish sir, you would practise this without me. I can't stay
dying here all night.
Richard Brinsley Sheridan 1751–1816: *The Critic* (1779)

8 'There is no terror, brother Toby, in its [death's] looks, but
   what it borrows from groans and convulsions—and the
   blowing of noses, and the wiping away of tears with the
   bottoms of curtains, in a dying man's room—Strip it of
   these, what is it?'—''Tis better in battle than in bed', said
   my uncle Toby.
   Laurence Sterne 1713–68: *Tristram Shandy* (1759–67)

9 Not die here in a rage, like a poisoned rat in a hole.
   Jonathan Swift 1667–1745: letter to Bolingbroke, 21 March 1730

10 Peace, peace, she cannot hear
   Lyre or sonnet,
   All my life's buried here,
   Heap earth upon it.
   Oscar Wilde 1854–1900: 'Requiescat' (1881)

11 Not a drum was heard, not a funeral note,
   As his corse to the rampart we hurried.
   Charles Wolfe 1791–1823: 'The Burial of Sir John Moore at Corunna'
   (1817)

Debt

1 These fellows . . . give themselves the sham military airs of
   retired colonels, travel around the country after all sorts of
   pleasures, and if one makes an inquiry, they haven't a
   penny, are laden with debts, and live in dread of the
   Encumbered Estates Court.
   of Irish landowners
   Friedrich Engels 1820–95: letter to Karl Marx, 23 May 1856

2 I couldn't imagine anything duller than a man with a
   regular income . . . I found financial insecurity a great
   aphrodisiac.
   Marian Keyes: *Lucy Sullivan is Getting Married* (1997)

3 I feel these days like a very large flamingo. No matter what way I turn, there is always a very large bill.
Joseph O'Connor 1963– : *The Secret World of the Irish Male* (1994)

4 One must have some sort of occupation nowadays. If I hadn't my debts I shouldn't have anything to think about.
Oscar Wilde 1854–1900: *A Woman of No Importance* (1893)

Democracy

1 This is the first time since 1918 in an act of self-determination that everyone on this island, on the one issue, has had the opportunity to pass their verdict.
opening the Fianna Fáil referendum campaign
Bertie Ahern 1951– : in *Irish Times* 9 May 1998 'This Week They Said'

2 I have yet to see a country without original sin, where there isn't electoral abuse, or bribery and corruption for that matter.
comment of the chief electoral officer for Northern Ireland
Pat Bradley: in *Irish Times* 27 June 1998 'This Week They Said'

3 The Dublin Parliament, that noisy side-show, so bizarre in its lineaments and so tragi-comic in its fate.
Daniel Corkery 1878–1964: *The Hidden Ireland* (1925)

4 The idea that those who shout loudest most often can claim to be the majority opinion reminds me of the woman who once, long ago, roared at me here in Galway in Devon Park, and said, 'God plus one is a majority.'
Michael D. Higgins 1941– : in *Irish Times* 23 June 1997

5 Democracy substitutes election by the incompetent many for appointment by the corrupt few.
George Bernard Shaw 1856–1950: *Man and Superman* (1903) 'Maxims: Democracy'

Determination

1 If our last cartridge had been fired, our last shilling spent, and our last man lying on the ground, with his enemies howling round him ready to plunge their bayonets into his body, that man should say, if asked to come into the British Empire, 'No I will not.' And he would not.
Cathal Brugha 1874–1922: in 1922, attributed

2 I have nothing to regret, to retract or take back. I can only say: God save Ireland!
statement from the dock during the trial of the Manchester Martyrs; the death sentence passed on Condon was commuted
Edward O'Meagher Condon: Robert Kee *The Bold Fenian Men* (1989);
cf. **Last Words 1**

3 Mr Churchill is proud of Britain's stand alone, after France had fallen, and before America had entered the war. Could he not find in his heart the generosity to acknowledge that there is a small nation that stood alone, not for one year or two, but for several hundred years, against aggression; that endured spoliation, famines, massacres in endless succession; that was clubbed many times into insensibility but each time, on returning consciousness, took up the fight anew; a small nation that could never be got to accept defeat and has never surrendered her soul?
Eamon de Valera 1882–1975: radio broadcast, 16 May 1945

4 To gain that which is worth having, it may be necessary to lose everything else.
Bernadette Devlin McAliskey 1947– : preface to *The Price of My Soul* (1969)

5 There is a moral electricity in the continuous expression of public opinion concentrated on a single point.
Daniel O'Connell 1775–1847: R. F. Foster *Modern Ireland* (1988)

6 This is not a stand-off. They don't know what a stand-off is yet.
Robert Saulters: at Drumcree, 5 July 1998

7 One man that has a mind and knows it can always beat ten
men who haven't and don't.
George Bernard Shaw 1856–1950: *The Apple Cart* (1930)

8 She's as headstrong as an allegory on the banks of the Nile.
Richard Brinsley Sheridan 1751–1816: *The Rivals* (1775)

9 'Tis known by the name of perseverance in a good cause,—
and of obstinacy in a bad one.
Laurence Sterne 1713–68: *Tristram Shandy* (1759–67)

10 I have neglected no step to which my duty called me, and,
in that conduct, I will persist to the end.
Wolfe Tone 1763–98: diary, June 1798

Eamon de Valera (1882–1975)

1 The Long Fellow.
Anonymous: popular nickname for Eamon de Valera

2 How could one argue with a man who was always drawing
lines and circles to explain his position?
Michael Collins 1890–1922: attributed

3 Whenever I wanted to know what the Irish people wanted,
I had only to examine my own heart and it told me straight
off what the Irish people wanted.
Eamon de Valera 1882–1975: in Dáil Éireann, 6 January 1922

4 [Looking like] a cross between a corpse and a cormorant.
Oliver St John Gogarty 1878–1957: attributed

5 Negotiating with de Valera . . . is like trying to pick up
mercury with a fork.
to which de Valera replied, 'Why doesn't he use a spoon?'
David Lloyd George 1863–1945: M. J. MacManus *Eamon de Valera* (1944)

6 The constitutional Houdini of his generation.
F. S. L. Lyons 1923–83: Diana Norman *Terrible Beauty* (1987)

7 So long as he can work his mystique over Irishmen in all
parts of the world, Mr de Valera does not have to worry
about the rest of humanity.
as British Ambassador in Dublin
John Maffey 1877–1969: letter, May 1945

Diaries

1 I've kept political diaries ever since I went into
politics . . . I'd love to do a political memoir, but a lot of
people will have to be dead first.
Máire Geoghegan-Quinn 1950– : in *Irish Times* 6 November 1997

2 I never travel without my diary. One should always have
something sensational to read in the train.
Oscar Wilde 1854–1900: *The Importance of Being Earnest* (1895)

Dictionaries

1 How could I resist a man who could find recipes in a
dictionary?
Katy Hayes: *Forecourt* (1995)

2 I'm too weary going from one word to another in this
heavy dictionary which leads me on a wild goose chase
from this word to that word and all because the people who
wrote the dictionary don't want the likes of me to know
anything.
Frank McCourt 1930– : *Angela's Ashes* (1996)

3 Grammarians always search the world and dictionaries for
the words you want least in a language and give them to
you to learn, and leave out the words that you want every
day. I can talk about hawks and flails, scythes, rye and

barley, magicians, kings and fairies; but I couldn't find out
how to ask for an extra blanket or a clean plate or fork.
while learning Gaelic
Constance Markievicz 1868–1927: in 1920; Diana Norman *Terrible Beauty*
(1987)

4 A bad business, opening dictionaries; a thing I very rarely
   do. I try to make it a rule never to open my mouth,
   dictionaries, or hucksters' shops.
   Flann O'Brien 1911–66: *The Best of Myles* (1968)

5 I suppose that so long as there are people in the world, they
   will publish dictionaries defining what is unknown in terms
   of something equally unknown.
   Flann O'Brien 1911–66: *Myles Away from Dublin* (1990)

6 The books that are available to me are trash. I'm going to
   ask for a dictionary tomorrow.
   Bobby Sands 1954–81: diary, 16 March, 1981 in *Writings from Prison*
   (1998)

Donegal

1 No one who has not seen them can imagine the intense
   desolation of these Donegal moors. Not a man, not a beast,
   not a cabin was visible.
   Dinah Craik 1826–87: *An Unknown Country* (1887)

2 You know what a pull that place has on all of us. Flying
   back home from Dublin, over the mountains before the
   plane comes down, I realize that the landscape is always
   with me, in my head, in my music.
   Enya: in *Times* 6 November 1997

3 They sing about the hills of Oklahoma,
   The big Swiss mountains where the yodellers call,
   They sing about the black hills of Dakota,

But I'll settle for the hills of Donegal.
Johnny McCauley 1925– : 'I'll Settle for Old Ireland'

Dress

1 We condemn English-made evening dress, but evening
dress of Irish manufacture is just as Irish as a Donegal
cycling suit. Some people think we cannot be Irish unless
we always wear tweeds and only occasionally wear collars.
view of the magazine of the Gaelic League, An Claidheamh
Soluis
Anonymous: D. P. Moran *The Philosophy of Irish Ireland* (1905)

2 He can't think without his hat.
Samuel Beckett 1906–89: *Waiting for Godot* (1956)

3 She wore high black boots and a black leather beret pulled
down the side of her head. It would have looked really good
with big chunky flashy earrings. But for Christmas Mass
Clodagh showed restraint. She was unaware that her aunt
knelt with her head in her hands and asked the Mother of
God why a girl so good and helpful as Clodagh should dress
like a prostitute.
Maeve Binchy 1940– : *Circle of Friends* (1990)

4 Dare to be dowdy! that's my motto, because it comes to us
all—the dirty acrylic jumpers and the genteel trickle of piss
down our support tights.
Anne Enright 1962– : *The Portable Virgin* (1991)

5 A lady, if undressed at Church, looks silly,
One cannot be devout in dishabilly.
George Farquhar 1678–1707: *The Stage Coach* (1704)

6 Golden stockings you had on
In the meadow where you ran.
Oliver St John Gogarty 1878–1957: 'Golden Stockings'

7 I'm not a prostitute ... When have you ever seen a
prostitute in a black suit? This is nineteen ninety-seven.
Day-glo jackets are standard issue for hookers now.
Katy Hayes: *Curtains* (1997)

8 Even though she was only about thirty-five she wore awful
tweed skirts and flowery frocks that looked like family
heirlooms.
Marian Keyes: *Lucy Sullivan is Getting Married* (1997)

9 Isn't it great that they have things like that to talk about? I
think that I have three trouser suits to my name, but
people think that when you wear them that that's all you
ever wear.
responding to reports that she had been criticized for wearing
trouser suits on formal occasions
Mary McAleese 1951– : in *Irish Times* 28 February 1998

10 She favoured sensible shades:
Moss Green, Mustard, Beige.
I dreamt a robe of a colour
so pure it became a word.
Paula Meehan 1955– : 'The Pattern' (1991)

11 I like curious clothes. Back in Dublin I stayed in my riding
breeches, bought at a cheap shop in Dublin, and wore
them for weeks after, as an enjoyable symbol of the Irish
habit of life, until someone tactfully suggested I looked like
a stable boy.
V. S. Pritchett 1900–97: *Midnight Oil* (1971)

12 O Lord, Sir—when a heroine goes mad she always goes
into white satin.
Richard Brinsley Sheridan 1751–1816: *The Critic* (1779)

13 A brilliant blue garment that was an offence alike to her
convictions and her complexion.
Edith Œ. Somerville 1858–1949 and **Martin Ross** 1862–1915: *Further*
Experiences of an Irish R.M. (1908)

14 It is a fit house for an outlaw, a meet bed for a rebel, and
an apt cloak for a thief.
of the traditional Irish mantle
Edmund Spenser c.1552–99: *A View of the Present State of Ireland* (1596)

15 She wears her clothes, as if they were thrown on her with
a pitchfork.
Jonathan Swift 1667–1745: *Polite Conversation* (1738)

Drink see Food and Drink

Dublin

1 In Dublin's fair city,
Where the girls are so pretty,
I first set my eyes on sweet Molly Malone.
Anonymous: 'Cockles and Mussels' (19th-century street song)

2 And that old triangle
Went jingle-jangle
Along the banks of the Royal Canal.
Brendan Behan 1923–64: *The Quare Fellow* (1964)

3 Your first day in Dublin is always your worst.
John Berryman 1914–72: *The Dream Songs* (1990)

4 But also, Dublin had by now [in 1916] become a modern
city—as such, she was destined to be the first to see the
modern illusion crack . . . more than cracked, it shivered
across; not again to be mended in our lifetime.
Elizabeth Bowen 1899–1973: *The Shelbourne* (1951)

5 As I walked down through Dublin City
At the hour of twelve in the night,
Who should I spy but a Spanish lady
Washing her feet by candlelight.
Joseph Campbell 1879–1944: 'The Spanish Lady'

6 The Irish are the niggers of Europe . . . An' Dubliners are
the niggers of Ireland . . . An' the northside Dubliners are
the niggers o' Dublin.
Roddy Doyle 1958– : *The Commitments* (1993)

7 How was I to know that Dublin would expand northwards?
It had always expanded southwards before. When I was
young, Dublin ended at Donnycarney village.
Charles Haughey 1925– : attributed

8 You had to go to London to be a proper yuppie. We weren't
the right material here. Too much religion. Not enough
dress designers.
Katy Hayes: *Curtains* (1997)

9 BOSWELL: Should you not like to see Dublin, Sir?
JOHNSON: No, sir; Dublin is only a worse capital.
Samuel Johnson 1709–84: James Boswell *Life of Samuel Johnson* (1791)

10 Strumpet city in the sunset
Suckling the bastard brats of Scots, of Englishry, or
    Huguenot.
Brave sons breaking from the womb, wild sons fleeing from
    their Mother.
Wilful city of savage dreamers.
So old, so sick with memories!
Denis Johnston 1901–84: *The Old Lady Says 'No'* (1929)

11 Dear dirty Dublin.
James Joyce 1882–1941: *Ulysses* (1922)

12 riverrun, past Eve and Adam's, from swerve of shore to
bend of bay, brings us by a commodious vicus of
recirculation back to Howth Castle and Environs.
James Joyce 1882–1941: *Finnegans Wake* (1939)

13 My intention was to write a chapter of the moral history of
my country and I chose Dublin for the scene because that
city seemed to me the centre of paralysis.
of Dubliners
James Joyce 1882–1941: letter to Grant Richards on *Dubliners,* 5 May 1905

14 Dublin is a state of mind as much as a city.
Tom MacDonagh 1934– : *My Green Age* (1986)

15 Dublin city, with its bay and pleasant villas—city of
bellowing slaves, villas of genteel dastards.
John Mitchel 1815–75: *Jail Journal* (1854)

16 The long decay of Dublin that began with the Union.
George Moore 1852–1933: *Hail and Farewell* (1911–14)

17 He'd . . . settled into a life of Guinness, sarcasm and late
late nights, the kind of life that American academics think
real Dubliners lead.
Joseph O'Connor 1963– : *Cowboys and Indians* (1991)

18 At its centre it is a Georgian city in every line. But it is
Georgian with a difference. It is certainly not, never was, a
part of Georgian England: not even on the face of it. It is
about as Hanoverian as the heel of my boot.
Sean O'Faolain 1900–91: *An Irish Journey* (1940)

19 My sentimental regard for Ireland does not include the
capital.
George Bernard Shaw 1856–1950: *Immaturity* (1931)

20 St Patrick was a gentleman,
He came of decent people.
He built a church in Dublin town
And on it put a steeple.
Zozimus 1794–1846: 'St Patrick was a Gentleman'

Easter 1916

1 [Like] watching a stream of blood coming from beneath a
closed door.
a contemporary expression of the feelings evoked by news of the
executions after the Easter Rising
Anonymous: Robert Kee *Ourselves Alone* (1976)

2 It is not an *Irish* rebellion. It would be a pity if *ex post facto*
it became one, and was added to the long and melancholy
list of Irish rebellions.
final report before resigning as Chief Secretary for Ireland, 30
April 1916
Augustine Birrell 1850–1933: Robert Kee *Ourselves Alone* (1976)

3 While it lasted, the Rising was unpopular with almost all
the people of Ireland: the insurgents were seen as reckless,
destructive, crazy. It was what came after that changed the
feelings . . . Executions, wholesale arrests, deportations,
savoured to Ireland of Cromwellian reprisals: they were to
combine to plough 1916 deep in among other race-
memories in the country's heart.
Elizabeth Bowen 1899–1973: *The Shelbourne* (1951)

4 I say I am proud of their courage and if you were not so
dense and stupid, as some of you English people are, you
could have had these men fighting for you . . . It is not
murderers who are being executed; it is insurgents who
have fought a clean fight, however misguided, and it would
have been a damned good thing for you if your soldiers
were able to put up as good a fight as did those men in
Dublin.
John Dillon 1851–1927: speech in the British House of Commons, 11 May
1916

5 Irish history records the Easter Uprising. Let us hope that
this Easter records the Irish Settlement.
John Major 1943- : in *Times* 11 April 1998

6 The 1916 myth, like malaria, is in my bloodstream.
Dervla Murphy 1931- : *A Place Apart* (1978)

7 And then one day a couple of hundred Dublin workmen, a
couple of score of students, a handful of intellectuals, came
out into the streets of Dublin, and proclaimed an Irish
Republic.
Peadar O'Donnell 1893–1986: *The Knife* (1930)

8 The founding act of the modern Irish state—the 1916
Rising—is a religious as much as a political act, and
conceived by its leader, Patrick Pearse, as such. Its
symbolic occurrence at Easter, its conscious imagery of
blood sacrifice and redemption, shaped a specifically
Catholic political consciousness that belied the secular
Republican aims of many of the Revolutionaries.
Fintan O'Toole 1958- : *Black Hole, Green Card* (1994)

9 People will say hard things of us now, but we shall be
remembered by posterity and blessed by unborn
generations.
two days before his execution
Patrick Pearse 1879–1916: letter to his mother, 1 May 1916

10 There was clamour and confusion, that there was a
destroying battle between Irish and Strangers in Dublin.
news of the Easter Rising reaches the Blaskets
Peig Sayers 1873–1958: *An Old Woman's Reflections* (translated by Séamus
Ennis, 1962)

11 The shot Irishmen will now take their places beside Emmet
and the Manchester Martyrs in Ireland, and beside the
heroes of Poland and Serbia and Belgium in Europe; and
nothing in heaven or earth can prevent it.
George Bernard Shaw 1856–1950: letter to the *Daily News* May 1916

12 People say: 'Of course, they will be beaten.' The statement is almost a query, and they continue, 'but they are putting up a decent fight.' For being beaten does not matter greatly in Ireland, but not fighting does matter.
James Stephens 1882–1950: *The Insurrection in Dublin* (1916)

13 At this time of year . . . it is prudent to expect, every time you open a quality English newspaper, to be confronted by an attack on the Irish revolution by a leading Irish intellectual—a ritual now almost as inevitable as Easter eggs . . . In the eyes of the British establishment . . . a willingness to attack the Easter Rising is evidence of an unquestionably modern disposition.
John Waters 1955– : in *Irish Times* 7 April 1998

14 I write it out in a verse—
MacDonagh and MacBride
And Connolly and Pearse
Now and in time to be,
Wherever green is worn,
Are changed, changed utterly:
A terrible beauty is born.
W. B. Yeats 1865–1939: 'Easter, 1916' (1921)

Education

1 Mother Bernard thought that Brother Healy had life easy. Boys were so simple and straightforward. They weren't devious like girls. Brother Healy thought it must be a very easy number just to have little girls in a uniform. They didn't write terrible words on the bicycle shed and beat each other black and blue in the yard.
Maeve Binchy 1940– : *The Glass Lake* (1994)

2 Example is the school of mankind, and they will learn at no other.
Edmund Burke 1729–97: *Two Letters on the Proposals for Peace with the Regicide Directory* (9th ed., 1796)

3 What is this fear of a Catholic University? . . . Do you think that the Catholics of Ireland will be worse off with the enlightenment of a university education than they are now when they are deprived of it?
Edward Carson 1854–1935: speech, March 1914

4 A boarding school is designed to distort its pupils' perspective. There are no outside concerns or demands to dilute the intensity of the school experience so everything which happens in it assumes an exaggerated importance.
Bob Geldof 1954– : *Is That It?* (1986)

5 Work, work, work. It's impossible to get the boys to do a decent day's work these days.
view of a school principal on why girls outstripped boys in the Leaving Certificate
J. J. Harvey: in *Irish Times* 23 August 1997 'Quotes of the Week'

6 It was then that Mr Furriskey surprised and, indeed, delighted his companions, not to mention our two friends, by a little act which at once demonstrated his resource and his generous urge to spread enlightenment. With the end of his costly malacca cane, he cleared away the dead leaves at his feet and drew the outline of three dials or clock faces on the fertile soil . . . How to read the gas-meter, he announced.
Flann O'Brien 1911–66: *At Swim-Two-Birds* (1939)

7 The most important thing I would learn in school was that almost everything I would learn in school would be utterly useless. When I was fifteen I knew the principal industries of the Ruhr Valley, the underlying causes of World War One and what Peig Sayers had for her dinner every day . . . What I wanted to know when I was fifteen was the best way to chat up girls. That is what I still want to know.
Joseph O'Connor 1963– : *The Secret World of the Irish Male* (1994)

8 He who can, does. He who cannot, teaches.
George Bernard Shaw 1856–1950: *Man and Superman* (1903)

9 Education is an admirable thing, but it is well to remember
from time to time that nothing that is worth knowing can
be taught.
Oscar Wilde 1854–1900: *Intentions* (1891)

Elegy

1 *Cad a dhéanfaimid feasta gan adhmad?*
Tá deireadh na gcoillte ar lár.
Níl trácht ar Chill Chais ná a teaghlach
Is ní cluinfear a cling go brách.

What shall we do for timber?
The last of the woods is down.
Kilcash and the house of its glory
And the bell of the house are gone.
Anonymous: 'Chill Chais [Kilcash]' (18th century poem translated by Frank
O'Connor)

2 Tara is grass, and see how Troy is now. And the English
themselves—maybe they might die!
Anonymous: 18th century (from the Irish)

3 They give birth astride a grave, the light gleams an instant,
then it's night once more.
Samuel Beckett 1906–89: *Waiting for Godot* (1953)

4 She stepped away from me, and she moved through the
fair.
Padraic Colum 1881–1972: 'She Moved Through the Fair'

5 I walked through Ballinderry in the springtime,
When the bud was on the tree,
And I said, in every fresh-ploughed field beholding
The sowers striding free,
Scattering broadcast forth the corn in golden plenty
On the quick, seed-clasping soil
Even such, this day, among the fresh-stirred hearts of Erin,

Thomas Davis, is thy toil.
Samuel Ferguson 1810–86: 'Lament for the Death of Thomas Davis'

6　I thought of you tonight, *a leanbh,* lying there in your long
　　barrow,
　colder and dumber than a fish by Francisco de Herrera.
　Paul Muldoon 1951– : 'Incantata' (1994)

7　*Ní dóigh liom go mbeidh mo leithéid arís ann.*
　I do not believe there will ever be the like of me again.
　Flann O'Brien 1911–66: *An Béal Bocht* (The Poor Mouth, 1941)

8　*Da mbeadh an codladh so i gCill na Dromad ort*
　no in uaigh san Iarthar
　mo bhrón do bhogfadh, cé gur mhór mo dhocar
　is ni bheinn id' dhiaidh air.

　If this sleep was on you in Cill na Dromad
　Or some grave in the West
　it would soften my sorrow, though great my affliction,
　and I'd not complain.
　Padraig O hEigeartaigh b. 1871: 'Ochón! A Dhonncha' (lament for a
　drowned child, *c.*1906); Fintan O'Toole *The Ex-Isle of Erin* (1997)

9　*Ní bheidh a leithéid aris ann.*
　Their likes won't be here again.
　Peig Sayers 1873–1958: expression customarily used by Peig Sayers and
　the other autobiographical Blasket writers, Maurice O'Sullivan and Tomás Ó
　Criomhthain

10　Oh my grief, I've lost him surely. I've lost the only Playboy
　　of the Western World.
　John Millington Synge 1871–1909: *The Playboy of the Western World*
　(1907)

11　Man is in love and loves what vanishes,
　　What more is there to say?
　W. B. Yeats 1865–1939: 'Nineteen Hundred and Nineteen' (1921)

Emigration see also Exile, Ireland and America

1 This was a distinguished crew for one ship; for it is indeed
certain that the sea had not supported, and the winds had
not wafted from Ireland, in modern times, a party of one
ship who would have been more illustrious, or noble in
point of genealogy, or more renowned for deeds, valour or
high achievements.
*of the Flight of the Earls (Hugh O'Neill, Earl of Tyrone, and
Rory O'Donnell, Earl of Tyrconnell) from Rathmullen, Donegal,
on 14 September 1607*
Annals of the Four Masters: compilation of annals recording events in
Ireland from the earliest times to 1616

2 *Anois tá an choill á gearradh,*
triallfaimíd thar caladh,
's a Sheáin Uí Dhuibhir a' Ghleanna
tá tú gan game.

Now the woods are being cut down
We'll sail over the sea,
And my Sean O'Dwyer of the Glen
Your game is gone.
Anonymous: 'Seán O Duibhir a' Ghleanna' (c.1650)

3 I lately took the notion
To cross the briny ocean
And I'm off to Philadelphia in the morning.
Anonymous: 19th century music-hall song

4 *Is chuaigh sé ar bórd loinge, 'sé Jimmy mo mhíle stór.*

And he went off by ship, my thousand-fold-loved Jimmy.
Anonymous: 19th century traditional song

5 They set my roof on fire with their cursed English spleen,
And that's another reason why I left old Skibbereen.
Anonymous: song, 19th century

6 To seek a home, far o'er the foam,
On the shores of Amerikay.
Anonymous: 'The Shores of Amerikay' (song, 19th century)

7 Imagine how they stood there, what they stood with
that their possessions may become our power.

Cardboard. Iron. Their hardships parcelled in them.
Eavan Boland 1944– : 'The Emigrant Irish'

8 As for us that are here, we are glad to see the day wherein
the countenance and majesty of the law and civil
government hath banished Tyrone out of Ireland, which
the best army in Europe, and the expense of two million
sterling pounds, had not been able to bring to pass.
John Davies 1569–1626: attributed; preface to *Annals of the Kingdom of
Ireland* (ed. John O'Donovan, 1851)

9 No longer shall our children, like our cattle, be brought up
for export.
Eamon de Valera 1882–1975: speech in Dáil Éireann, 1934

10 Is the cabin still left standing? Has the rich man need of all?
Is the children's birthplace taken now within the new park
wall?
Helen, Lady Dufferin 1807–67: 'The Emigrant Ship'

11 The country wears their going like a scar.
Today their relatives save to support and
Send others in planes for the new diaspora.
Sean Dunne 1956–97: 'Letter from Ireland' (1991)

12 It was her settled purpose to make the Irish and Ireland
ridiculous and contemptible to Lord Colambre; to disgust
him with his native country; to make him abandon the
wish of residing on his own estate. To confirm him an
absentee was her object.
Maria Edgeworth 1767–1849: *The Absentee* (1812)

13 The Irish were not English. God had sent them to Canada
to keep people from marrying Protestants.
Mavis Gallant 1922– : *Across the Bridge* (1993)

14 No one who has any self-respect stays in Ireland, but flees
afar as though from a country that has undergone the
visitation of an angered Jove.
James Joyce 1882–1941: *Ireland, Island of Saints and Sages*, lecture, 27
April 1907

15 Asked me was it true I was going away and why. Told him
the shortest way to Tara was *via* Holyhead.
James Joyce 1882–1941: *A Portrait of the Artist as a Young Man* (1916)

16 For many, emigration still means getting on the boat with
a tenner in your pocket.
John M. Kelly 1931– : comment, 1989

17 Disappearance & death
of a world, as down Lough Swilly
the great ship, encumbered with nobles,
swells its sails for Europe:
The Flight of the Earls.
John Montague 1929– : *The Rough Field* (1971)

18 Why Brownlee left, and where he went,
Is a mystery even now.
Paul Muldoon 1951– : 'Why Brownlee Left' (1980)

19 Emigration is an utterly ingrained part of the Irish psyche.
Growing up in Dublin, you expect emigration to happen to
you, like puberty.
Joseph O'Connor 1963– : *The Secret World of the Irish Male* (1994)

20 I've said and written a lot about emigration. But maybe
soon I'll be writing The Flight of Earls in reverse—about
everyone coming back home again.
Liam Reilly: in *Irish Post* 23 August 1997

21 I brought up my children to read and write, and there
never were children with cleverer heads for their books;
but there was no place for them in Ireland, and they have
all gone to America but one, and soon he too will be gone.
Peig Sayers 1873–1958: *The Western Island* (1944)

22 It'd be a pity surely to have your like sailing from Mayo to
the Western World.
John Millington Synge 1871–1909: *The Playboy of the Western World*
(1907)

Endurance

1 You must go on, I can't go on, life goes on.
Samuel Beckett 1906–89: *The Unnamable* (1975)

2 And this the burthen of his song,
For ever used to be,
I care for nobody, not I,
If no one cares for me.
Isaac Bickerstaffe 1733–c.1808: *Love in a Village* (1762)

3 The true man spurns the helot's song:
The freeman's friend is self-reliance!
Thomas Davis 1814–45: 'Self-Reliance' (1845)

4 Half-pleased, contented will I be,
Contented, half to please.
Frances Greville c.1724–89: 'A Prayer for Indifference' (1759)

5 If they keep me here for may years I will forget what the
fair outer world is like. Gazing on grey stones, my eyes will
grow stony.
John Mitchel 1815–75: *Jail Journal* (1854)

6 I did not come here to complain.
in prison, c.1870, while serving a sentence for subversion
John O'Leary 1830–1907: Nicholas Mansergh *The Irish Question*
(ed. 3, 1975)

7 The stoical scheme of supplying our wants, by lopping off
our desires, is like cutting off our feet when we want shoes.
Jonathan Swift 1667–1745: *Thoughts on Various Subjects* (1711)

Enemies see also Hate

1 He that wrestles with us strengthens our nerves, and
sharpens our skill. Our antagonist is our helper.
Edmund Burke 1729–97: *Reflections on the Revolution in France* (1790)

2 Next to the British government, the worst enemy Ireland
ever had—or rather the most fatal friend.
of Daniel O'Connell
John Mitchel 1815–75: *The Last Conquest of Ireland (Perhaps)* (1861)

3 When a man takes a farm from which another has been
evicted, you must show him on the roadside when you
meet him; you must show him in the streets of the town;
you must show him in the fair and the market-place; and
even in the house of worship, by leaving him severely
alone—by putting him into a moral Coventry, by isolating
him from his kind as if he were a leper of old.
initiation of the practice of boycotting
Charles Stewart Parnell 1846–91: speech, 19 September 1880

4 A man cannot be too careful in the choice of his enemies.
Oscar Wilde 1854–1900: *The Picture of Dorian Gray* (1891)

England and the English see also Britain,
Ireland and
England

1 But praise God that we are white,
And better still are English,
Tea and toast and muffin rings,
Old ladies with stern faces,
And the captains and the kings.
Brendan Behan 1923–64: 'The Captains and the Kings'

2 The English always have their wars in someone else's
country.
Brendan Behan 1923–64: attributed

3 Tonight
with London's ghost
I walk the streets
As easy as November fog
Among the reeds.
Patrick Galvin 1927– : 'Christ in London'

4 The English don't have a culture, not any more. The place
is full of traditions from other countries; Irish, West Indian,
Indian.
Shane McGowan 1957– : in *Irish Times* 13 November 1997

5 The people of England are never so happy as when you tell
them they are ruined.
Arthur Murphy 1727–1805: *The Upholsterer, or What News* (1757)

6 The Englishman has all the qualities of a poker except its
occasional warmth.
Daniel O'Connell 1775–1847: attributed

7 The captain is in his bunk, drinking bottled ditch-water;
and the crew is gambling in the forecastle. She will strike
and sink and split. Do you think the laws of God will be
suspended in favour of England because you were born in
it?
George Bernard Shaw 1856–1950: *Heartbreak House* (1919)

8 Englishmen never will be slaves: they are free to do
whatever the Government and public opinion allow them
to do.
George Bernard Shaw 1856–1950: *Man and Superman* (1903)

9 There is nothing so bad or so good that you will not find
Englishmen doing it; but you will never find an Englishman
in the wrong. He does everything on principle. He fights
you on patriotic principles; he robs you on business

principles; he enslaves you on imperial principles; he
bullies you on manly principles; he supports his king on
loyal principles and cuts off his king's head on republican
principles.
George Bernard Shaw 1856–1950: *The Man of Destiny* (1898)

10 The real weakness of England lies, not in incomplete
armaments or unfortified coasts, not in the poverty that
creeps through sunless lanes, or the drunkenness that
brawls in loathsome courts, but simply in the fact that her
ideals are emotional and not intellectual.
Oscar Wilde 1854–1900: *The Critic as Artist* (1891) pt. 2

11 The English have a miraculous power of turning wine into
water.
Oscar Wilde 1854–1900: *In Conversation*

Envy

1 Familiarity breeds envy, and that conspiracy, and that
skulduggery.
Sean O'Faolain 1900–91: *Foreign Affairs* (1976)

2 I will not stand for the ill-informed criticism and the
unctuous envy of these people who failed to make it to
these benches, and made it to the columns of a certain
newspaper instead.
*as Finance Minister, addressing the Press Gallery in Leinster
House*
Ruairi Quinn 1946– : speech in the Dáil, 1996

3 An invariable hallmark of the begrudger is that he can
create nothing.
Albert Reynolds 1933– : in 1991, attributed

4 But was there ever dog that praised his fleas?
W. B. Yeats 1865–1939: 'To a Poet, Who would have Me Praise certain bad
Poets, Imitators of His and of Mine' (1910)

Epitaphs

1 That volley which we have just heard is the only speech
which it is proper to make over the grave of a dead Fenian.
at the funeral of Thomas Ashe in 1917
Michael Collins 1890–1922: Ulick O'Connor *The Troubles* (rev. ed., 1996)

2 Let no man write my epitaph . . . When my country takes
her place among the nations of the earth, *then*, and *not till
then*, let my epitaph be written.
Robert Emmet 1778–1803: speech from the dock when condemned to
death, 19 September 1803. cf. **Independence 5**

3 Maguire, I believe, suggested a blackbird
And over your grave a phrase from Euripides
Which suits you down to the ground, like this churchyard
With its play of shadows, its humane perspective.
at the grave of Louis MacNeice
Derek Mahon 1941– : 'In Carrowdore Churchyard'

4 Where fierce indignation can no longer tear his heart.
Swift's epitaph
Jonathan Swift 1667–1745: S. Leslie *The Skull of Swift* (1928)

5 On limestone quarried near the spot
By his command these words are cut:
*Cast a cold eye
On life, on death.
Horseman, pass by!*
W. B. Yeats 1865–1939: 'Under Ben Bulben' (1939)

Excess and Moderation

1 You overdo it with your carrots.
Samuel Beckett 1906–89: *Waiting for Godot* (1955)

2 I know many have been taught to think that moderation,
in a case like this, is a sort of treason.
Edmund Burke 1729–97: *Letter to the Sheriffs of Bristol* (1777)

3 It is the nature of all greatness not to be exact.
Edmund Burke 1729–97: *On American Taxation* (1775)

4 She lays it on with a trowel.
William Congreve 1670–1729: *The Double Dealer* (1694)

5 I hadn't meant to overdo it, I had simply overestimated the quality of the cocaine I had taken.
Marian Keyes: *Rachel's Holiday* (1997)

6 Moderation is fatal. Too much is as good as a banquet, enough is as bad as a meal.
Mícheál Mac Liammóir 1899–1978: *An Oscar of No Importance* (1968)

7 Let your precept be, Be Easy.
Richard Steele 1672–1729: in *The Tatler* 11 July 1710

8 Moderation is a fatal thing, Lady Hunstanton. Nothing succeeds like excess.
Oscar Wilde 1854–1900: *A Woman of No Importance* (1893)

Execution

1 In Mountjoy jail one Monday morning
High upon the gallows tree,
Kevin Barry gave his young life
For the cause of liberty.
Kevin Barry (1902–20), the first IRA man to be executed in the Anglo-Irish War
Anonymous: 'Kevin Barry', 20th century ballad

2 They have murdered Henry Joy.
Henry Joy McCracken (1767–98), United Irishman, executed 17 July 1798
Anonymous: 'Henry Joy' (Belfast street ballad, c.1800)

3 When he came to the nubbling chit,
He was tucked up so neat and so pretty.
The rumbler jogged off from his feet,

And he died with his face to the city.
Anonymous: 'The Night Before Larry was Stretched' (song, 19th century)

4 How hard is my fortune, and vain my repining.
The strong rope of fate for this young neck is twining.
Jeremiah John Callanan 1795–1829: 'The Convict of Clonmel'

5 Young Rody MacCorley goes to die
On the Bridge of Toome today.
Ethna Carbery 1866–1902: 'Rody MacCorley' (1902)

6 It is a strange, strange fate, and now, as I stand face to face
with death, I feel just as if they were going to kill a boy. For
I feel like a boy—and my hands are so free from blood and
my heart always so compassionate and pitiful that I cannot
comprehend that anyone wants to hang me.
Roger Casement 1864–1916: diary note found after his execution, 3
August 1916

7 It seems perfectly simple and inevitable, like lying down
after a long day's work.
Erskine Childers 1870–1922: letter to his wife, November 1922

8 There are certain things which are not jokes, Gogarty, and
one of them is my hanging.
*after Lord Dunsany's arrest by the Black and Tans in 1921,
Oliver St John Gogarty had joked about the peer's privilege of
being hanged with a silken rope*
Lord Dunsany 1878–1957: Ulick O'Connor *Oliver St John Gogarty*

9 *Fils de Saint Louis, montez au ciel.*
Son of Saint Louis, ascend to heaven.
to Louis XVI as he mounted the steps of the guillotine, 1793
L'Abbé Edgeworth de Firmont 1745–1807: attributed

10 No more hanging? . . . What's this country coming to!
Patrick McCabe 1955– : *The Butcher Boy* (1992)

11 I wish you had the decency to shoot me.
on hearing of the commutation of her death sentence
Constance Markievicz 1868–1927: Diana Norman *Terrible Beauty* (1987)

Execution

12 This is the death I should have asked for if God had given me the choice of all deaths—to die a soldier's death for Ireland and freedom.
Patrick Pearse 1879–1916: letter to his mother, May 1916

13 I am sorry it was necessary.
on the execution of Louis XVI, 21 January 1793
Wolfe Tone 1763–98: Oliver Knox *Rebels and Informers* (1997)

14 But it is not sweet with nimble feet
To dance upon the air!
Oscar Wilde 1854–1900: *The Ballad of Reading Gaol* (1898)

15 For the man they hanged at Downpatrick Gaol
Was the Man from God-knows-where!
Thomas Russell (1767–1803), United Irishman, executed 21 October 1803
Florence M. Wilson: 'The Man from God-Knows-Where'

Exile see also Emigration, Ireland and America

1 Adieu to Belashanny! where I was bred and born;
Go where I may, I'll think of you as sure as night and morn.
William Allingham 1824–89: 'The Winding Banks of Erne'

2 And over the seas are Ireland's best,
The Dukes and the Burkes, Prince Charlie and the rest,
And Captain Talbot their ranks adorning,
And Patrick Sarsfield, Ireland's darling.
Anonymous: 'Farewell to Patrick Sarsfield' (1691, translated Frank O'Connor)

3 There was a wild colonial boy,
Jack Duggan was his name,
He was born and reared in Ireland,
In a place called Castlemaine.
Anonymous: 'The Wild Colonial Boy', 19th century Australian song

4 But the land of their heart's hope they never saw more,
   For in far, foreign fields, from Dunkirk to Belgrade
   Lie the soldiers and chiefs of the Irish Brigade.
   Thomas Davis 1814–45: 'The Battle-Eve of the Brigade' (1845)

5 Blinding in Paris, for his party-piece
   Joyce named the shops along O'Connell Street
   And on Iona Colmcille sought ease
   By wearing Irish mould next to his feet.
   Seamus Heaney 1939– : 'Gravities' (1980)

6 Yet like Lir's children banished to the waters
   our hearts still listen to the landward bells.
   John Hewitt 1907–87: 'An Irishman in Coventry'

7 She said, 'Not mine, not mine, that fame;
   Far over sea, far over land,
   Cast forth like rubbish from my shores,
   They won it yonder, sword in hand.'
   Emily Lawless 1845–1913: 'After Aughrim'

8 An exile in my circumstances is a branch cut from its tree;
   it is dead but it has an affectation of life.
   John Mitchel 1815–75: *Jail Journal* (1854)

9 She is far from the land where her young hero sleeps,
   And lovers are round her, sighing:
   But coldly she turns from their gaze, and weeps,
   For her heart in his grave is lying.
   of Sarah Curran, sweetheart of Robert Emmet
   Thomas Moore 1779–1852: *Irish Melodies* (1807) 'She is far from the land'

10 Antrim hills and the wet rain fallin'
   Whiles ye are nearer than snow-tops keen:
   Dreams o' the night and a night-wind callin',
   What is the half o' the world between?
   Moira O'Neill 1870?–1951: 'Lookin' Back'

Exile

11 Deep in Canadian woods we've met,
   From one bright island flown.
   Timothy Daniel Sullivan 1827–1914: 'Song from the Backwoods'

12 What captivity was to the Jews, exile has been to the Irish.
   America and American influence has educated them.
   Oscar Wilde 1854–1900: in *Pall Mall Gazette* 13 April 1889

Experience

1 And anything that happened to me afterwards, I never felt
   the same about again.
   Frank O'Connor 1903–66: *Guests of the Nation* (1931)

2 Experience is the name every one gives to their mistakes.
   Oscar Wilde 1854–1900: *Lady Windermere's Fan* (1892)

Failure

1 For you must rise up early
   In the clear grey light of dawn,
   And I know you won't be able
   To plough the rocks of Bawn.
   Anonymous: 'The Rocks of Bawn', 19th century song

2 It is the usual thing for a herd led by a mare to find itself
   strayed and destroyed.
   *comment of Fergus Mac Roich on the defeat of Queen Medb's
   Connacht forces*
   Anonymous: *Táin Bó Cuailnge* ('Cattle Raid of Cooley', central poem of the
   Ulster Cycle)

3 Events of great formal brilliance but indeterminate purport.
Samuel Beckett 1906–89: *Watt* (1953)

4 Ever tried. Ever failed. No matter. Try again. Fail again. Fail better.
Samuel Beckett 1906–89: *Worstward Ho* (1983)

5 Come forth, Lazarus! And he came fifth and lost the job.
James Joyce 1882–1941: *Ulysses* (1922)

6 Nothing in life brings you back to reality like arriving at a bookshop in a rainy Northern English town [on an author tour] to find the pallid and overworked staff trying to spread out and look like a crowd.
Joseph O'Connor 1963– : *The Secret World of the Irish Male* (1994)

7 Do not remember my failures,
But remember my fate.
Patrick Pearse 1879–1916: 'The Fool'

8 I did not realise, as Connolly and the others did, the power that an intrepid failure has to rouse Ireland.
Esther Roper 1868–1938: *The Prison Letters of Constance Markievicz* (1934)

9 The triumph of failure.
of the Easter Rising
Desmond Ryan 1893–1964: *The Rising* (1949); closing line

Fame

1 'Damned to fame' like in the Dunciad.
of himself
Samuel Beckett 1906–89: letter to James Knowlson, 20 May 1981

2 There's no such thing as bad publicity except your own obituary.
Brendan Behan 1923–64: Dominic Behan *My Brother Brendan* (1965)

3 I've put in so many enigmas and puzzles that it will keep
the professors busy for centuries arguing over what I
meant, and that's the only way of insuring one's
immortality.
of Ulysses
James Joyce 1882–1941: Richard Ellmann *James Joyce* (1982)

4 Ireland is so hard up for celebrities that it wildly over-uses
the few it has, and, as far as her treasured privacy was
concerned, I was a much a local landmark as the
proverbial begging ass.
Hugh Leonard 1926– : *Rover and Other Cats* (1992)

5 Oh! breathe not his name, let it sleep in the shade,
Where cold and unhonoured his relics are laid.
Thomas Moore 1779–1852: *Irish Melodies* (1807) 'Oh! breathe not his
name'

6 This Peter was a mouthful among the parishes. He was
important.
Peig Sayers 1873–1958: *An Old Woman's Reflections* (translated by Séamus
Ennis, 1962)

7 Martyrdom . . . the only way in which a man can become
famous without ability.
George Bernard Shaw 1856–1950: *The Devil's Disciple* (1901)

8 We carved not a line, and we raised not a stone—
But we left him alone with his glory.
Charles Wolfe 1791–1823: 'The Burial of Sir John Moore at Corunna'
(1817)

The Family see also Parents

1 We begin our public affections in our families. No cold
relation is a zealous citizen.
Edmund Burke 1729–97: *Reflections on the Revolution in France* (1790)

2 There is no more sombre enemy of good art than the pram
in the hall.
Cyril Connolly 1903–74: *Enemies of Promise* (1938)

3 Except for Margaret, who hadn't got past the qualifying
rounds, the position of Least Favourite Daughter passed
round from one of us to the next on a rotating basis, like
the presidency of the EU.
Marian Keyes: *Rachel's Holiday* (1997)

4 The black dog was the only intelligent member of the
family. He died a few years later. He was poisoned, and no
one will convince me it wasn't suicide.
Hugh Leonard 1926– : *Da* (1973)

5 I suppose it's very embarrassing to have a relation that gets
into jail and fights in revolutions that you are not in
sympathy with.
Constance Markievicz 1868–1927: Diana Norman *Terrible Beauty* (1987)

6 The typical west of Ireland family consists of father,
mother, twelve children and resident Dutch anthropologist.
Flann O'Brien 1911–66: attributed

7 I decided at an early age that my own family—whom I
loved very much—wasn't Irish enough for me so I adopted
a family to supply the missing Irish ingredient.
Kate Cruise O'Brien 1948–98: 'The Missing Ingredient'

8 Then the sniper turned over the dead body and looked into
his brother's face.
Sean O'Faolain 1900–91: 'The Sniper'

9 I call it a criminal thing in anyone's great-great-
grandfather to rear up a preposterous troop of sons and
plant them all out in his own country . . . I detest
collaterals. Blood may be thicker than water, but it is also a
great deal nastier.
Edith Œ. Somerville 1858–1949 and **Martin Ross** 1862–1915: *Some
Experiences of an Irish R.M.* (1899)

10 I wish either my father or my mother, or indeed both of them, as they were in duty both equally bound to it, had minded what they were about when they begot me.
Laurence Sterne 1713–68: *Tristram Shandy* (1759–67)

11 Relations are simply a tedious pack of people, who haven't got the remotest knowledge of how to live, nor the smallest instinct about when to die.
Oscar Wilde 1854–1900: *The Importance of Being Earnest* (1895)

Famine

1 Those who governed in London at the time failed their people through standing by while a crop failure turned into a massive human tragedy. We must not forget such a dreadful event. It is also right that we should pay tribute to the ways in which the Irish people have triumphed in the face of this catastrophe.
Tony Blair 1953– : official statement, 1 June 1997, read at the Famine commemoration at Millstreet, County Cork.

2 Read your own hearts and Ireland's present story,
Then feed her famine fat with Wellesley's glory.
Lord Byron 1788–1824: *Don Juan* (1819–24)

3 Clay is the word and clay is the flesh
Where the potato-gatherers like mechanized scarecrows move
Along the side-fall of the hill—Maguire and his men.
Patrick Kavanagh 1904–67: 'The Great Hunger' (1947)

4 The cry of the whole people is loud for bread; God knows what will be the consequence; many are starved, and I am afraid many more will be.
view of the Archbishop of Dublin in 1720
William King 1650–1729: Daniel Corkery *The Hidden Ireland* (1925)

5 There's famine in the land, its grip is tightening still!
There's trouble, black and bitter, on every side I glance.
Emily Lawless 1845–1913: 'An Exile's Mother'

6 Families, when all was eaten and no hope left, took their
last look at the sun, built up their cottage doors, that none
might see them die nor hear their groans, and were found
weeks afterwards, skeletons on their own hearth.
John Mitchel 1815–75: *Jail Journal* (1854)

7 A NATION is starving.
Daniel O'Connell 1775–1847: in 1846; Charles Chevenix Trench *The Great Dan* (1984)

8 Take it from us, every grain,
We were made for your to drain;
Black starvation let us feel,
England must not want a meal!

When our rotting roots shall fail,
When the hunger pangs assail,
Ye'll have of Irish corn your fill—
We'll have grass and nettles still!
John O'Hagan 1822–90: 'Famine and Exportation' (*c.*1847)

9 Out of every corner of the woods and glens they came
creeping forth upon their hands, for their legs could not
bear them; they looked like anatomies of death, they spake
like ghosts crying out of their graves; they did eat the dead
carrions . . . insomuch as the very carcases they spared not
to scrape out of their graves; and, if they found a plot of
watercresses or shamrocks, there they flocked as to a feast.
Edmund Spenser *c.*1552–99: *A View of the Present State of Ireland* (1596)

10 If the Devil himself had exercised all his ingenuity to invent
a scheme which should destroy the country, he could not
have contrived anything more effectual than the principles

and practices upon which landed property has been held and managed.

to John Bright in 1849, after working for famine relief in the West of Ireland

Count Strzelecki: R. A. J. Walling (ed.) *The Diaries of John Bright* (1930)

11 I will venture to affirm, that the three seasons wherein our corn has miscarried did not more contribute to our present misery, than one spoonful of water thrown upon a rat already drowned would contribute to his death.

Jonathan Swift 1667–1745: *A Proposal that all the Ladies and Women of Ireland should appear constantly in Irish Manufactures* (1729)

12 Weary men, what reap ye?—'Golden corn for the
    stranger.'
What sow ye?—'Human corses that wait for the Avenger.'
Fainting forms, all hunger-stricken, what see you in the
    offing?
'Stately ships to bear our food away amid the stranger's
    scoffing.'

Jane Francesca Wilde ('Speranza') 1821–96: 'The Famine Year'

Fate

1 Hanging and marriage, you know, go by Destiny.
George Farquhar 1678–1707: *Love and a Bottle* (1698)

2 Fate is not an eagle, it creeps like a rat.
Elizabeth Bowen 1899–1973: *The House in Paris* (1935)

3 I am ready for my fourteen years' ordeal, and for whatsoever the same may bring me—toil, sickness, ignominy, death. Fate, thou art defied.
John Mitchel 1815–75: *Jail Journal* (1854)

4 A shudder in the loins engenders there
The broken wall, the burning roof and tower
And Agamemnon dead.
W. B. Yeats 1865–1939: 'Leda and the Swan' (1928)

5 Why, what could she have done being what she is?
   Was there another Troy for her to burn?
   W. B. Yeats 1865–1939: 'No Second Troy' (1910)

Fear

1 No passion so effectually robs the mind of all its powers of
   acting and reasoning as fear.
   Edmund Burke 1729–97: *On the Sublime and Beautiful* (1757)

2 Pity is the feeling which arrests the mind in the presence of
   whatsoever is grave and constant in human sufferings and
   unites it with the human sufferer. Terror is the feeling
   which arrests the mind in the presence of whatsoever is
   grave and constant in human sufferings and unites it with
   the secret cause.
   James Joyce 1882–1941: *A Portrait of the Artist as a Young Man* (1916)

The Fenians

1 Glory O, Glory O, to the bold Fenian men!
   Anonymous: 'The Bold Fenian Men'

2 Didn't the bishops and priests . . . denounce the Fenian
   movement from the pulpit and in the confession box?
   James Joyce 1882–1941: *A Portrait of the Artist as a Young Man* (1916)

3 But God (Who our nurse declared
   Guards British dominions)
   Sent down a deep fall of snow
   And scattered the Fenians.
   Alice Milligan 1866–1953: 'When I Was a Little Girl'

4 But one little rebel there,
   Watching all with laughter,
   Thought 'When the Fenians come
   I'll rise and go after.'
   Alice Milligan 1866–1953: 'When I Was a Little Girl'

5 Eternity is not long enough nor hell hot enough for such
  miscreants.
  view of the Bishop of Kerry
  David Moriarty 1814–77: sermon, February 1867

6 I do not believe, and I never shall believe, that any murder
  was committed at Manchester.
  objecting to the expression 'the Manchester murders' in alluding
  to the escape of the Fenians, Kelly and Deasy, in 1867
  Charles Stewart Parnell 1846–91: in the House of Commons, June 1876

Flags and Emblems

1 It's old but it is beautiful, its colours they are fine,
  It was worn at Derry, Aughrim, Enniskillen and the Boyne.
  My father wore it when a youth in bygone days of yore,
  So on the Twelfth I proudly wear the sash my father wore.
  Anonymous: 'The Sash My Father Wore', traditional Orange song

2 The National Flag is an uncrowned gold harp on a plain
  green background.
  Anonymous: in *Irish Volunteer* 18 March 1916

3 The shamrock is by law forbid to grow on Irish ground.
  Anonymous: 'The Wearin' o' the Green' (*c.*1795 ballad)

4 No symbols where none intended.
  Samuel Beckett 1906–89: *Watt* (1953)

5 Now may be the time to show whether all those ceremonies
  and forms which are practised by the Orange Lodges are
  really living symbols or only idle meaningless ceremonies.
  Lord Randolph Churchill 1849–94: in 1886; Nicholas Mansergh *The Irish
  Question* (ed. 3, 1975)

6 The people's flag is deepest red;
  It shrouded oft our martyred dead.
  James M. Connell 1852–1929: 'The Red Flag' (1889)

7 Viva la the New Brigade!
   Viva la the Old One, too!
   Viva la, the Rose shall fade,
   And the shamrock shine for ever new.
   Thomas Davis 1814–45: 'Clare's Dragoons' (1845)

8 I have decided that, apart from the shamrock, the President
   should not wear emblems or symbols of any kind.
   *on her decision not to wear a poppy at her inauguration on 11
   November 1997*
   Mary McAleese 1951– : in *Guardian* 6 November 1997

9 Green . . . is associated with too many national tragedies,
   including 1798, the Famine and the current Irish rugby
   team.
   Frank McNally: in *Irish Times* 11 March 1998

10 Flags and emblems are strange things and are as lethal to
    toy with as a mercury switch booby trap.
    Kevin Myers 1947– : in *Irish Times* 5 March 1985

11 Men and women who have quarrelled can learn through
    suffering how to live together and apart, as France and
    Germany have learned. People can wake up in the morning
    and find an imprisoning myth no longer imprisoning but
    just plain silly. Cathleen ní Houlihan and King Billy are not
    necessarily immortal.
    Conor Cruise O'Brien 1917– : *States of Ireland* (1972)

12 This party will continue to fly the flag and it is in no doubt
    of the flag that it is flying, unlike the Ulster Unionist Party
    who are flying the white flag of surrender.
    view of the Democratic Unionist Party deputy leader
    Peter Robinson: in *Irish Times* 20 June 1998 'This Week They Said'

13 Far-off, most secret and inviolate Rose.
    W. B. Yeats 1865–1939: 'The Secret Rose' (1899)

Flowers

1 Have I stooped so low as to lyricise about heather,
adjusting my love
to fit elegantly
within the terms of disinterested discourse?
Moya Cannon 1956– : 'Hills' (1997)

2 But in Kildare there was no lion's tooth,
Just the dandelion: Brigid's flower.
Neil Curry 1937– : *Ships in Bottles* (1988) 'In a Calendar of Saints'

3 And the gold-dust coming up
From the trampled buttercup.
Oliver St John Gogarty 1878–1957: 'Golden Stockings'

4 Of meadow grass and river flags, the bulrush and
waterweed, and of falling griefs of weeping willow.
James Joyce 1882–1941: *Finnegans Wake* (1939) 'Anna Livia Plurabelle'

5 I am travelling from one April to another.
It is the same train between the same embankments.
Gorse fires are smoking, but primroses burn
And celandines and white may and gorse flowers.
Michael Longley 1939– : 'Gorse Fires' (1991)

6 At the brush of your palm, all my herbs
and spices spill open

frond by frond, lured to unfold
and exhale in the heat;
wild strawberries rife, and pimpernels
flagrant and scarlet.
Nuala Ní Dhomhnaill 1952– : 'Blodewedd' (1990, translated by John
Montague)

7 Oh! a delight to my heart was the smell of your heather.
Peig Sayers 1873–1958: *An Old Woman's Reflections* (translated by Séamus
Ennis, 1962)

Food and Drink see also Alcohol

1 [Tar water] is of a nature so mild and benign and
   proportioned to the human constitution, as to warm
   without heating, to cheer but not inebriate.
   George Berkeley 1685–1753: *Siris* (1744)

2 My mother tells me she's worn out pouring tinned sauce
   over the frozen chicken.
   Maeve Binchy 1940– : *Evening Class* (1996)

3 The Great Northern Fry comes, almost invariably, with one
   egg. There isn't room on the plate for two.
   Ciaran Carson 1948– : *Last Night's Fun* (1996)

4 Your Irish ortolans are famous good eating.
   Maria Edgeworth 1767–1849: *The Absentee* (1812)

5 I don't often eat boys. Never Celts. They're stringy.
   Jennifer Johnston 1930– : *The Captains and the Kings* (1972)

6 When I makes tea I makes tea, as old mother Grogan said.
   And when I makes water I makes water . . . *Begob, ma'am,*
   says Mrs Cahill, *God send you don't make them in the one pot.*
   James Joyce 1882–1941: *Ulysses* (1922)

7 Mr Leopold Bloom ate with relish the inner organs of beasts
   and fowls. He liked thick giblet soup, nutty gizzards, a
   stuffed roast heart, liverslices fried with crustcrumbs, fried
   hencod's roes. Most of all he liked grilled mutton kidneys
   which gave to his palate a fine tang of faintly scented urine.
   James Joyce 1882–1941: *Ulysses* (1922)

8 My culinary hinterland—a place where the traditional
   approach to food was: if you want to eat something make
   sure you boil the hell out of it first. All you needed was a
   large pot of boiling water . . . and if you really wanted to
   spice things up a bit you could always throw in a bit of salt.
   of traditional Ulster cookery
   John Kelly: in *Irish Times* 15 November 1997

9 Her cooking verged on the poisonous . . . I have known no other woman who could make fried eggs taste like perished rubber.
Hugh Leonard 1926– : *Home Before Night* (1979)

10 Sushi, crab claws, caviar, little heaps of pink glop . . . A taste of dank rock pools fills my mouth.
Liz McManus 1947– : 'Dwelling Below the Skies' (1997)

11 Yet, who can help loving the land that has taught us
Six hundred and eighty-five ways to dress eggs?
Thomas Moore 1779–1852: *The Fudge Family in Paris* (1818)

12 A mountainous dish of trifle, in whose veins ran honey instead of jam, and to whose enlightenment a bottle at least of whisky had been dedicated.
Edith Œ. Somerville 1858–1949 and **Martin Ross** 1862–1915: *Further Experiences of an Irish R.M.* (1908)

13 While I live I shall not forget her potato cakes. They came in hot, and hot from the pot oven, they were speckled with caraway seed, they swam in salt butter, and we ate them shamelessly and greasily, and washed them down with hot whiskey and water.
Edith Œ. Somerville 1858–1949 and **Martin Ross** 1862–1915: *Some Experiences of an Irish R.M.* (1899)

14 I have been assured by a very knowing American of my acquaintance in London, that a young healthy child well nursed is at a year old a most delicious, nourishing, and wholesome food, whether stewed, roasted, baked, or boiled, and I make no doubt that it will equally serve in a fricassee, or a ragout.
Jonathan Swift 1667–1745: *A Modest Proposal for Preventing the Children of Ireland from being a Burden to their Parents or Country* (1729)

15 When I ask for a watercress sandwich, I do not mean a loaf
with a field in the middle of it.
Oscar Wilde 1854–1900: Max Beerbohm, letter to Reggie Turner, 15 April
1893

16 If you dine out of tins, you should have the labels served up
with the grub.
Jack B. Yeats 1871–1957: *The Charmed Life* (1938)

Friendship

1 Who can I tear to pieces, if not my friends? ... If they were
not my friends, I could not do such violence to them.
Francis Bacon 1902–92: John Russell *Francis Bacon* (1979)

2 Friendship is a disinterested commerce between equals;
love, an abject intercourse between tyrants and slaves.
Oliver Goldsmith 1728–74: *The Good-Natured Man* (1768)

3 He's an oul' butty o' mine—oh, he's a darlin' man, a
daarlin' man.
Sean O'Casey 1880–1964: *Juno and the Paycock* (1925)

4 We helped each other and lived in the shelter of each other.
Friendship was the fastest root in our hearts.
Peig Sayers 1873–1958: *An Old Woman's Reflections* (translated by Séamus
Ennis, 1962)

5 Think where man's glory most begins and ends
And say my glory was I had such friends.
W. B. Yeats 1865–1939: 'The Municipal Gallery Re-visited' (1937)

The Future

1 People will not look forward to posterity, who never look
backward to their ancestors.
Edmund Burke 1729–97: *Reflections on the Revolution in France* (1790)

2   We have trained them [men] to think of the Future as a
    promised land which favoured heroes attain—not as
    something which everyone reaches at the rate of sixty
    minutes an hour.
    C. S. Lewis 1898–1963: *The Screwtape Letters* (1942)

3   Let me make a prediction now: the twenty-first century will
    be the Age of the Irish.
    Mary McAleese 1951– : in *Irish Post* 1 November 1997

4   The day of the dinosaurs is over. The future belongs to the
    bridge-builders, not the wreckers.
    on the election to the Northern Ireland Assembly
    Mary McAleese 1951– : in *Irish Times* 27 June 1998

5   Now the time has arrived to give thought to the future, to
    consider how best the Office of President can serve the Irish
    people as the new millennium approaches.
    announcing that she would not seek a second term of office
    Mary Robinson 1944– : in *Irish Times* 13 March 1997

6   And so we are to beggar ourselves for fear of vexing
    posterity! Now, I would ask the honourable gentleman,
    and still more honourable House, why should we put
    ourselves out of our way to do anything for posterity; for
    what has posterity done for us?
    debate in the Irish House of Commons
    Boyle Roche 1743–1807: Jonah Barrington *Personal Sketches and
    Recollections of his own Times* (1827)

7   Make me a beautiful word for doing things tomorrow; for
    that surely is a great and blessed invention.
    George Bernard Shaw 1856–1950: *Back to Methuselah* (1921)

8   The darkness drops again but now I know
    That twenty centuries of stony sleep
    Were vexed to nightmare by a rocking cradle,
    And what rough beast, its hour come round at last,
    Slouches towards Bethlehem to be born?
    W. B. Yeats 1865–1939: 'The Second Coming' (1921)

Future

Gadgets

1 Is it about a bicycle?
Flann O'Brien 1911–66: *The Third Policeman* (1940)

2 Father had a secret of making inanimate objects appear to
possess malevolent life of their own, and sometimes it was
hard to believe that his tools and materials were not really
in a conspiracy against him.
Frank O'Connor 1903–66: *An Only Child* (1961)

3 Make me a handle as straight as the mast of a ship.
Eoghan Rua Ó Súilleabháin 1748–84: 'To the Blacksmith with a Spade'
(translated by Frank O'Connor)

4 The photographer is like the cod which produces a million
eggs in order that one may reach maturity.
George Bernard Shaw 1856–1950: introduction to the catalogue for Alvin
Langdon Coburn's exhibition at the Royal Photographic Society, 1906

5 A crank is a small engine that causes revolutions.
on being described as a crank
Francis Sheehy-Skeffington 1878–1916: Owen Dudley Edwards and Fergus
Pyle *1916: the Easter Rising* (1968)

6 It is only the unimaginative who ever invents. The true
artist is known by the use he makes of what he annexes.
Oscar Wilde 1854–1900: review, 30 May 1885

Galway

1 If you ever go across the sea to Ireland,
Then maybe at the closing of your day,
You will sit and watch the moon rise over Claddagh,

And watch the sun go down on Galway Bay.
Anonymous: 'Galway Bay', 19th century song

2 Galway city . . . is to the discoverer of Ireland something
like what Chapman's *Homer* was to Keats. It is a clue, a
provocation, an enticement.
Robert Lynd 1879–1949: 'Galway of the Races'

Gardening

1 We are a strange secret society with mysterious rituals, like
the Freemasons, except our sign of mutual recognition is
grime under the fingernails and a lingering odour of
something in the compost.
on allotment holders
Michael Leapman: in *Irish Times* 28 February 1998 'This Week They Said'

2 A good Nationalist should look upon slugs in the garden in
much the same way as she looks on the English in Ireland.
Constance Markievicz 1868–1927: in *Bean na hÉireann* November 1908

3 There was a bed of mignonette . . . and Michael, once
second in command of many a filibustering expedition, was
now on his knees, ingloriously tying carnations to little
pieces of cane.
Edith Œ. Somerville 1858–1949 and **Martin Ross** 1862–1915: *Some
Experiences of an Irish R.M.* (1899)

Garryowen

1 Where'er we go they fear the name
Of Garryowen in glory.
Anonymous: 19th century song (official marching tune of Custer's Seventh
Cavalry)

2 The girl I love is beautiful, she's fairer than the dawn;
She lives in Garryowen, and she's called the Colleen Bawn.
Dion Boucicault 1820–90: *The Colleen Bawn* (1860)

Genius

1 A man of genius makes no mistakes. His errors are
   volitional and are the portals of discovery.
   James Joyce 1882–1941: *Ulysses* (1922)

2 He's on the border-line of genius, but he never trespasses
   over it.
   Patrick Kelly: Maurice Healy *The Old Munster Circuit* (1939)

3 The problem with Ireland is that it's a country full of
   genius but with absolutely no talent.
   Hugh Leonard 1926– : in *The Times* 1977

4 When a true genius appears in the world, you may know
   him by this sign, that the dunces are all in confederacy
   against him.
   Jonathan Swift 1667–1745: *Thoughts on Various Subjects* (1711)

5 Good God! what a genius I had when I wrote that book.
   of A Tale of a Tub
   Jonathan Swift 1667–1745: Sir Walter Scott (ed.) *Works of Swift* (1814)

6 I have nothing to declare except my genius.
   at the New York Custom House
   Oscar Wilde 1854–1900: Frank Harris *Oscar Wilde* (1918)

God

1 Let us pray to God . . . the bastard! He doesn't exist!
   Samuel Beckett 1906–89: *Endgame* (1958)

2 How can one better magnify the Almighty than by
   sniggering with him at his little jokes, particularly the
   poorer ones.
   Samuel Beckett 1906–89: *Happy Days* (1961)

3 I had a very special relationship with God. I regarded him
as a friend, and Irish, and somebody who knew me well.
Maeve Binchy 1940– : *A Portrait of the Artist as a Young Girl* (1986)

4 I had long stopped believing that the God who had been
assigned to me was a benign old lad with long hair and a
beard. He was more like a celestial Jeremy Beadle, and my
life was the showcase he used to amuse the other Gods.
Marian Keyes: *Rachel's Holiday* (1997)

5 My physical landscape in Belfast was one in which God was
male, Irish and Catholic, his mother having presumably
emigrated to Nazareth from Ireland after the famine. My
Protestant friends meanwhile also understood God to be
male, but Protestant and British. Reared between these two
parochial Gods who carried their crosses like lances in a
jousting tournament, we were all introduced young to the
Ya-boo school of theology—the my-God-is-bigger-than-
your-God school of theological bully boys.
Mary McAleese 1951– : in *Guardian* 16 January 1998

6 I began to think that God wasn't quite what he was
cracked up to be.
Frank O'Connor 1903–66: 'My Oedipus Complex'

7 God made the grass, the air and the rain; and the grass, the
air and the rain made the Irish; and the Irish turned the
grass, the air and the rain back into God.
Sean O'Faolain 1900–91: in *Holiday* June 1958

8 I see his blood upon the rose
And in the stars the glory of his eyes.
Joseph Mary Plunket 1887–1916: 'I see His Blood Upon the Rose'

9 Man . . . must regard God as a helpless Longing, which
longed him into existence by its desperate need for an
executive organ.
George Bernard Shaw 1856–1950: letter to Lady Gregory, 19 August 1909

God

Good and Evil

1 These two men [the victims] . . . in a sense symbolized the future in Northern Ireland and these gunmen—in the evil atrocity they committed—symbolized the past.
of the Poyntzpass murders
Tony Blair 1953– : in *Irish Times* 7 March 1998 'This Week They Said'

2 It is necessary only for the good man to do nothing for evil to triumph.
Edmund Burke 1729–97: attributed (in a number of forms) to Burke, but not found in his writings

3 All these years we were told the Irish were always noble and they made brave speeches before the English hanged them. Now Hoppy O'Halloran is saying the Irish did bad things. Next thing he'll be saying the English did good things.
Frank McCourt 1930– : *Angela's Ashes* (1996)

Government

1 If I could unsay that interview, I would. I would not use the word 'government'.
the Minister for Foreign Affairs regretting that he had described the proposed North-South executive body as 'not unlike a government' in a BBC interview
David Andrews 1936– : in *Irish Times* 6 December 1997 'This Week They Said'

2 Going about persecuting civil servants.
assessment by one unidentified senator of how politicians spend their time
Anonymous: R. F. Foster *Modern Ireland* (1988)

3 For righteous monarchs,
Justly to judge, with their own eyes should see;
To rule o'er freemen, should themselves be free.
Henry Brooke 1703–83: *Earl of Essex* (performed 1750, published 1761)

4 Those who have been once intoxicated with power, and have derived any kind of emolument from it, even though for but one year, can never willingly abandon it.
Edmund Burke 1729–97: *Letter to a Member of the National Assembly* (1791)

5 The time has come to reform altogether the absurd and wicked anachronism known as Dublin Castle.
Joseph Chamberlain 1836–1914: speech, 17 June 1885

6 Dáil Éireann is the only place in Ireland where the Civil War is still going on.
John B. Keane 1928– : *Many Young Men of Twenty* (1961)

7 Dublin Castle, if it did not know what the Irish people want, could not so infallibly have maintained its tradition of giving them the opposite.
Thomas Kettle 1880–1916: Ulick O'Connor *The Troubles* (rev. ed., 1996)

8 Your restless nation gives us a great deal of trouble in parliament.
David Ricardo 1772–1823: letter to Maria Edgeworth, 26 May 1823

9 That fatal and dreary policy of giving Ireland everything except that which she wants and that which according to every principle of Liberalism . . . she has a right to obtain.
Lord Rosebery 1847–1929: speech, 1885

10 Her control was as fast and as firm over those who were under her hand as the control of Queen Maeve of Connaught long ago.
Peig Sayers 1873–1958: *An Old Woman's Reflections* (translated by Séamus Ennis, 1962)

11 The art of government is the organization of idolatry.
George Bernard Shaw 1856–1950: *Man and Superman* (1903) 'Maxims: Idolatry'

12 It is the folly of too many, to mistake the echo of a London coffee-house for the voice of the kingdom.
Jonathan Swift 1667–1745: *The Conduct of the Allies* (1711)

13 It is alleged indeed, that the high heels are most agreeable
to our ancient constitution: but however this be, his
Majesty hath determined to make use of only low heels in
the administration of the government.
Jonathan Swift 1667–1745: *Gulliver's Travels* (1726) 'A Voyage to Lilliput'

14 This is not East Timor or Peking. A government which uses
the Army against its own people makes one of the greatest
mistakes in public life that is possible.
John Taylor: in *Daily Telegraph* 8 July 1998

15 A Sinn Fein president in a government of Northern
Ireland? That's like Hitler in a synagogue.
*discounting the view that Gerry Adams might take a seat on the
Ulster Executive*
David Trimble 1944– : in *Daily Telegraph* 17 April 1998

16 I am not saying 'absolutely never' with regard to that
individual, but he has a long, long way to go.
*on the prospect of sitting in the Ulster Executive with Gerry
Adams*
David Trimble 1944– : in *Irish Times* 9 May 1998 'This Week They Said'

Graveyards

1 Personally, I have no bone to pick with graveyards.
Samuel Beckett 1906–89: 'First Love' (1974)

2 So many belonging to me lay buried in Kilbarrock, the
healthiest graveyard in Ireland, they said, because it was so
near the sea.
Brendan Behan 1923–64: *Borstal Boy* (1958)

3 There in pinnacled protection,
One extinguished family waits
A Church of Ireland resurrection
By the broken, rusty gates.

Sheepswool, straw and droppings cover,
Graves of spinster, rake and lover,
Whose fantastic mausoleum
Sings its own seablown Te Deum,
In and out the slipping slates.
John Betjeman 1906–84: 'Ireland with Emily' (1945)

4 The skeleton of a village, cruelly distinct in its structure,
neatly laid out on the sombre slope as if for an anatomy
lesson . . .
   No bombed city, no artillery-raked village ever looked
like this. In limitless patience time and the elements have
eaten away everything not made of stone, and from the
earth have sprouted cushions on which these bones lie like
relics, cushions of moss and grass.
of a deserted village on Achill Island
Heinrich Böll 1917–85: *Irish Journal* (1957, translated Leila Vennewitz)

5 In Bodenstown Churchyard there is a green grave,
And freely around it let winter winds rave.
Thomas Davis 1814–45: 'Tone's Grave'

6 You lay
three fields away

in collegelands
graveyard, in land
so wet you weren't so much
buried there as drowned.
Paul Muldoon 1951– : 'The Fox' (1987)

7 It was like a miracle; but before our very eyes, and almost
in the drawing of a breath, the whole body crumbled into
dust and passed from our sight.
Bram Stoker 1847–1912: *Dracula* (1897)

8 I've the cold earth's dark odour
   And I'm worn from the weather.
   Edward Walsh 1805–50: *Irish Popular Songs* (1847)

Guilt

1 Women feel guilty about everything—about the house if it
   isn't clean, about their children, their father, their mother,
   everything . . .
   Kathleen Lynch: in *Irish Times* 1 February 1997

2 One thing that the Roman Catholic Church and the West
   Midlands Serious Crimes Squad have in common—well,
   one of many things actually—is the shrewd professional
   understanding that given the right circumstances people
   will always want to confess, whether guilty or not.
   Joseph O'Connor 1963– : *The Secret World of the Irish Male* (1994)

3 When I was a 17-year-old student in Paris, I thought it the
   height of decadence to see a film at ten in the morning.
   Mary Robinson 1944– : opening the Dublin Film Festival in 1991

4 The more things a man is ashamed of, the more respectable
   he is.
   George Bernard Shaw 1856–1950: *Man and Superman* (1903)

Happiness

1 Philip nailed a smile to his face and wondered whether any
   other young man of his age was having such an appalling
   Saturday night.
   Maeve Binchy 1940– : *The Glass Lake* (1994)

2 Happiness is a rare plant, that seldom takes root on earth: few ever enjoyed it, except for a brief period; the search after it is rarely rewarded by the discovery. But, there is an admirable substitute for it, which all may hope to attain, as its attainment depends wholly on self—and that is, a contented spirit.
Lady Blessington 1789–1849: *The Victims of Society* (1837)

3 I felt the rush of happiness and warmth coming out of the people and I was carried out among them on a surge of joy. I suppose when you die and go to heaven you get a feeling like that.
Gerry Conlon 1954– : *Proved Innocent* (1990)

4 I felt better. Not happy or anything like that. I still felt we were all doomed and that the future was a vast wasteland of bleak greyness, but that it mightn't hurt if I got up for half an hour to watch *Eastenders*.
Marian Keyes: *Lucy Sullivan is Getting Married* (1997)

5 But a lifetime of happiness! No man alive could bear it: it would be hell on earth.
George Bernard Shaw 1856–1950: *Man and Superman* (1903)

6 Happiness is no laughing matter.
Richard Whately 1787–1863: *Detached Thoughts and Apophthegms* (1854)

7 When we are happy we are always good, but when we are good we are not always happy.
Oscar Wilde 1854–1900: *The Picture of Dorian Gray* (1891)

8 Land of Heart's Desire,
Where beauty has no ebb, decay no flood,
But joy is wisdom, Time an endless song.
W. B. Yeats 1865–1939: *The Land of Heart's Desire* (1894)

Hate see also Enemies

1 *Your Hatred to Orangemen*: . . . These men, who are so very
  hateful in your eyes, are our brethren in Christ; they are
  each of them as dear to him as the apple of his eye.
  James Warren Doyle 1786–1834: 'Pastoral Address to the Deluded and
  Illegal Association of Ribbonmen' (1822)

2 Hapless Nation! hapless Land
  Heap of uncementing sand!
  Crumbled by a foreign weight:
  And by worse, domestic hate.
  William Drennan 1754–1820: 'The Wake of William Orr'

3 Though little fields and scraping poverty do not lead to
  grand flaring passions, there was plenty of fire and an
  amount of vicious neighbourly hatred to keep us awake.
  Patrick Kavanagh 1904–67: *The Green Fool* (1938)

4 Sacred Heart o' Jesus, take away our hearts o' stone, and
  give us hearts o' flesh! Take away this murdherin' hate,
  an' give us Thine own eternal love!
  Sean O'Casey 1880–1964: *Juno and the Paycock* (1924)

5 Almost all his loyalties in the colours and enjoyments of life
  had been burned away, leaving but a slender, intense flame
  of hatred to what he knew to be England.
  of Tom Clarke
  Sean O'Casey 1880–1964: Ulick O'Connor *The Troubles* (rev. ed., 1996)

6 The worst sin towards our fellow creatures is not to hate
  them, but to be indifferent to them: that's the essence of
  inhumanity.
  George Bernard Shaw 1856–1950: *The Devil's Disciple* (1901)

7 William or James, need we still hate each other?
  Dora Sigerson 1866–1918: *Sixteen Dead Men* (1919) 'A Catholic to his
  Ulster Brother'

8 We had fed the heart on fantasies,
   The heart's grown brutal from the fare,
   More substance in our enmities
   Than in our love; Oh, honey-bees
   Come build in the empty house of the stare.
   W. B. Yeats 1865–1939: 'Meditations in Time of Civil War' no. 6 'The Stare's
   Nest by my Window' (1928)

9 Out of Ireland have we come.
   Great hatred, little room,
   Maimed us at the start.
   I carry from my mother's womb
   A fanatic heart.
   W. B. Yeats 1865–1939: 'Remorse for Intemperate Speech' (1933)

Health and Sickness

1 It is like the crescendo of a train I used to listen to in the
   night at Ussy, interminable, starting up again just when
   one thinks it is over and silence restored for ever.
   of his mother's last illness
   Samuel Beckett 1906–89: letter to Henri Hayden, 31 July 1950

2 Meningitis. It was a word you had to bite on to say it. It
   had a fright and a hiss in it.
   Seamus Deane 1940– : *Reading in the Dark* (1996)

3 The doctors found, when she was dead,—
   Her last disorder mortal.
   Oliver Goldsmith 1728–74: 'An Elegy on that Glory of her Sex, Mrs Mary
   Blaize'

4 *O áit go háit ba bhreá mo shiúl,*
   Is dob árd mo léim ar bhárr an tsléibh.

   Strong was my stride from place to place,

And I jumped high on the mountain top.
Douglas Hyde 1860–1949: 'An Gleann 'nar tógadh mé'

5　I told him to consult a vet.
of a fellow lawyer worried about his health
Matt Kenny 1861–1942: Maurice Healy *The Old Munster Circuit* (1939)

6　He took me into his surgery . . . He gave me one of those
looks of his, redolent of the cemetery, and said that I should
buy day-returns from now on instead of season tickets.
Hugh Leonard 1926– : *A Life* (1986)

7　Nearly every sickness is from the teeth.
Flann O'Brien 1911–66: *The Third Policeman* (1940)

8　I commend him on his resilience and stamina and the fact
that he has kept his figure after all those lunches, dinners
and receptions.
of the Taoiseach, Bertie Ahern, after his trip to Canada
Nora Owen: in *Irish Times* 28 March 1998 'This Week They Said'

9　There is at bottom only one genuinely scientific treatment
for all diseases, and that is to stimulate the phagocytes.
George Bernard Shaw 1856–1950: *The Doctor's Dilemma* (1911)

10　The many friends of Mr John A. Robinson, who was
involved in a recent boating accident, will be pleased to
hear that he is alive and well.
notification, according to Emergency Censorship rules, that the
Irish Times *journalist had survived the sinking of the* Prince of
Wales (*the paragraph was headed* 'Accident in the Pacific')
Robert Maire Smyllie: in *Irish Times* 17 December 1941

11　We are so fond of one another, because our ailments are
the same.
Jonathan Swift 1667–1745: *Journal to Stella* (in *Works*, 1768) 1 February
1711

12 Ah, well, then, I suppose that I shall have to die beyond my
means.
at the mention of a huge fee for a surgical operation
Oscar Wilde 1854–1900: R. H. Sherard *Life of Oscar Wilde* (1906)

Heaven

1 I will ask my God to let me make my heaven,
In that dear land across the Irish sea.
Anonymous: 'Galway Bay', 19th century song

*when his son reminded him that he would soon visit a better
land, as he looked out of his window at his Irish estate:*
2 I doubt it.
Edward Pennefeather Croker d. 1830: attributed; T. Toomey and H.
Greensmith *An Antique and Storied Land* (1991)

3 You forget that the kingdom of heaven suffers violence: and
the kingdom of heaven is like a woman.
James Joyce 1882–1941: *Exiles* (1918)

4 Brian O'Lynn and his last hour was due.
'Repent or St Peter will not let you through!'
'I've a trick up my sleeve if he won't let me in,
So give me a jemmy,' said Brian O'Lynn.
Patrick MacDonogh 1902–61: 'Brian O'Lynn'

5 Bright the vision that delighted
Once the sight of Judah's seer;
Sweet the countless tongues united
To entrance the prophet's ear.
Richard Mant 1776–1848: 'Bright the vision that delighted' (1837 hymn)

6 I shall not go to Heaven when I die,
But if they let me be
I think I'll take the road I used to know
That goes by Shere-na-garagh and the sea.
Helen Waddell 1889–1965: 'I Shall Not Go To Heaven'

History

1 This is not a time for soundbites. We've left them at home. I
feel the hand of history upon our shoulders . . . I'm here to
try.
*arriving in Belfast for the final stage of the Northern Irish
negotiations, 8 April 1998*
Tony Blair 1953– : in *Irish Times* 11 April 1998 'This Week They Said'

2 I could wish that the English kept history in mind more,
that the Irish kept it in mind less.
Elizabeth Bowen 1899–1973: 'Notes on Eire' 9 November 1949

3 There is the squeeze of pain in every episode, and although
people sometimes say that the Irish are great lickers of
wounds, they have had many to lick.
Polly Devlin 1944– : *All of Us There* (1983)

4 Living in history is a bit like finding oneself in a shuttered
mansion to which one has been brought blindfold, and
trying to imagine what it might look like from the outside.
Garret Fitzgerald 1926– : in *Irish Times* 9 May 1998

5 We are all revisionists now. But who will revise the
revisionists?
R. F. Foster 1949– : in *Irish Review* 1986

6 It is not the literal past, the 'facts' of history, that shape us,
but images of the past embodied in language . . . we must
never cease renewing those images; because once we do,
we fossilize.
Brian Friel 1929– : *Translations* (1980)

7 I could, as others have done, have sent your Highness some
small pieces of gold, falcons, or hawks with which the
island abounds. But since I thought that a high-minded
prince would place little value on such things that easily
come to be—and just as easily perish—I decided to send to
your Highness those things rather which cannot be lost. By

them I shall, through you, instruct posterity. For no age can destroy them.
dedication of his History *to Henry II*
Giraldus Cambrensis *c.*1146–1223: *The History and Topography of Ireland*

8 History, Stephen said, is a nightmare from which I am trying to awake.
James Joyce 1882–1941: *Ulysses* (1922)

9 We feel in England that we have treated you rather unfairly. It seems history is to blame.
James Joyce 1882–1941: *Ulysses* (1922)

10 Every one of the new Galls who writes on Ireland writes . . . in imitation of Cambrensis . . . because it is Cambrensis who is as the bull of the herd for them for writing the false history of Ireland, wherefore they had no choice of guide.
Geoffrey Keating 1570?–1644?: *History of Ireland* (Irish Texts Society, 1902)

11 Mr de Valera has been talking non-stop since eight o'clock this morning, filling me in on the background to the Irish fight for freedom. And after eight hours and sixteen minutes he hasn't even reached the Norman invasion of Ireland yet.
during the 1921 peace negotiations
David Lloyd George 1863–1945: attributed, probably apocryphal

12 Books about Ireland that begin with its history have a tendency to remain unread. The misunderstandings are so many.
Frank O'Connor 1903–66: attributed

13 SWINDON: What will history say?
BURGOYNE: History, sir, will tell lies as usual.
George Bernard Shaw 1856–1950: *The Devil's Disciple* (1901)

14 It is necessary that Irish history should be known and studied, for we are persuaded that *there* only are the secret springs of Irish discontent to be traced.
Samuel Smiles 1812–1904: *History of Ireland and the Irish People, under the Government of England* (1844)

Holidays

1 I would love . . . a one-year break doing absolutely nothing. Now whether, as I say to my friends, I will take to the gin bottle at 11 o'clock in the morning, and drink myself or smoke myself to death, I don't know—but I'd love to find out.
Gay Byrne 1934– : in *Irish Post* 16 May 1998

2 What kind of holiday can you take when you live in almost continual sunshine in an olive grove in the mountains, which is only twenty minutes away from the beaches and the sea?
Patrick Campbell 1913–80: *Gullible Travels* (1969)

3 I suppose we all have our recollections of our earlier holidays, all bristling with horror.
Flann O'Brien 1911–66: *Myles Away from Dublin* (1990)

4 A perpetual holiday is a good working definition of hell.
George Bernard Shaw 1856–1950: *Parents and Children* (1914)

5 Cultivated leisure is the aim of man.
Oscar Wilde 1854–1900: in *Fortnightly Review* February 1890

Home Rule see also Independence

1 When it comes I shall not be sorry. Only let us have separation as well as Home Rule: England cannot afford to go on with the Irishmen in her Parliament.
Arthur James Balfour 1848–1930: Wilfrid Scawen Blunt *The Land War in Ireland* (1912)

2 We do not want a sentence of death with a stay of execution for six years.
rejecting the suggestion that the Home Rule Bill should allow the temporary exclusion of Ulster for six years
Edward Carson 1854–1935: speech, March 1914

3 I decided some time ago that if the G.O.M. [Gladstone] went for Home Rule, the Orange card would be the one to play. Please God it may turn out the ace of trumps and not the two.
Lord Randolph Churchill 1849–94: letter to Lord Justice FitzGibbon, 16 February 1886

4 Mr Gladstone has reserved for his closing days a conspiracy against the honour of Britain and the welfare of Ireland more startlingly base and nefarious than any of those numerous designs and plots which, during the last quarter of a century, have occupied the imagination.
Lord Randolph Churchill 1849–94: speech, 20 June 1886

5 The Irish leader who would connive in the name of Home Rule at the acceptance of any measure which alienated for a day—for an hour—for one moment of time—a square inch of the soil of Ireland would act the part of a traitor and would deserve a traitor's fate.
Arthur Griffith 1871–1922: in *Sinn Féin* 21 February 1914

6 You may reject this Bill, but its record will remain. The history of England and Ireland can never be as if this offer had never been made. You may kill it now, but its ghost will ever haunt your festivals of coercion.
to the Unionists
William Harcourt 1827–1904: speech in the House of Commons, 1885

7 In theory I suppose I am a separatist, in practice I would accept any settlement that would enable Irishmen to freely control their own affairs.
Eoin MacNeill 1867–1945: in 1904; R. F. Foster *Modern Ireland* (1988)

explaining that nationalists were ready to go to almost any
lengths to accommodate the needs of Ulster in regard to Home
Rule:

8 With one exception—that is, the partition of our country.
William O'Brien 1852–1928: in the House of Commons, 1913

9 The man who killed Home Rule.
of Joseph Chamberlain, after the defeat of the first Home Rule
Bill in 1885
Charles Stewart Parnell 1846–91: J. L. Garvin *The Life of Joseph
Chamberlain* (1932–4)

in the spring of 1914 Redmond was asked by a friend, a priest
from Tipperary, if anything could now rob them of Home Rule:
10 A European war might do it.
John Redmond 1856–1918: in *Dictionary of National Biography* (1917–)

11 The English people say that if we got Home Rule we should
cut each other's throats. Who has a better right to cut
them?
George Bernard Shaw 1856–1950: speech in London, December 1912

12 His haste in dropping it is only equalled by the celerity with
which he takes it up again as soon as he sees he cannot live
as a minister without the votes of the Irish party.
of Asquith's support for Home Rule
F. E. Smith 1872–1930: speech in the House of Commons, 7 August 1911

13 Uncle says if Home Rule comes there won't be a fox or a
Protestant left in Ireland in ten years' time; and he said,
what's more, that if *he* had to choose it mightn't be the
Protestants he'd keep.
Edith Œ. Somerville 1858–1949 and **Martin Ross** 1862–1915: *Further
Experiences of an Irish R.M.* (1908)

Hope see also Optimism

1 He had the boys school to do still. Serious warnings on the
evils of drink and self abuse.
    Father John sometimes wondered whether any of it did
any good at all. But he reminded himself that thinking
along those lines was almost a sin against Hope.
Maeve Binchy 1940– : *The Glass Lake* (1994)

2 Those, who have much to hope and nothing to lose, will
always be dangerous, more or less.
Edmund Burke 1729–97: letter to Charles James Fox, 8 October 1777

3 Expectation of good news from the British government is
never something I have lived with easily. And yet I have it
and I appreciate it. Maybe I should have more faith.
*on the decision by the British Government not to extradite her
daughter, Róisín, to Germany*
Bernadette Devlin McAliskey 1947– : in *Irish Times* 14 March 1998 'This
Week They Said'

4 It is no exaggeration to say that a ray of light shines across
the entire island of Ireland and will lift the hearts of all its
inhabitants.
on the setting up of all-party talks in Northern Ireland
John O'Donoghue: in *Irish Times* 27 September 1997 'Quotes of the Week'

5 He who has never hoped can never despair.
George Bernard Shaw 1856–1950: *Caesar and Cleopatra* (1901)

Hospitality

1 It was a nice lunch, and the company was good.
*of a St Patrick's Day banquet at the British Embassy in
Washington*
Gerry Adams 1948– : in *Guardian* 17 March 1998

2 'Ah Dan, my dear, you're welcome here.'
'Thank you ma'am', says Dan.
Anonymous: '"Thank you ma'am", says Dan', 19th century ballad

3 Night after night the revel afforded uninterrupted pleasure
to the joyous gentry: the festivity being subsequently
renewed at some other mansion, till the gout thought
proper to put the whole party *hors de combat*—having the
satisfaction of making cripples for a few months such as he
did not kill.
Jonah Barrington 1760–1834: *Personal Sketches and Recollections of his
own Time* (1827)

4 You can tell Mother Clare that it damn' well won't suit the
Community to have her here just because her own lot
above in Dublin want to be shot of her for Christmas.
Maeve Binchy 1940– : *Circle of Friends* (1990)

5 Come in the evening, or come in the morning,
Come when you're looked for, or come without warning.
Thomas Davis 1814–45: 'The Welcome' (1846)

6 He gave the finest entertainment ever was heard of in the
country—not a man could stand after supper but Sir
Patrick himself, who could sit out the best man in Ireland,
let alone the three kingdoms itself.
Maria Edgeworth 1767–1849: *Castle Rackrent* (1800)

7 There is a tavern in the town.
Wellington Guernsey 1817–85: title of song

8 There is perpetual kindness in the Irish cabin—butter-milk,
potatoes—a stool is offered or a stone is rolled so your
honour may sit down and be out of the smoke, and those
who beg everywhere seem desirous to exercise free
hospitality in their own houses.
Sir Walter Scott 1771–1832: J. G. Lockhart *Life of Sir Walter Scott*
(1837–8)

9 Philippa's genius for hospitality here saw its chance, and
   broke forth into unbridled tea-party in connection with the
   sports, even involving me in the hire of a tent, the
   conveyance of chairs and tables, and other large
   operations.
   Edith Œ. Somerville 1858–1949 and **Martin Ross** 1862–1915: *Some
   Experiences of an Irish R.M.* (1899)

10 He showed me his bill of fare to tempt me to dine with him;
   poh, said I, I value not your bill of fare, give me your bill of
   company.
   Jonathan Swift 1667–1745: *Journal to Stella* 2 September 1711

11 I'm sure I don't know half the people who come to my
   house. Indeed, for all I hear, I shouldn't like to.
   Oscar Wilde 1854–1900: *An Ideal Husband* (1895)

Houses see also Architecture

1 Cullenaghmore . . . exhibited altogether an uncouth mass,
   warring with every rule of symmetry in architecture. The
   original castle had been demolished, and its materials
   converted to a much worse purpose; the front of the edifice
   was particularly ungraceful—a Saracen's head, our crest,
   in coloured brickwork being its only ornament.
   Jonah Barrington 1760–1834: *Personal Sketches and Recollections of his
   own Time* (1827)

2 In February, before those leaves had visibly budded, the
   death—execution rather—of the three houses,
   Danielstown, Castle Trent, Mount Isabel, occurred in the
   same night. A fearful scarlet ate up the hard spring
   darkness.
   Elizabeth Bowen 1899–1973: *The Last September* (1929)

3 Oh, to have a little house!
   To own the hearth and stool and all!
   The heaped-up sods upon the fire,
   The pile of turf against the wall!

. . . a little house—a house of my own—
Out of the wind's and the rain's way.
Padraic Colum 1881–1972: 'An Old Woman of the Roads' (*c.*1907)

4 Laughterless now the sweet demesne,
And the gaunt house looks blank on Sligo Bay
A nest decayed, an eagle flown . . .
of Lissadell House
C. Day-Lewis 1904–72: 'Remembering Con Markievicz' (1970)

5 The long, long house in the ultimate land of the
undiscovered West.
of Renvyle House
Oliver St John Gogarty 1878–1957: *As I Was Going Down Sackville Street*
(1937)

6 Nothing left but a charred oak beam quenched in the well
beneath the house. And ten tall square towers, chimneys,
stand bare on Europe's extreme verge.
of Renvyle House, burned down in the Civil War
Oliver St John Gogarty 1878–1957: *As I Was Going Down Sackville Street*
(1937)

7 The roof, the floors are gone.
Stolen your sea-green slates
And smith-work from Gort.
P. J. Kavanagh 1931– : 'Yeats's Tower' (1958)

8 There was too much beauty round Aragon, and too much
beauty is dangerous . . . Rising above the river banks and
stone flights of fox-watched steps, the house had the lonely
quality of bird flight.
Molly Keane 1904–96: *Two Days in Aragon* (1941)

9 I am a product of long corridors, empty sunlit rooms . . .
attics explored in solitude, distant noises of gurgling
cisterns and pipes.
C. S. Lewis 1898–1963: *Surprised by Joy* (1955)

10 *Bothán gan áit chun suidhe ann,*
 Ach súgh sileáin is fáscadh aníos ann,
 Fiadhaile ag teacht go fras gan choímse
 Is rian na gcearc air treasna scríobtha,
 Lag ina dhrom 's na gabhla ag lúbadh
 Is clagarnach dhonn go trom ag túirlint.

 A cabin with no place to sit down,
 But dripping soot from above and oozings from below,
 No end of weeds growing riotously,
 And the scrapings of hens across it,
 Its roof-tree sagging, its couples bending
 And brown rain falling heavily.
 Brian Merriman ?1745–1805: *Cúirt an Mheadhon Oidhche* [The Midnight Court] (1780)

11 It was . . . as though the sun going down beyond the Clare
 hills had clenched his fist and shaken it at the porch, and
 the porch, like some great beast driven to bay, dug its
 columns deeper into the ground and snarled back at it.
 Frank O'Connor 1903–66: *Irish Miles* (1947)

12 Georgian architects, ironic
 Deists, crossed over from the mainland
 To build a culture brick by brick,
 And graft their reason to a state
 The rain is washing out of shape.
 Tom Paulin 1949– : 'Going in the Rain' (1980)

13 The tenement houses of Dublin are so rotten that they
 periodically collapse upon their inhabitants, and if the
 inhabitants collect in the street to discuss the matter, the
 police baton them to death.
 during the 'Dublin lockout' labour dispute of 1913
 Patrick Pearse 1879–1916: *Patrick Pearse: Political Writings and Speeches* (1962)

14 A great stone box . . . full of Italian mantelpieces and
    decayed eighteenth-century furniture and carpets all in
    holes.
    of Bowen's Court
    Virginia Woolf 1882–1941: letter to Vanessa Bell, 3 May 1934

15 The light of evening, Lissadell,
    Great windows open to the south.
    W. B. Yeats 1865–1939: 'In Memory of Eva Gore-Booth and Con Markiewicz'
    (1933)

16 I, the poet William Yeats,
    With old mill boards and sea-green slates,
    And smithy work from the Gort forge,
    Restored this tower for my wife George;
    And may these characters remain
    When all is ruin once again.
    W. B. Yeats 1865–1939: 'To be Carved on a Stone at Thoor Ballylee' (1918)

The Human Race

1 There was one small bird to shoot: it sang
   'Better Beast and know your end, and die
   Than Man with murderous angels in his head.'
   Denis Devlin 1908–59: 'The Tomb of Michael Collins' (c.1956)

2 I got disappointed in human nature as well and gave it up
   because I found it too much like my own.
   J. P. Donleavy 1926– : *A Fairy Tale of New York* (1973)

3 Physically there is nothing to distinguish human society
   from the farmyard except that children are more
   troublesome and costly than chickens and calves and that
   men and women are not so completely enslaved as farm
   stock.
   George Bernard Shaw 1856–1950: preface to *Getting Married* (1908)

4 I cannot but conclude the bulk of your natives to be the
   most pernicious race of little odious vermin that nature
   ever suffered to crawl upon the surface of the earth.
   Jonathan Swift 1667–1745: *Gulliver's Travels* (1726) 'A Voyage to
   Brobdingnag'

5 Principally I hate and detest that animal called man;
   although I heartily love John, Peter, Thomas, and so forth.
   Jonathan Swift 1667–1745: letter to Pope, 29 September 1725

6 Nor dread nor hope attend
   A dying animal;
   A man awaits his end
   Dreading and hoping all.
   W. B. Yeats 1865–1939: 'Death' (1933)

Humour

1 Humour is the safety-valve of the nation.
   Anonymous: slogan of the satirical journal *Dublin Opinion*

2 About lunchtime on every April 1st, people start falling
   around with laughter and saying wasn't it all wonderful
   and some eejits really believed it and wasn't the paper so
   clever? And I sit there with darkening brow and sense of
   humour failure written all over me, unable to find anything
   remotely funny about printing lies.
   Maeve Binchy 1940– : in *Irish Times* 4 April 1998

3 There is nothing more unbecoming a man of quality than
   to laugh; Jesu, 'tis such a vulgar expression of the passion!
   William Congreve 1670–1729: *The Double Dealer* (1694)

4 We don't try to make jokes in Ulster. We say serious things
   in a way that makes them appear funny when you see how
   serious they are.
   Lynn C. Doyle 1873–1961: *The Ballygunnion Bus* (1957)

5 The Irish have wit but little humour. They cannot laugh at
   the battle while they are involved in the broil of life.
   Oliver St John Gogarty 1878–1957: *Tumbling in the Hay* (1939)

6 Full well they laughed with counterfeited glee,
   At all his jokes, for many a joke had he.
   Oliver Goldsmith 1728–74: *The Deserted Village* (1770)

7 If 'tis a thing I ever find out you were telling jokes to Jesuits
   I'll tear the bloody kidneys outa you.
   Frank McCourt 1930– : *Angela's Ashes* (1996)

8 Another day gone and no jokes.
   Flann O'Brien 1911–66: *The Best of Myles* (1968)

9 I don't try to explain my jokes . . . any more than Picasso
   tries to explain his pictures.
   Flann O'Brien 1911–66: *c.*1940; Tony Gray *The Lost Years: the Emergency in
   Ireland 1939–45* (1997)

10 That's the Irish people all over—they treat a joke as a
   serious thing and a serious thing as a joke.
   Sean O'Casey 1880–1964: *The Shadow of a Gunman* (1923)

11 'A cause to laugh for us, wife,' said he, 'as Peter said long
   ago when he found the ass drowned!'
   Peig Sayers 1873–1958: *An Old Woman's Reflections* (translated by Séamus
   Ennis, 1962)

12 My way of joking is to tell the truth. It's the funniest joke in
   the world.
   George Bernard Shaw 1856–1950: *John Bull's Other Island* (1907)

13 For every ten jokes, thou hast got an hundred enemies.
   Laurence Sterne 1713–68: *Tristram Shandy* (1769)

Hunting

1 Hunt the hare and turn her down the rocky road
And all the way to Dublin, wack-folall-de-da!
Anonymous: 'The Rocky Road to Dublin' (song, 19th century)

2 There is nothing like going out hunting with your best
friends, to teach you how little you matter to them.
Countess of Fingall 1860–1944: *Seventy Years Young* (1937)

3 When a man wants to murder a tiger he calls it sport;
when a tiger wants to murder him he calls it ferocity.
George Bernard Shaw 1856–1950: *Man and Superman* (1903)

4 It is my belief that six out of every dozen people who go out
hunting are disagreeably conscious of a nervous system,
and two out of six are in what is brutally called 'a blue
funk'.
Edith Œ. Somerville 1858–1949 and **Martin Ross** 1862–1915: *Some
Experiences of an Irish R.M.* (1899)

5 The English country gentleman galloping after a fox—the
unspeakable in full pursuit of the uneatable.
Oscar Wilde 1854–1900: *A Woman of No Importance* (1893)

Ignorance

1 Let us hope and trust that there are sufficient proud and
ignorant people left in this country to stand up to the
intellectuals who are out to destroy faith and fatherland.
Oliver J. Flanagan 1920–87: *c.*1985, attributed

2 Ignorance is like a delicate flower: touch it and the bloom is gone.
Oscar Wilde 1854–1900: *The Importance of Being Earnest* (1895)

Image see also **People, Politicians**

1 I am against this Treaty, not because I am a man of war, but because I am a man of peace.
Eamon de Valera 1882–1975: in 1921

2 I was reared in a labourer's cottage here in Ireland. I have not lived solely among intellectuals.
Eamon de Valera 1882–1975: in 1922

3 My family was in politics while de Valera's was still bartering budgerigars in the back streets of Barcelona.
James Dillon 1902– : comment of the leader of Fine Gael, 1950s

4 I expect that I was rather objectionable—always late and perhaps a bit arrogant. Bumptious, that's the word to describe me.
on his student days
Garret Fitzgerald 1926– : attributed

5 I'm not a vindictive person. Now people might say I'd cut your throat with barbed wire but I'm not deliberately vindictive.
Padraig Flynn 1939– : comment, 1990s

6 I am not Santa Claus.
Charles Haughey 1925– : as Taoiseach, 1991

7 I'm practical, I'm from Kerry.
Con Houlihan: in *Irish Times* 2 January 1997

8 It is not my fault that the odour of ashpits and old weeds and offal hangs round my stories. I seriously believe that you will retard the course of civilization in Ireland by

preventing the Irish people from having/one good look at
themselves in my nicely polished looking-glass.
James Joyce 1882–1941: letter, 23 June 1906

9 I think very highly of myself. I have grasped more of the
truth than almost any other man.
James Stephens 1824–1901: Desmond Ryan *The Fenian Chief* (1967)

Independence see also Home Rule

1 Profiting by the weakness of England, Ireland had raised
herself within an ace of independence. It was her
quinquennium; it was her golden age: by universal
confession, it was an age of concord, tranquillity, morality,
festivity, and happiness.
Jeremy Bentham 1748–1832: draft of historical preface intended for *A
Fragment on Government*, ed. 2

2 Self-government is our right, a thing born in us at birth, a
thing no more to be doled out to us, or withheld from us,
by another people than the right to life itself—than the
right to feel the sun, or smell the flowers, or to love our
kind.
Roger Casement 1864–1916: statement at the conclusion of his trial, the
Old Bailey, London, 29 June 1916

3 The time for Ireland's battle is NOW, the place for Ireland's
battle is HERE.
James Connolly 1868–1916: in *The Workers' Republic* 22 January 1916

4 And then I prayed I yet might see
Our fetters rent in twain,
And Ireland, long a province, be
A Nation once again.
Thomas Davis 1814–45: 'A Nation Once Again' (1846)

5 Let no man write my epitaph . . . When my country takes
her place among the nations of the earth, *then,* and *not till
then,* let my epitaph be written.
Robert Emmet 1778–1803: speech from the dock when condemned to
death, 19 September 1803; cf. **Epitaphs 2**

6 We had an opportunity of building up a worthy State that
would attract and, in time, absorb and assimilate the
[Unionist] elements. We preferred to burn our own houses,
blow up our own bridges, rob our own banks . . . Generally
we preferred to practise upon ourselves worse iniquities
than the British had practised on us since Cromwell and
Mountjoy, and now we wonder why the Orangemen are
not hopping like so many fleas across the Border in their
anxiety to come within our fold.
Kevin O'Higgins 1892–1927: Robert Kee *The Green Flag* (1972)

7 None of us, whether we are in America or Ireland, or
wherever we may be, will be satisfied until we have
destroyed the last link which keeps Ireland bound to
England.
Charles Stewart Parnell 1846–91: speech at Cincinnati, 20 February 1880

8 The fools, the fools, the fools, they have left us our Fenian
dead, and while Ireland holds these graves Ireland unfree
shall never be at peace.
Patrick Pearse 1879–1916: oration over the grave of the Fenian Jeremiah
O'Donovan Rossa, 1 August 1915

9 Irishmen and Irishwomen: In the name of God and of the
dead generations from which she receives her old tradition
of nationhood, Ireland, through us, summons her children
to her flag and strikes for her freedom.
*signed 'on behalf of the provisional government' by Thomas J.
Clarke, Sean MacDiarmada, Thomas MacDonagh, P. H. Pearse,
Eamonn Ceannt, James Connolly, and Joseph Plunket*
Poblacht na hÉireann 1916: *Proclamation of the Republic* (1916)

I

Invasion

1 A single legion, with a moderate band of auxiliaries, would
be enough to finish the conquest of Ireland.
Gnaeus Julius Agricola AD 40–93: Tacitus *Histories*

2 Light as a blackbird on a green bough swinging
Would my heart be if the French would come—
O the broken ranks and the trumpets ringing
On the sunny side of Slievenamon!
Anonymous: 'Sliabh na mBan' (*c.*1798, translated by Frank O'Connor)

3 O! The French are in the bay,
They'll be here by break of day,
And the Orange will decay,
Says the Sean-Bhean bhocht.
Anonymous: 'The Sean-Bhean Bhocht' (traditional song, *c.*1798)

4 I will never despair, but that the parliament of England, if it
may perceive, that this action is not a flash, but a solid and
settled pursuit, will give aid to a work so religious, so
politic, and so profitable.
Francis Bacon 1561–1626: *Certain Considerations Touching the Plantation
in Ireland* (1606)

5 At length an invader more welcome comes o'er,
And without opposition sets foot on the shore;
No war trumpet sounds her approach to declare,
'Tis the horn's merry note that invites to Kildare.
Rowland Eyles Egerton-Warburton 1804–91: 'On the Visit of the Empress
of Austria to Kildare' (February, 1879)

6 The devouring demon of Anglicization in Ireland . . . with
its foul jaws has devoured, one after another, everything
that was hereditary, national, instructive, ancient,
intellectual and noble in our race, our language, our
music, our songs, our industries, our dances, and our

pastimes—I **know**, I say, that you will plant your feet
firmly, and say with us, 'Back, Demon, back!'
Douglas Hyde 1860–1949: speaking on behalf of the Gaelic League in
America, 1904

7 If someone were to tell me now that the Germans were
coming in over our back wall, I wouldn't lift up a finger to
stop them. They could come!
after the Easter Rising executions
Francis Ledwidge 1891–1917: Alice Curtayne *Francis Ledwidge* (1972)

8 The sons of Ulster will rise and lay their enemy low, as they
did at the Boyne, as they did at the Somme, against any
invader who will trespass on to their homeland.
Frank McGuinness 1953– : *Observe the Sons of Ulster Marching Towards the
Somme* (1985)

9 The Norman walled this town against the country
To stop his ears to the yelping of his slave
And built a church in the form of a cross but denoting
The list of Christ on the cross in the angle of the nave.
Louis MacNeice 1907–63: 'Carrickfergus' (1937)

Ireland see also Ireland and America, Ireland and
England

1 Icham of Irlaunde
Ant of the holy londe of irlonde
Gode sir pray ich ye
for of saynte charite,
come ant daunce wyt me,
in irlaunde.
Anonymous: fourteenth century; cf. **Dance 1, The Presidency 8**

2 I met wid Napper Tandy, and he took me by the hand,
And he said, 'How's poor ould Ireland, and how does she
stand?'
She's the most disthressful country that iver yet was seen,

For they're hangin' men an' women for the wearin' o' the
  Green.
Anonymous: 'The Wearin' o' the Green' (c.1795 ballad)

3 For this island being another Britain, as Britain was said to
  be another world, is endowed with so many dowries of
  nature, considering the fruitfulness of the soil, the ports,
  the rivers, the fishings, the quarries, the woods, and other
  materials . . . as it is not easy, no not upon the continent, to
  find such confluence of commodities, if the hand of man did
  join with the hand of nature.
  Francis Bacon 1561–1626: *Certain Considerations Touching the Plantation
  in Ireland* (1606)

4 Do you not feel that this island is moored only lightly to the
  sea-bed, and might be off for the Americas at any moment?
  Sebastian Barry 1955– : *Prayers of Sherkin* (1991)

5 This island is a region of dreams and trifles.
  George Berkeley 1685–1753: *The Querist* (1735)

6 Bells are booming down the bohreens,
  White the mist along the grass.
  Now the Julias, Maeves and Maureens
  Move between the fields to Mass.
  John Betjeman 1906–84: 'Ireland with Emily' (1945)

7 An overwhelmingly Catholic country, then, in which
  strikes flourish as obedience does elsewhere.
  Heinrich Böll 1917–85: *Irish Journal* (1957, translated Leila Vennewitz)

8 She could not conceive of her country emotionally: it was a
  way of living, an abstract of several landscapes, or an
  oblique frayed island, moored at the north but with an air
  of being detached and washed out west from the British
  coast.
  Elizabeth Bowen 1899–1973: *The Last September* (1929)

9 Ireland is one of the few countries—perhaps the last—
where the boundaries between politics and art have never
been fixed.
George Dangerfield 1904–86: *The Strange Death of Liberal England* (1935)

10 This country of ours is no sand-bank, thrown up by some
recent caprice of earth. It is an ancient land, honoured in
the archives of civilisation, traceable into antiquity by its
piety, its valour, and its sufferings. Every great European
race has sent its stream to the river of Irish mind.
Thomas Davis 1814–45: *Literary and Historical Essays* (1846)

11 That Ireland which we dreamed of would be the home of a
people who valued material wealth only as a basis of right
living, of a people who were satisfied with frugal comfort
and devoted their leisure to the things of the spirit; a land
whose countryside would be bright with cosy homesteads,
whose fields and villages would be joyous with sounds of
industry, the romping of sturdy children, the contests of
athletic youths, the laughter of comely maidens; whose
firesides would be the forums of the wisdom of serene old
age.
Eamon de Valera 1882–1975: St Patrick's Day broadcast, 1943

12 The plains of lovely Ireland flow with honey and milk.
Donatus *c.*829–876: 'The Land Called Scotia'; Thomas Kinsella (ed.) *The
New Oxford Book of Irish Verse* (1986)

13 There lay the green shore of Ireland, like some coast of
plenty. We could see towns, towers, churches, harvests;
but the curse of eight hundred years we could not discern.
Ralph Waldo Emerson 1803–82: *English Traits* (1856)

14 Ireland is at all points like a young wench that hath a
greensickness. She is very fair of visage, and hath a smooth
skin of tender grass.
Luke Gerson fl. 1620: *Ireland Delineated*

15 Ireland is the old sow that eats her farrow.
James Joyce 1882–1941: *A Portrait of the Artist as a Young Man* (1916)

16 Ireland is a small but insuppressible island half an hour
nearer the sunset than Great Britain.
Thomas Kettle 1880–1916: 'On Crossing the Irish Sea'

17 The land of scholars and saints:
Scholars and saints my eye, the land of ambush,
Purblind manifestoes, never-ending complaints
The born martyr and the gallant ninny.
Louis MacNeice 1907–63: *Autumn Journal* (1938)

18 What we call our country is not a poetical abstraction . . .
There is no such person as Caitlin Ni Uallachain or Roisin
Dubh or the Sean-bhean Bhocht, who is calling on us to
save her.
Eoin MacNeill 1867–1945: in February, 1916; Robert Kee *The Bold Fenian
Men* (1989)

19 In Ireland the inevitable never happens and the unexpected
constantly occurs.
John Pentland Mahaffy 1839–1919: W. B. Stanford and R. B. McDowell
Mahaffy (1971)

20 I know tolerably well what Ireland was, but have a very
imperfect idea of what Ireland *is*.
John Stuart Mill 1806–73: letter to J. E. Cairnes, 29 July 1864

21 Spenser's Ireland
has not altered;—
a place as kind as it is green,
the greenest place I've never seen.
Marianne Moore 1887–1972: 'Spenser's Ireland' (1941)

22 I remember arriving home from Baltistan last year and
feeling that I'd come from the Third World to some dotty
Fourth World consisting only of Ireland.
Dervla Murphy 1931– : *A Place Apart* (1978)

23 A country fit for Protestants to live in.
on the 'yes' vote given in the divorce referendum, 1995
Conor Cruise O'Brien 1917– : Mary Kenny *Goodbye to Catholic Ireland*
(1997)

24 Everything seemed so ancient, the connection to the land intimate and personal, the people bilingual. I'd never met peasants before.
an American's view
Tim O'Grady: in *Irish Post* 1 November 1997

25 Why should Ireland be treated as a geographical fragment of England . . . Ireland is not a geographical fragment, but a nation.
Charles Stewart Parnell 1846–91: in the House of Commons, 26 April 1875

26 *Mise Éire!*
I am Ireland:
I am older than the hag of Beara.
Patrick Pearse 1879–1916: 'I am Ireland'

27 Ireland is a unit . . . The two nations theory is to us an abomination and a blasphemy.
John Redmond 1856–1918: speech, October 1913

28 John Bull's other island.
George Bernard Shaw 1856–1950: title of play, 1907

29 I reckon no man is throughly miserable unless he be condemned to live in Ireland.
Jonathan Swift 1667–1745: letter to Ambrose Philips, 30 October 1709

30 I think it manifest that whatever circumstances can possibly contribute to make a country poor and despicable, are all united with respect to Ireland.
Jonathan Swift 1667–1745: letter to the Earl of Peterborough, 28 April 1726

31 Sarsfield and the siege-train, he thought, the Island of Saints and Scholars, the Famine Queen bejasus and the Fenian dead, bold Robert Emmet the darling of Erin and Kevin Barry gave his young life for the cause of libertee.
William John White 1920–80: *The Devil You Know* (1962)

Ireland and America

1 In whatever quarter of the world an Irishman sets his foot,
  there stands a bitter, an implacable enemy of England . . .
  There are hundreds of thousands—I suppose there are
  millions—of the population of the United States of America
  who are Irish by birth, or by immediate descent; and be it
  remembered, Irishmen settled in the United States have a
  large influence in public affairs.
  John Bright 1811–89: in the House of Commons, 25 August 1848

2 America is a very big place; but I think I was in most towns
  of it anyway. Philadelphia, Chicago I was . . .
  Joe Cooley 1924–73: attributed, 1973

3 It took 115 years and 6,000 miles and three generations to
  make this trip, but I'm proud to be here.
  John Fitzgerald Kennedy 1917–63: at New Ross, Wexford, while visiting
  Ireland in 1963

4 Being Irish in New York has a perennial cachet, but while I
  lived there it was actually groovy.
  Marian Keyes: *Rachel's Holiday* (1997)

5 None of this would have been possible without the industry
  of my ancestors, the canny Irishmen who immigrated in
  1824 from County Down . . . I bless them with every
  breath.
  of his publishing company, New Directions
  James Laughlin 1914–97: in 1992; in *Guardian* 18 November 1997,
  obituary

6 Ireland is passing forth. It is wending its way to the North
  American States . . . to ask for an empty space of ground.
  Prince Metternich 1773–1859: in the mid 19th century; Nicholas Mansergh
  The Irish Question (ed. 3, 1975)

7 For the first time, the discontent in Ireland rests on a
  background of several millions of Irish across the
  Atlantic . . . The number of Irish in America is constantly

increasing. Their power to influence the political conduct of the United States is increasing and will daily increase; and is there any probability that the American-Irish will come to hate this country less than they do at the present moment?
John Stuart Mill 1806–73: in the House of Commons, 12 March 1868

8 Our cause for the present among the Irish here is a lost one. They have blood in their eyes when they look our way.
as British Ambassador in Washington, commenting on the effect of the Easter Rising executions
Cecil Spring-Rice 1859–1918: letter, 16 June 1916

9 Until recently, Irish-Americans, if they made money, disappeared into WASP-dom in Connecticut.
Kevin Whelan: in *Irish Times* 10 June 1998

Ireland and England

1 Thank God we're surrounded by water!
Dominic Behan 1928– : 'The Sea Around Us' (song, 1960s)

2 We are sorry if we have offended Irish people and we have no wish to misrepresent them.
British Broadcasting Corporation: apology for the portrayal of Ireland in an episode of *Eastenders*, September 1997

3 England and Ireland may flourish together. The world is large enough for us both. Let it be our care not to make ourselves too little for it.
Edmund Burke 1729–97: attributed

4 Thus you have a starving population, an absentee aristocracy, and an alien Church, and in addition the weakest executive in the world. That is the Irish Question.
Benjamin Disraeli 1804–81: speech in the House of Commons, 16 February 1844

5 Ireland may be regarded as the first English colony and as one which because of its proximity is still governed in the old way, and here one can already observe that the so-called liberty of English citizens is based on the oppression of the colonies.
Friedrich Engels 1820–95: letter to Karl Marx, 23 May 1856

6 He is . . . blissfully ignorant of the emotions which prejudice normal English politicians' attitudes towards Ireland. His heart pounds neither at the cry of 'No Surrender' nor at the memory of the plough and the stars.
of Tony Blair
Roy Hattersley 1932– : in *Guardian* 1 December 1997

7 It seems that the historic inability in Britain to comprehend Irish feelings and sensitivities still remains.
Charles Haughey 1925– : in *Observer* February 1988

8 She was Irish and had a huge inferiority complex and thought that everything English people suggested had to be right.
Marian Keyes: *Lucy Sullivan is Getting Married* (1997)

9 Isn't it a very curious thing that St Patrick drove the snakes out of Ireland an' the English brought in the fleas.
Frank McCourt 1930– : *Angela's Ashes* (1996)

10 The Irish are still the people the English understand least. And we're just not sure . . . if they will ever really forgive us for the unspeakable sin of not wanting to be like them.
Joseph O'Connor 1963– : *The Secret World of the Irish Male* (1994)

11 You've had that problem at your very door for 300 years. What is the matter that you don't solve it.
the American Ambassador to A. J. Balfour on England's failure to solve the Irish Question, 1916
Walter H. Page: Nicholas Mansergh *The Irish Question* (ed. 3, 1975)

12 The English look down on other races. We, the Irish, must never look up to them. We must despise their vices.
Charles Stewart Parnell 1846–91: Ulick O'Connor *The Troubles* (rev. ed., 1996)

13 England sees in the faults and vices of Irishmen the true explanation of their misfortunes; Ireland deems the cruelty and tyranny of the English to be the real and only cause of her unhappiness.
L. Paul-Dubois 1868–1938: *Contemporary Ireland* (1908)

14 Now dream
of that sweet
equal republic
where the juniper
talks to the oak,
the thistle,
the bandaged elm,
and the jolly, jolly chestnut.
Tom Paulin 1949– : 'The Book of Juniper' (1983)

15 That stretch of water, it's always
There for you to cross over
To the other side.
Tom Paulin 1949– : 'States' (1977)

16 I would have the two sisters embrace like one brother.
Boyle Roche 1743–1807: speech in favour of the Act of Union, 1799

17 Gladstone . . . spent his declining years trying to guess the answer to the Irish Question; unfortunately whenever he was getting warm, the Irish secretly changed the Question.
W. C. Sellar 1898–1951 and **R. J. Yeatman** 1898–1968: *1066 and All That* (1930)

18 The moment the very name of Ireland is mentioned, the English seem to bid adieu to common feeling, common prudence, and common sense, and to act with the barbarity of tyrants, and the fatuity of idiots.
Sydney Smith 1771–1845: *Letters of Peter Plymley* (1807)

19 When Spenser wrote of Ireland he wrote as an official, and
    out of the thoughts and emotions that had been organized
    by the state. He was the first of many Englishmen to see
    nothing but what he was desired to see.
    W. B. Yeats 1865–1939: 'Edmund Spenser' (1902)

The Irish Language see also Languages

1 If they really want to revive the Irish language, all they
   have to do is ban it.
   Anonymous: comment of a dentist in County Tipperary; Tony Gray
   St Patrick's People (1996)

2 In the bolder species of composition it is distinguished by a
   freedom of expression, a sublime dignity, and rapid energy,
   which it is scarcely possible for any translation fully to
   convey.
   Charlotte Brooke ?1740–93: *Reliques of Irish Poetry* (1789)

3 There is a disease after breaking out in the North among
   Irish speakers. The name of the disease is the 'Way to Make
   Irish Attractive to the Protestant Community in Northern
   Ireland.'
   view of the president of the Gaelic League
   Gearóid Ó Cairealláin: in *Irish Times* 13 December 1997 'This Week They
   Said'

4 The lovely, glorious tongue.
   Roger Casement 1864–1916: Ulick O'Connor *The Troubles* (rev. ed., 1996)

5 A people without a language of its own is only half a
   nation. To lose your native tongue and learn that of an
   alien, is the worst badge of conquest—it is the chain on the
   soul. To have lost entirely the national language is death;
   the fetter has worn through.
   Thomas Davis 1814–45: 'The National Language'

6 If I were told tomorrow, 'You can have a united Ireland if you give up the idea of restoring the national language to be the spoken language of the majority of the people,' I would for myself say no.
Eamon de Valera 1882–1975: speech in the Dáil, 1939

7 Even if I did speak Irish I'd always be an outsider here, wouldn't I? I may learn the password but the language of the tribe will always elude me, won't it?
Brian Friel 1929– : *Translations* (1980)

8 As long as there is English spoken in the home, what is taught in the morning will be undone in the evening by the parents, and the greatest enthusiast has not suggested the shooting of mothers of English-speaking children.
Oliver St John Gogarty 1878–1957: on the Gaeltacht Commission Report in the Senate, March 1927

9 The rhinoceros and the Irish language are both relics of the splendid diversity that life used to offer before we all became engulfed in this terrible tidal wave of cement and plastic and Coca Cola prosperity.
Tony Gray 1928– : comment, 1965; *St Patrick's People* (1996)

10 In order to de-Anglicise ourselves we must at once arrest the decay of the language.
Douglas Hyde 1860–1949: 'The Necessity for de-Anglicising Ireland' (1892)

11 The tide gone out for good,
Thirty-one words for seaweed
Whiten on the foreshore.
Aidan Carl Mathews 1956– : 'The Death of Irish'

12 '*A Ghaela,*' *adúirt sé,* '*cuireann sé gliondar ar mo chroi Gaelach a bheith annso inniu ag caint Gaeilge libh-se ar an fheis Ghaelaí seo i lár na Gaeltachta.*'
'Gaels,' he said, 'it puts joy in my Gaelic heart to be here today talking Gaelic with you at this Gaelic feis in the heart of the Gaeltacht.'
Flann O'Brien 1911–66: *An Béal Bocht* (The Poor Mouth, 1941)

13 In Donegal there are native speakers who know so many million words that it is a matter of pride with them never to use the same word twice in a life-time.
Flann O'Brien 1911–66: *The Best of Myles* (1968)

14 It is worth remembering that if Irish were to die completely, the standard of English here, both in the spoken and written word, would sink to a level probably as low as that obtaining in England and it would stop there only because it could go no lower.
Flann O'Brien 1911–66: *The Best of Myles* (1968)

15 Although the Irish language is connected with many recollections which twine round the hearts of Irishmen, yet the superior utility of the English tongue as a medium of all modern communication is so great that I can witness without a sigh the gradual disuse of Irish.
Daniel O'Connell 1775–1847: Charles Chevenix Trench *The Great Dan* (1984)

16 There are only two dialects of Irish, plain Irish and toothless Irish, and, lacking a proper acquaintance with the latter, I think I missed the cream of the old man's talk.
Frank O'Connor 1903–66: *Leinster, Munster and Connaught* (1950)

17 How do you say 'I am sad' in Irish? *Ta brón órm*, which means literally, 'sadness is upon me'; that is, I am the passive recipient of an emotion which is outside me . . . Irish features categories of passivity which other languages don't even dream about.
Joseph O'Connor 1963– : *The Irish Male at Home and Abroad* (1996)

18 Getting Jeremiah O'Donovan to screech in Irish down the holes in the fort, for fear old O'Reilly's hounds had no English.
Edith Œ. Somerville 1858–1949 and **Martin Ross** 1862–1915: *Further Experiences of an Irish R.M.* (1908)

19 There is no language like the Irish for soothing and quieting.
John Millington Synge 1871–1909: *The Aran Islands* (1907)

Irishness

1 To the voice which urges that I am mainly Irish by blood, I make the round reply that, nonsense, my blood is entirely Group O. I don't believe in 'blood' in that sense any more than I believe in leprechauns. But it is true that my exact sociological situation is too complex to allow me to make the simple assertion that I am English.
Brigid Brophy 1929–95: 'Am I an Irishwoman?' (1966)

2 What is called 'Irishness' can be understood only in relation to the homeland. There is a saying that you can take a boy out of Ireland but you cannot take Ireland out of the boy. In the long run, I believe geography counts for more than genes.
E. Estyn Evans 1905– : *Irish Folk Ways* (1957)

3 Varieties of Irishness.
R. F. Foster 1949– : prologue heading in *Modern Ireland* (1988)

4 I may appear Planter's Gothic, but there is a Round Tower somewhere inside and needled through every sentence that I utter.
John Hewitt 1907–87: 'Planter's Gothic' (autobiographical essay)

5 I believe it is our Gaelic past which, though the Irish race does not recognize it just at present, is really at the bottom of the Irish heart, and prevents us becoming citizens of the empire.
Douglas Hyde 1860–1949: address to the Irish National Literary Society, November 1897

6 When the soul of a man is born in this country, there are
   nets flung at it to hold it back from flight. You talk to me of
   nationality, language, religion. I shall try to fly by those
   nets.
   James Joyce 1882–1941: *A Portrait of the Artist as a Young Man* (1916)

7 My only programme for Ireland consists, in equal parts, of
   Home Rule and the Ten Commandments. My only counsel
   to Ireland is, that in order to become deeply Irish, she must
   become European.
   Thomas Kettle 1880–1916: 'Apology'

8 'Are you a plastic paddy?'
   'I was born here,' I admitted. 'But I *feel* Irish.'
   Marian Keyes: *Lucy Sullivan is Getting Married* (1997)

9 The 'real' Irishman is neither essentially a Celt nor
   essentially a Catholic. He is merely a man who has had the
   good or bad fortune to be born in Ireland or of Irish
   parents, and who is interested in Ireland more than in any
   other country in the world.
   Robert Lynd 1879–1949: *Home Life in Ireland* (1908)

10 There is more to being Irish than merely living in the island
   of Ireland. To me, there is no distinction between the Irish
   at home and the Irish abroad.
   Mary McAleese 1951– : in *Irish Post* 1 November 1997

11 Why do we like being Irish? Partly because
   It gives us a hold on the sentimental English
   As members of a world that never was,
   Baptized with fairy water.
   Louis MacNeice 1907–63: *Autumn Journal* (1938)

12 Since Grattan's time every popular leader, O'Connell, Butt,
   Parnell, Dillon and Redmond, has perpetuated this primary
   contradiction. They threw over Irish civilisation whilst they
   professed—and professed in perfectly good faith—to fight
   for Irish nationality.
   D. P. Moran 1871–1936: *The Philosophy of Irish Ireland* (1905)

Irishness

13 Irishness is not primarily a question of birth or blood or language: it is the condition of being involved in the Irish situation, and usually of being mauled by it. On that definition Swift is more Irish than Goldsmith or Sheridan, although by the usual tests they are Irish and he is pure English.
Conor Cruise O'Brien 1917– : *Writers and Politics* (1965)

14 You are Irish you say lightly, and allocated to you are the tendencies to be wild, wanton, drunk, superstitious, unreliable, backward, toadying and prone to fits, whereas you know that in fact a whole entourage of ghosts resides in you, ghosts with whom the inner rapport is as frequent, as perplexing, as defiant as with any of the living.
Edna O'Brien 1932– : *Mother Ireland* (1976)

15 The best way we can contribute to a new integrated Europe of the 1990s is by having a confident sense of our Irishness.
Mary Robinson 1944– : inaugural speech as President, 1990

16 Nationalism must now be added to the refuse pile of superstitions. We are now citizens of the world; and the man who divides the race into elect Irishmen and reprobate foreign devils (especially Englishmen) had better live on the Blaskets where he can admire himself without much disturbance.
George Bernard Shaw 1856–1950: in *Irish Statesman* 15 September 1925

The Irish People

1 *Hibernicis ipsis Hibernior.*
More Irish than the Irish themselves.
applied to the 'Old English' in Ireland from the 14th century
Anonymous: traditional saying

2 Query: whether there be upon earth any Christian or civilised people so beggarly, wretched and destitute as the common Irish.
George Berkeley 1685–1753: *The Querist* (1735–7)

3 The Irish have the thickest ankles in the world & the best
   complexions.
John Berryman 1914–72: *77 Dream Songs* (1964)

4 To every Irishman on earth
  Arrest comes soon or late.
George A. Birmingham 1865–1950: *The Search Party* (1906)

5 The people of this country are not idle. Let no man tell me
  this, when I see a peasant from Connaught going over to
  reap the harvest in England.
Isaac Butt 1813–79: speech in defence of Thomas F. Meagher, 1848

6 For the great Gaels of Ireland
  Are the men that God made mad,
  For all their wars are merry,
  And all their songs are sad.
G. K. Chesterton 1874–1936: *The Ballad of the White Horse* (1911)

7 I'll never understand this country. I thought I was going off
  to bloody combat, and instead I found myself in Mick
  Sullivan's feather bed in Kilnamartyr.
  while on the run, in 1922
Erskine Childers 1870–1922: Jim Ring *Erskine Childers* (1996)

8 The concept of the Gael as propagated by the extreme wing
  of the movement, is of a man approximately six feet and
  five inches in height, noble-browed and with the faraway
  look in his eyes which comes through perusing Erin's past
  glories. His wife is serene, beautiful and the mother of
  eleven children. In view of the mandatory chastity of the
  couple, conception, it will be understood, occurs non-
  sexually—through the medium, as it were.
Tim Pat Coogan 1935– : *Ireland Since the Rising* (1966)

9 The race of the Rackrents has long since been extinct in
  Ireland, and the drunken Sir Patrick, the litigious Sir
  Murtagh, the fighting Sir Kit, and the slovenly Sir Condy,
  are characters which would no more be met with at

present in Ireland, than Squire Western or Parson Trulliber in England.
Maria Edgeworth 1767–1849: preface to *Castle Rackrent* (1800)

10 This is a filthy people, wallowing in mire. Of all peoples it is the least instructed in the rudiments of the faith.
Giraldus Cambrensis *c.*1146–1223: *The History and Topography of Ireland*

11 When a Southern Irishman says 'Not an inch', he means no more than four or five inches, and certainly not, at any rate for the next five or six years. But when an Ulsterman says 'Not an inch', that's it: he means not the tiniest fraction of an inch, from now until the last syllable of recorded time. And when he says 'No Surrender' he means just that, no surrender, ever.
Tony Gray 1928– : *St Patrick's People* (1996)

12 By the real people of Ireland I mean the people who have their dinner in the middle of the day.
Jackie Healy-Rae: comment, 1997

13 I am troubled, I'm dissatisfied, I'm Irish.
Marianne Moore 1887–1972: 'Spenser's Ireland' (1941)

14 It's part of our national inferiority complex that when someone pays us a compliment, we take it as an insult.
Michael Noonan: comment, 1984

15 Attitudes don't change, the psyche of a country is not changed by wealth, change is not about getting milking machines . . . The Irish still feed off the human weaknesses and failures of others.
Edna O'Brien 1932– : in *Irish Times* 12 September 1992

16 The Plain People of Ireland.
Flann O'Brien 1911–66: customary reference in 'Cruiskeen Lawn' column of *Irish Times*, 1940–66

17 Deferential to a stranger, they evoked in themselves a sympathetic mood, changing gears in conversation to suit his beliefs and half believing them in sympathy whilst he

was present. Afterwards when they checked up on themselves it might be different; they would laugh at the stranger's outlandish opinions when their mood had hardened.

Ernie O'Malley 1898–1957: *On Another Man's Wound* (1936)

18 There are 70 million people living on this globe who claim Irish descent. I will be proud to represent them.

Mary Robinson 1944– : inaugural speech as President, 1990

19 An Irishman's heart is nothing but his imagination.

George Bernard Shaw 1856–1950: *John Bull's Other Island* (1907)

20 He gave the little wealth he had
To build a house for fools and mad;
And showed, by one satiric touch,
No nation wanted it so much.

Jonathan Swift 1667–1745: 'Verses on the Death of Dr Swift' (1731)

21 These people have all the divine virtues. They have the faith. No one is a better Christian than the Irishman. Their morals are pure. Their crimes are very rarely premeditated. But they lack essentially the civil virtues. They are without foresight, without prudence. Their courage is instinctive . . . They are changeable, love excitement, combat. The Englishman, on the other hand, coldly calculates the odds, approaches danger slowly, and withdraws only after having succeeded.

Alexis de Tocqueville 1805–59: *Voyage en Angleterre et en Irlande de 1835* (ed. J. P. Mayer, 1958)

22 We Irish, born into that ancient sect
But thrown upon this filthy modern tide
And by its formless spawning, fury wrecked,
Climb to our proper dark, that we may trace
The lineaments of a plummet-measured face.

W. B. Yeats 1865–1939: 'The Statues' (1939)

23 Cast your mind on other days
That we in coming days may be
Still the indomitable Irishry.
W. B. Yeats 1865–1939: 'Under Ben Bulben' (1939)

Justice

1 You have been acquitted by a Limerick jury, and you may now leave the court without any other stain upon your character.
Richard Adams 1846–1908: Maurice Healy *The Old Munster Circuit* (1939)

2 One of the thieves was saved. (*Pause*) It's a reasonable percentage.
Samuel Beckett 1906–89: *Waiting for Godot* (1955)

3 The life sentence goes on. It's like a runaway train that you can't just get off.
Gerry Conlon 1954– : in *Irish Post* 13 September 1997

4 Ireland, Ireland! that cloud in the west, that coming storm, the minister of God's retribution upon cruel and inveterate and but half-atoned injustice.
William Ewart Gladstone 1809–98: letter to his wife, 12 October 1845

5 Zero tolerance was to mean whatever John O'Donoghue said it meant, depending on whether there was a full moon and how Jackie Healy-Rae was feeling.
view of the spokesman for Fine Gael
Jim Higgins: in *Irish Times* 13 June 1998 'This Week They Said'

6 Are you talking about the new Jerusalem? says the citizen. I'm talking about injustice, says Bloom.
James Joyce 1882–1941: *Ulysses* (1922)

7 In England, justice is open to all—like the Ritz Hotel.
James Mathew 1830–1908: R. E. Megarry *Miscellany-at-Law* (1955)

8 He likes the slogan so much that even though he has
   redefined it beyond any reasonable meaning, he sticks to it
   like a barnacle on the keel of a sunken wreck.
   *of the Minister for Justice John O'Donoghue's fondness for the
   expression 'zero tolerance'*
   Fintan O'Toole 1958– : in *Irish Times* 14 November 1997

9 But, since we didn't reform ourselves,
   since we had to be caught
   red-handed, justice is something
   we have to be taught.
   James Simmons 1933– : 'Ulster Says Yes'

Kerry

1 Are 'oo from Kerry?
   I am. Are 'oo?
   Anonymous: traditional exchange between Kerrymen

2 When I return to Kerry, like a Roman back to Rome,
   I sometimes get the feeling that I am coming home.
   Charles Haughey 1925– : written for the Festival of Kerry; in *Irish Times* 1
   July 1997

3 She's off with her dear bridegroom towards Kerry's hills so
      fair.
   Robert Dwyer Joyce 1830–83: 'The Spalpeen'

4   I want to see on a Kerry moor
    The purple turf smoke, coil, and soar.
    Dora Sigerson 1866–1918: *The Sad Years* (1918) 'Home'

Kildare

1   As I travelled once in the county of Kildare in Ireland, in
    the summer-time, I came into a land of flowers and
    blossoms, hills, woods, and shades.
    Thomas Amory ?1691–1788: *The Life of John Buncle, Esq.* (1756–66)

2   And straight I will repair
    To the Curragh of Kildare,
    For it's there I'll find tidings of my dear.
    Anonymous: 'The Curragh of Kildare' (19th century song)

3   *Life*, the story goes,
    Was the daughter of Cannan,
    And came to the plain of Kildare.
    She loved the flat-lands and the ditches
    And the unreachable horizon.
    She asked that it be named for her.
    Eavan Boland 1944– : *In a Time of Violence* (1994) 'Anna Liffey'

Knowledge

1   Sweet is the scholar's life,
    engaged on his learning:
    the pleasantest fate in Ireland
    as you people know well.
    Anonymous: 'Beatha an Scoláire' (16th century poem)

2 We have first raised a dust and then complain we cannot
see.
George Berkeley 1685–1753: *A Treatise Concerning the Principles of Human Knowledge* (1710) introduction

3 I'll know the library in a city
Before I know there is a slum.
I could wish the weight of
Learning would bring me down
To where things are done.
Seamus Deane 1940– : 'Scholar II' (1977)

4 Can knowledge have no bounds, but must advance
So far, to make us wish for ignorance?
John Denham 1615–59: *Cooper's-Hill* (1709)

5 And still they gazed, and still the wonder grew,
That one small head could carry all he knew.
Oliver Goldsmith 1728–74: *The Deserted Village* (1770)

6 My speciality is omniscience.
Charles Haughey 1925– : attributed

7 There is a North-west passage to the intellectual World.
Laurence Sterne 1713–68: *Tristram Shandy* (1759–67)

8 As I stroll the city, oft I
Spy a building large and lofty,
Not a bow-shot from the College,
Half a globe from sense and knowledge.
Jonathan Swift 1667–1745: 'A Character, Panegyric and description of the Legion Club' (1736)

9 All shuffle there; all cough in ink;
All wear the carpet with their shoes;
All think what other people think;
All know the man their neighbour knows.
Lord, what would they say

Knowledge

Did their Catullus walk that way?
W. B. Yeats 1865–1939: 'Sailing to Byzantium' (1928)

Language see Speech and Language

Languages see also The Irish Language

1 She could curse fluently, so she boasted, in four
languages—in the English, the Gaelic of Donegal, the
Gaelic of Rachery, and the Gaelic of the Isles.
Margaret Barrington 1896–1982: *My Cousin Justin* (1939)

2 AIMWELL: Then you understand Latin, Mr Bonniface?
BONNIFACE: Not I, Sir, as the saying is, but he talks it so
very fast that I'm sure it must be good.
George Berkeley 1685–1753: *The Beaux' Stratagem* (1707)

3 I can speak English when it suits me.
Con Houlihan: in *Irish Post* 4 July 1998

4 To kill a language is to kill a people.
Pearse Hutchinson 1927– : *The Frost is All Over* (1975)

5 Writing in English is the most ingenious torture ever
devised for sins committed in previous lives. The English
reading public explains the reason why.
James Joyce 1882–1941: letter, 5 September 1918

6 If Berkeley and Swift, Goldsmith and Sheridan, Grattan and
Burke, had been compelled to write in Irish for the sake of
official promotion, or to soothe national sensibilities, not

only would the English-speaking world but Ireland herself, have suffered unreasonable damage.
John Pentland Mahaffy 1839–1919: in *Nineteenth Century* 1896

7   To grow
a second tongue, as
harsh a humiliation
as twice to be born.
John Montague 1929– : 'A Grafted Tongue' (1972)

8 A dry shank bone in the dust heap of Empire.
of the English language
George Moore 1852–1933: Ulick O'Connor *The Troubles* (rev. ed., 1996)

9 Waiting for the German verb is surely the ultimate thrill.
Flann O'Brien 1911–66: *The Hair of the Dogma* (1977)

10 It has been held that the teaching of subjects other than fishing not through Irish but through the medium of Irish leads to a generation 'illiterate in two languages'.
Flann O'Brien 1911–66: attributed

11 England and America are two countries divided by a common language.
George Bernard Shaw 1856–1950: attributed in this and other forms, but not found in Shaw's published writings

12 As the chirpings of a cock-sparrow on the houseroof to the soft cooing of the gentle cushat by the southern Blackwater.
English compared with Irish
Edward Walsh 1805–50: in *Dictionary of National Biography* (1917–)

13 We have really everything in common with America nowadays except, of course, language.
Oscar Wilde 1854–1900: *The Canterville Ghost* (1887)

Last Words

1 God save Ireland!
called out from the dock by the Manchester Martyrs, 1867,
repeating the words of Edward Condon (cf. Determination 2)
William Allen d. 1867, **Michael Larkin** d. 1867, and **William O'Brien**
d. 1867: Robert Kee *The Bold Fenian Men* (1989); cf. **3** below, **Sacrifice 15**

2 Come closer, boys. It will be easier for you.
to the firing squad at his execution
Erskine Childers 1870–1922: Burke Wilkinson *The Zeal of the Convert*
(1976)

3 God be with you, Irishmen and Irish women.
last words spoken from the dock after sentence of death was
passed
Michael Larkin d. 1867: Robert Kee *The Bold Fenian Men* (1989);
cf. **1** above

4 I am no traitor; I die a persecuted man for a persecuted
country.
William Orr 1768–97: speech before his execution at Carrickfergus;
cf. **Political Sayings and Slogans 7**

5 Would to God this wound had been for Ireland.
on being mortally wounded at the battle of Landen, 19 August
1693, while fighting for France
Patrick Sarsfield *c.*1655–93: attributed

6 I find, then, I am but a bad anatomist.
cutting his throat in prison, he severed his windpipe instead of
his jugular, and lingered for several days
Wolfe Tone 1763–98: Oliver Knox *Rebels and Informers* (1998)

of the wallpaper in the room where he was dying:
7 One of us must go.
Oscar Wilde 1854–1900: attributed, probably apocryphal

The Law see also **Justice**

1 When I came back to Dublin, I was courtmartialled in my absence and sentenced to death in my absence, so I said they could shoot me in my absence.
Brendan Behan 1923–64: *Hostage* (1958)

2 Bad laws are the worst sort of tyranny.
Edmund Burke 1729–97: *Speech at Bristol, previous to the Late Election* (1780)

3 Laws, like houses, lean on one another.
Edmund Burke 1729–97: *A Tract on the Popery Laws* (planned *c.*1765)

4 Make him a bishop, or even an archbishop, but not a Chief Justice.
an Irish Lord Chancellor's view of the proposed appointment of Lord Norbury as Chief Justice of Ireland
Lord Clare 1749–1802: in *Dictionary of National Biography* (1917–)

5 As for the law, I believe no man, dead or alive, ever loved it so well as Sir Murtagh . . . Everything upon the face of the earth furnished him good matter for a suit. He used to boast that he had a law-suit for every letter of the alphabet.
Maria Edgeworth 1767–1849: *Castle Rackrent* (1800)

6 You might as well try to employ a boa constrictor as a tape-measure as to go to a lawyer for legal advice.
Oliver St John Gogarty 1878–1957: *Tumbling in the Hay* (1939)

7 The Polis as Polis, in this city, is Null an' Void!
Sean O'Casey 1880–1964: *Juno and the Paycock* (1925)

8 Nothing advances an Irish barrister more than the talent of ridicule.
Daniel O'Connell 1775–1847: Charles Chevenix Trench *The Great Dan* (1984)

9 Of all the cubs being suckled by the Celtic Tiger, by far the fattest, sleekest and best-nurtured are the lawyers.
Pat Rabbitte: in *Irish Times* 20 December 1997 'This Week They Said'

10 As to Coercion Acts, the worst English one on record is a perfect Magna Carta compared with the one imposed by the Free State . . . The little finger of the Free State is thicker than the loins of the Castle; but the Irish stand it because it is their own government.
George Bernard Shaw 1856–1950: in *Irish Statesman* 15 September 1925

11 Laws are like cobwebs, which may catch small flies, but let wasps and hornets break through.
Jonathan Swift 1667–1745: *A Critical Essay upon the Faculties of the Mind* (1709)

Liberty

1 The people never give up their liberties but under some delusion.
Edmund Burke 1729–97: speech at County Meeting of Buckinghamshire, 1784; attributed

2 Apostles of freedom are ever idolised when dead, but crucified when alive.
James Connolly 1868–1916: in *Workers' Republic* August 1898

3 The condition upon which God hath given liberty to man is eternal vigilance; which condition if he break, servitude is at once the consequence of his crime, and the punishment of his guilt.
John Philpot Curran 1750–1817: speech on the right of election of the Lord Mayor of Dublin, 10 July 1790

4 Freedom. In this place. Never was, never would be. What was it, anyway? Freedom to do what you liked, that was one thing. Freedom to do what you should, that was another.
Seamus Deane 1940– : *Reading in the Dark* (1996)

5 The thing he proposes to buy is what cannot be sold—liberty.
Henry Grattan 1746–1820: in *Dictionary of National Biography* (1917–)

6 Union! Liberty! The Irish Republic!—such is your shout.
Let us march. Our hearts are devoted to you; our glory is in
your happiness.
Jean Joseph Humbert 1755–1823: proclamation at Ballina, 23 August
1798

7 *Is níl laistigh d'aon daoirse*
Ach saoirse ó'n daoirse sin.

And only the unfree
Can know what freedom is.
Seán Ó Ríordáin 1916–77: 'Daoirse' ['Unfreedom']

8 Liberty means responsibility. That is why most men dread
it.
George Bernard Shaw 1856–1950: *Man and Superman* (1903) 'Maxims:
Liberty and Equality'

9 Fair LIBERTY was all his cry.
Jonathan Swift 1667–1745: 'Verses on the Death of Dr Swift' (1731)

10 Our freedom must be held at all hazards; if the men of
property will not help us they must fall; we will free
ourselves by the aid of that large and respectable class of
the community—the men of no property.
Wolfe Tone 1763–98: Marianne Elliott *Wolfe Tone* (1989)

11 Parnell came down the road, he said to a cheering man:
'Ireland shall get her freedom and you still break stone.'
W. B. Yeats 1865–1939: 'Parnell' (1938)

Lies and Lying

1 Falsehood has a perennial spring.
Edmund Burke 1729–97: *On American Taxation* (1775)

2 What you take for lying in an Irishman is only his attempt
to put an herbaceous border on stark reality.
Oliver St John Gogarty 1878–1957: *Going Native* (1940)

3 Mr Butler ... was not all full of his high discourse in praise
of Ireland, whither he and his whole family is going ... But
so many lies I never heard in praise of anything as he told
of Ireland.
Samuel Pepys 1633–1703: diary, 28 July 1660

4 The Right Honourable gentleman is indebted to his
memory for his jests, and to his imagination for his facts.
in reply to Mr Dundas
Richard Brinsley Sheridan 1751–1816: in the House of Commons; T. Moore
Life of Sheridan (1825) vol. 2

5 He replied that I must needs be mistaken, or that I *said the
thing which was not*. (For they have no word in their
language to express lying or falsehood.)
Jonathan Swift 1667–1745: *Gulliver's Travels* (1726)

6 I never expect sincerity from any man; and am no more
angry at the breach of it, than at the colour of his hair.
Jonathan Swift 1667–1745: letter to Charles Ford, 8 September 1711

7 As one knows the poet by his fine music, so one can
recognize the liar by his rich rhythmic utterances, and in
neither case will the casual inspiration of the moment
suffice. Here, as elsewhere, practice must precede
perfection.
Oscar Wilde 1854–1900: *Intentions* (1891)

Life

1 Beauing, belle-ing, dancing, drinking,
Breaking windows, damning, sinking,
Ever raking, never thinking,
Live the rakes of Mallow.
Anonymous: song, 19th century

2 We're waiting for Godot.
Samuel Beckett 1906–89: *Waiting for Godot* (1955)

3 The transience of life has always exasperated me.
Beatrice Behan 1921–93: *My Life with Brendan* (1973)

4 The Wise Woman would get on with her life and stop
dreaming. Then she thought how tiring it was going to be
for the rest of her life trying to be the Wise Woman all the
time. It would be great to be the very Unwise Woman on
occasions.
Maeve Binchy 1940– : *Circle of Friends* (1990)

5 The world is only a blue bag. Knock a squeeze out of it
when you can.
Eric Cross 1905–80: *The Tailor and Ansty* (1942)

6 When you don't have any money, the problem is food.
When you have money, it's sex. When you have both it's
health.
J. P. Donleavy 1926– : *The Ginger Man* (1955)

7 Man wants but little here below,
Nor wants that little long.
Oliver Goldsmith 1728–74: 'Edwin and Angelina, or the Hermit' (1766)

8 Welcome, O life! I go to encounter for the millionth time
the reality of experience and to forge in the smithy of my
soul the uncreated conscience of my race . . . Old father, old
artificer, stand me now and ever in good stead.
James Joyce 1882–1941: *A Portrait of the Artist as a Young Man* (1916)

9 That was how his life happened.
No mad hooves galloping in the sky,
But the weak, washy way of true tragedy—
A sick horse nosing around the meadow for a clean place to
die.
Patrick Kavanagh 1904–67: 'The Great Hunger' (1947)

Life

10 My life was the Reduced-Male variety, the Male Lite life.
Marian Keyes: *Lucy Sullivan is Getting Married* (1997)

11 World is crazier and more of it than we think,
Incorrigibly plural. I peel and portion
A tangerine and spit the pips and feel
The drunkenness of things being various.
Louis MacNeice 1907–63: 'Snow'

12 By a high star our course is set.
Our end is Life. Put out to sea.
Louis MacNeice 1907–63: 'Thalassa'

13 So this is life, the ranger said:
A bald brush for a bald head.
Blanaid Salkeld 1880–1959: 'Optimism'

14 I never wake without finding life a more insignificant thing
than it was the day before.
Jonathan Swift 1667–1745: letter to Lord Bolingbroke and Alexander
Pope, 5 April 1729

15 She bid me take life easy, as the grass grows on the weirs;
But I was young and foolish, and now am full of tears.
W. B. Yeats 1865–1939: 'Down by the Salley Gardens' (1889)

Literature

1 His writing is not *about* something; it is that something
itself.
Samuel Beckett 1906–89: *Our Exagmination Round the Factification for
Incamination of Work in Progress* (1929)

2 The country folk of Ulster are not much given to literature.
Lynn C. Doyle 1873–1961: *An Ulster Childhood* (1921)

3 I should like to see the day of what might be called, without
   any disrespect to Davis, the de-Davisisation of Irish
   literature.
   John Eglinton 1868–1961: in *United Irishman* 31 March 1902

4 Wordsworth? . . . no, I'm afraid we're not familiar with
   your literature, Lieutenant. We feel closer to the warm
   Mediterranean. We tend to overlook your island.
   Brian Friel 1929– : *Translations* (1980)

5 The celebrated Anglo-Irish stew.
   Michael Hartnett 1941– : 'A Farewell to English' (1978)

6 If we turn to early Irish literature, as we naturally may, to
   see what sort of people the Irish were in the infancy of the
   race, we find ourselves wandering in delighted
   bewilderment through a darkness shot with lightning and
   purple flame.
   Sean O'Faolain 1900–91: *The Irish* (1948)

7 The things I like to find in a story are punch and poetry.
   Sean O'Faolain 1900–91: *The Short Story* (1948) foreword

8 A literary movement is five or six people who live in the
   same town and hate each other.
   George William Russell (Æ) 1867–1935: attributed

9 In literature the ambition of the novice is to acquire the
   literary language: the struggle of the adept is to get rid of it.
   George Bernard Shaw 1856–1950: Hesketh Pearson *Bernard Shaw* (1942)

10 I think it is the art of the glimpse. If the novel is like an
   intricate Renaissance painting, the short story is an
   Impressionist painting. It *should* be an explosion of truth.
   William Trevor 1928– : in *Paris Review* 1989

11 Literature always anticipates life.
   Oscar Wilde 1854–1900: *Intentions* (1891)

12 Alone, perhaps, among the nations of Europe we are in our
ballad or epic age . . . Our poetry is still a poetry of the
people in the main, for it still deals with the tales and
thoughts of the people.
W. B. Yeats 1865–1939: 'Nationality and Literature', lecture 19 May 1893

13 The old literature of Ireland . . . has been the chief
illumination of my imagination all my life.
W. B. Yeats 1865–1939: speech in the Irish Senate on Irish manuscripts,
1923

Logic

1 My chief desire is to let you see that there is that which is
rational, that which is irrational and that which is non-
rational—and to leave you weltering in the morass
thereafter.
Seamus Deane 1940– : *Reading in the Dark* (1996)

2 I said, 'It is most extraordinary weather for this time of
year!' He replied, 'Ah, it isn't this time of year at all.'
Oliver St John Gogarty 1878–1957: *It Isn't This Time of Year at All* (1954)

3 I would not like to leave contraception on the long finger
too long.
Jack Lynch 1917– : in *Irish Times* 23 May 1971

4 The conclusion of your syllogism, I said lightly, is
fallacious, being based upon licensed premises.
Flann O'Brien 1911–66: *At Swim-Two-Birds* (1939)

5 I can stand brute force, but brute reason is quite
unbearable. There is something unfair about its use. It is
hitting below the intellect.
Oscar Wilde 1854–1900: *The Picture of Dorian Gray* (1891)

6 The only business of the head in the world is to bow a
ceaseless obeisance to the heart.
W. B. Yeats 1865–1939: letter, 1886

Loss

1 I will cry my fill, but not for God, but because Finn and Fianna are not living.
Oisín to St Patrick
Anonymous: 'The Fenian Cycle', translated by Lady Gregory as *Gods and Fighting Men* (1904)

2 I would like my love to die
and the rain to be falling on the graveyard
and on me walking the streets
mourning she who sought to love me.
Samuel Beckett 1906–89: 'I would like my love to die'

3 But 'tis my grief that Parnell should be lying cold and low
And Michael Davitt underneath the sod in far Mayo.
Stephen Lucius Gwynn 1864–1950: 'Davitt's Grave'

4 My heart's wound
Why was I not with you
When you were shot
That I might take the bullet
In my own body?
Eibhlin Dubh Ni Chonaill *c.*1748–*c.*1800: 'Lament for Art O'Leary'

5 I know you don't love me anymore
you used to hold my hand when the plane took off
two years ago there just seemed so much more
and I don't know what happened to our love.
Sinéad O'Connor 1966– : 'The Last Day of Our Acquaintance' (1990)

6 The entire Fianna Fáil front bench is in need of counselling following their loss of power.
Pat Rabbitte: in February 1995, attributed

7 To lose one parent, Mr Worthing, may be regarded as a misfortune; to lose both looks like carelessness.
Oscar Wilde 1854–1900: *The Importance of Being Earnest* (1895)

Lough Derg

1 With mullioned Europe shattered, this Northwest
Rude-sainted island would pray it whole again.
Denis Devlin 1908–59: 'Lough Derg'

2 From Cavan and from Leitrim and from Mayo,
From all the thin-faced parishes where hills
Are perished noses running peaty water,
They come to Lough Derg to fast and pray and beg.
Patrick Kavanagh 1904–67: 'Lough Derg' (1972)

3 Sad my visit to Loch Dearg.
Donnchadh Mór Ó Dálaigh fl. 1220: attributed; Douglas Hyde *The Religious Songs of Connacht* (1906)

4 'I thought of an old island, with old gray ruins, and old holly trees and rhododendrons down to the water, a place where old monks would live.'
   They saw tall buildings like modern hotels rising by the island's shore, an octagonal basilica big enough for a city, four or five bare, slated houses, a long shed like a ballroom. Another bus drew up beside them and people peered out through the wiped glass.
   'O God!' she groaned. 'I hope this isn't going to be like Lourdes.'
Sean O'Faolain 1900–91: 'Lovers of the Lake'

Love

1 My grief on the sea,
How the waves of it roll!
For they heave between me
And the love of my soul.
Anonymous: 'Mo bhrón ar an bhfarraige' ('My grief on the sea'), 18th century Irish poem translated by Douglas Hyde

2 My one affection left me is my love for Ireland.
after the death of his wife in 1913
Edward Carson 1854–1935: Montgomery Hyde *Carson* (1953)

3 O Susan Chaplin was the maid
That I loved late and early,

My Kildare's bonny Susan
With her glossy raven hair.
John Clare 1793–1864: 'Sweet Susan Chaplin was a Maid' (poems written in
Northampton Asylum, 1842–64)

4 And O! She was the Sunday
In every week.
Austin Clarke 1896–1974: 'The Planter's Daughter' (1929)

5 Love is like an old tree. It is very easily killed by cruelty or
neglect; but it takes a long time to die, and it goes on dying
a long time after it is dead.
Cyril Connolly 1903–74: *The Unquiet Grave* (1944)

6 Adrian was showing no signs of wanting to ravish me but
this was not due to his Protestant self-control, I believed,
but rather to his state of being helplessly in love.
Ita Daly 1945– : *Ellen* (1986)

7 Love seemed to be blighted in Ireland, in another deadly
kind of famine. Even the words used for the progression of
courtship and love are diminishing and unsympathetic . . .
the recognition of anyone of the opposite sex as being
special, is called 'having a notion of' and is regarded as a
foolish state.
Polly Devlin 1944– : *All of Us There* (1983)

8 Our Irish blunders are never blunders of the heart.
Maria Edgeworth 1767–1849: *Essay on Irish Bulls* (1802)

9 If you want them to run after you, just walk the other way,
For they're mostly like the Pride of Petravore.
Percy French 1854–1920: 'Eileen Oge'

10 And here is love
like a tinsmith's scoop
sunk past its gleam
in the meal-bin.
Seamus Heaney 1939– : 'Mossbawn Sunlight'

11 My heart's like a battlefield–what's left of it.
Con Houlihan: in *Irish Post* 4 July 1998

12 Love is never defeated, and I could add, the history of
Ireland proves it.
John Paul II 1920– : speech by the Pope in Galway, 30 September 1979

13 Force, hatred, history, all that. That's not life for men and
women, insult and hatred. And everybody knows that it's
the very opposite of that that is really life.
What? says Alf.
Love, says Bloom. I mean the opposite of hatred.
James Joyce 1882–1941: *Ulysses* (1922)

14 Oh I loved too much, and by such, by such,
Is happiness thrown away.
Patrick Kavanagh 1904–67: 'On Raglan Road'

15 What I say is what business have the likes of us with love?
It is enough to have to find the bite to eat.
speech of the matchmaker, Thomasheen Seán Rua
John B. Keane 1928– : *Sive* (1959)

16 Love is a very strange idea. I never know what it is. When
you were young it seemed to be all intensity and no
opportunity. Later when you did have the opportunity the
fire had gone out of it.
Bernard MacLaverty 1942– : *Cal* (1983)

17 Oh! there was lightning in my blood,
Red lightning lightened through my blood,
My Dark Rosaleen!
James Clarence Mangan 1803–49: 'Dark Rosaleen'

18 No, the heart that has truly loved never forgets,
But as truly loves on to the close.
Thomas Moore 1779–1852: *Irish Melodies* (1807) 'Believe me, if all those endearing young charms'

19 *Mo ghrá go daingean thú*
Lá dá bhfaca thú
Ag ceann tí an mhargaidh.

You were my love irremovably
From the day I saw you
At the end of the market-house.
Eibhlin Dubh Ni Chonaill *c.*1748–*c.*1800: 'Lament for Art O'Leary'

20 It isn't human to love, you know. It's foolish, it's a folly, a divine folly. It's beyond all reason, all limits.
Sean O'Faolain 1900–91: 'Lovers of the Lake'

21 Amo, amas, I love a lass,
As a cedar tall and slender;
Sweet cowslip's grace
Is her nom'native case,
And she's of the feminine gender.
John O'Keeffe 1747–1833: *The Agreeable Surprise* (1781)

22 Have you ever been in love, me boys,
Or have you felt the pain?
I'd rather be in jail, I would,
Than be in love again.
Johnny Patterson 1840–89: 'The Garden Where the Praties Grow'

23 Be wise, be wise, and do not try
How he can court, or you be won;
For love is but discovery:
When that is made, the pleasure's done.
Thomas Southerne 1660–1746: *Sir Anthony Love* (1690)

Love

24 Love is exactly like war, in this; that a soldier, though he
has escaped three weeks complete o'Saturday night, may
nevertheless be shot through his heart on Sunday morning.
Laurence Sterne 1713–68: *Tristram Shandy* (1759–67)

25 To say a man is fallen in love,—or that he is deeply in
love,—or up to the ears in love,—and sometimes even over
head and ears in it,—carries an idiomatical kind of
implication, that love is a thing below a man.
Laurence Sterne 1713–68: *Tristram Shandy* (1759–67)

26 Amn't I after seeing the love-light of the star of knowledge
shining from her brow, and hearing words would put you
thinking on the holy Brigid speaking to the infant saints.
John Millington Synge 1871–1909: *The Playboy of the Western World*
(1907)

27 Well, the heart's a wonder; and, I'm thinking, there won't
be our like in Mayo, for gallant lovers, from this hour
today.
John Millington Synge 1871–1909: *The Playboy of the Western World*
(1907)

28 Yet each man kills the thing he loves.
Oscar Wilde 1854–1900: *The Ballad of Reading Gaol* (1898)

29 To love oneself is the beginning of a lifelong romance.
Oscar Wilde 1854–1900: *An Ideal Husband* (1895)

30 The Irish men are reckoned terrible heart stealers—but I do
not find them so very formidable.
Mary Wollstonecraft 1759–97: letter, 11 May 1787

31 A woman can be proud and stiff
When on love intent;
But Love has pitched his mansion in
The place of excrement;
For nothing can be sole or whole
That has not been rent.
W. B. Yeats 1865–1939: 'Crazy Jane Talks with the Bishop' (1932)

32 Down by the salley gardens my love and I did meet;
She passed the salley gardens with little snow-white feet.
She bid me take love easy, as the leaves grow on the tree;
But I, being young and foolish, with her would not agree.
W. B. Yeats 1865–1939: 'Down by the Salley Gardens' (1889)

33 Tread softly because you tread on my dreams.
W. B. Yeats 1865–1939: 'He Wishes for the Cloths of Heaven' (1899)

Love of Country

1 *Is maith an t-ancoire an t-iarta.*
The hearth is a good anchor.
Anonymous: traditional saying; Daniel Corkery *The Hidden Ireland* (1925)

2 Oh hand in hand let us return to the dear land of our birth,
the bays, the bogs, the moors, the glens, the lakes, the
rivers, the streams, the brooks, the mists, the—er—fens,
the—er—glens, by tonight's mail-train.
Samuel Beckett 1906–89: *Murphy* (1938)

3 An author's first duty is to let down his country.
Brendan Behan 1923–64: in an interview, 1960

4 Come all you young rebels
And list while I sing,
For the love of one's country
Is a terrible thing.
Dominic Behan 1928– : 'The Patriot Game'

5 The man who is bubbling over with love and affection for
'Ireland' and can pass unmoved through our streets and
witness all the sorrow and suffering . . . without burning to
end it, is a fraud and a liar in his heart, no matter how
much he loves that combination of chemical elements he is
pleased to call 'Ireland'.
James Connolly 1868–1916: Desmond Ryan *James Connolly* (1924)

6 She said, 'God knows, they owe me nought,
   I tossed them to the foaming sea,
   I tossed them to the howling wastes,
   Yet still their love comes home to me.'
   Emily Lawless 1845–1913: 'After Aughrim'

7 O my dark Rosaleen,
   Do not sigh, do not weep!
   The priests are on the ocean green,
   They march along the deep.
   James Clarence Mangan 1803–49: 'Dark Rosaleen', after the 18th century
   Irish poem 'An Róisín Dubh'

8 My native heath is brown beneath,
   My native waters blue;
   But crimson red o'er both shall spread,
   Ere I am false to you,
   Dear land!
   Ere I am false to you.
   John O'Hagan 1822–90: 'Dear Land' (1845)

9 The savage loves his native shore.
   James Orr 1770–1816: 'The Irishman'

10 I want to go to the Leinster hills,
   To the Dublin hills by the rocky shore.
   I want to climb to Ben-Edar's heights—
   I want to be home once more.
   Dora Sigerson 1866–1918: *The Sad Years* (1918) 'Home'

Loyalism

1 O Child! thou must remember that bleak day in December
   When the 'Prentice-boys of Derry rose up and shut the
   gates.
   Cecil Frances Alexander 1818–95: 'The Siege of Derry'

2 We'll fight to the last in the honest old cause,
   And guard our religion, our freedom, and laws;
   We'll fight for our country, our king, and his crown,
   And make all the traitors and croppies lie down.
   Anonymous: 'Croppies Lie Down'

3 And, blow as he would, though it made a great noise,
   The flute would play only 'The Protestant Boys'.
   Anonymous: 'The Old Orange Flute'

4 The Protestant boys are loyal and gay,
   The Protestant boys will carry the day.
   Anonymous: 'The Protestant Boys'

5 So on the Twelfth I proudly wear the sash my father wore.
   Anonymous: 'The Sash My Father Wore', traditional Orange song

6 I do not come here to preach any doctrines of passive
   obedience or non-resistance. You have had to fight for your
   liberties before. I pray God you may never have to fight for
   them again. I do not believe that you ever will have to fight
   for them, but I admit that the tyranny of majorities may be
   as bad as the tyranny of Kings . . . and I do not think that
   any rational or sober man will say that what is justifiable
   against a tyrannical King may not under certain
   circumstances be justifiable against a tyrannical majority.
   watching the Belfast march past of Ulster Loyalists in 1893
   A. J. Balfour 1848–1930: in *Times* 5 April 1893

7 The great thing I have discovered about Orangemen is that
   they have feelings.
   Brendan Behan 1923–64: attributed

8 There are things stronger than parliamentary majorities. I
   can imagine no length of resistance to which Ulster will not
   go, in which I shall not be ready to support them.
   at a Unionist meeting at Blenheim in 1912
   Andrew Bonar Law 1858–1923: Robert Blake *The Unknown Prime Minister*
   (1955)

9 I now enter into compact with you, and with the help of
God you and I joined together . . . will yet defeat the most
nefarious conspiracy that has ever been hatched against a
free people . . . We must be prepared . . . the morning Home
Rule passes, ourselves to become responsible for the
government of the Protestant Province of Ulster.
Edward Carson 1854–1935: speech at Craigavon, 23 September 1911

10 Ulster will fight; Ulster will be right.
Lord Randolph Churchill 1849–94: public letter, 7 May 1886

11 The yeomanry are in the style of the Loyalists in America,
only much more numerous and powerful, and a thousand
times more ferocious. These men have saved the country,
but they now take the lead in rapine and murder.
Lord Cornwallis 1738–1805: letter, 24 July 1798

12 We swore by King William there'd never be seen
An all-Irish parliament at College Green,
So at Stormont we're nailing the flag to the mast:
May the Lord in His mercy be kind to Belfast.
based on the traditional refrain; cf. **Belfast 2**
Maurice James Craig 1919– : 'Ballad to a Traditional Refrain' (1974)

13 People don't march as an alternative to jogging. They do it
to assert their supremacy. It is pure tribalism, the cause of
troubles all over the world.
Gerry Fitt 1926– : in *The Times* 5 August 1994

14 The truth is that Ulster Unionists are not loyal to the
crown, but to the half-crown.
John Hume 1937– : in *Irish Times* 23 August 1969 'This Week They Said'

15 What answer from the North?
One Law, one Land, one Throne.
If England drive us forth,
We shall not fall alone.
Rudyard Kipling 1865–1936: 'Ulster' (1912)

16 Their case was 'Let us remain with you.' Our case was 'Out you go or we fight you.' We could not have done it . . . The first axiom is whatever happened we could not coerce Ulster.
of the 1921 peace negotiations
David Lloyd George 1863–1945: Thomas Jones *Whitehall Diary* (1971)

17 I have never and never will accept the right of a minority who happen to be a majority in a small part of the country to opt out of a nation.
Jack Lynch 1917– : in *Irish Times* 14 November 1970 'This Week They Said'

18 Trusting in the God of our fathers and confident that our cause is just, we will never surrender our heritage.
Ian Paisley 1926– : in *Guardian* 21 August 1968

19 One Protestant Ulsterman
wants to confess this:
we frightened you Catholics, we gerrymandered,
we applied injustice.
James Simmons 1933– : 'Ulster Says Yes'

20 Derry's sons alike defy
Pope, traitor, or pretender.
Peal to heaven their 'prentice cry
Their patriot—'No surrender!'
Charlotte Elizabeth Tonna 1790–1846: 'No Surrender'

21 I must say to the Portadown brethren that the only way in which they can clearly distance themselves from these murders . . . is to come down off the hill.
appealing to the local Orange Lodge to end their protest at Drumcree
David Trimble 1944– : in *Guardian* 13 July 1998

22 If serious trouble arises on the frontier between the Six Counties and the Twenty-Six Counties, I hope that the government will not restrain the military from crossing the frontier in their own self-defence.
Henry Wilson 1864–1922: in 1922; Diana Norman *Terrible Beauty* (1987)

Loyalism

Manners

1 Compliments pass when the quality meet.
Brendan Behan 1923–64: *Borstal Boy* (1958)

2 Manners are of more importance than laws . . . Manners
are what vex or soothe, corrupt or purify, exalt or debase,
barbarize or refine us, by a constant, steady, uniform,
insensible operation, like that of the air we breathe.
Edmund Burke 1729–97: *Letters of a Regicide Peace* (1796)

3 A naturally free, familiar, good-natured, precipitate, Irish
manner, had been schooled, and schooled late in life, into a
sober, cold, still, stiff deportment, which she mistook for
English.
Maria Edgeworth 1767–1849: *The Absentee* (1812)

4 Your people of refined sentiments are the most troublesome
creatures in the world to deal with.
Hugh Kelly 1739–77: *False Delicacy* (performed 1768)

5 The trouble with a gentleman's agreement is that it has to
be between gentlemen.
Michael McDowell: comment, 1993

6 People assumed I was a lot stronger than I was because I
had a big mouth and a shaved head. I acted tough to cover
the vulnerability.
Sinéad O'Connor 1966– : in *Irish Times* 22 November 1997 'This Week They
Said'

7 The great secret . . . is not having bad manners or good
manners or any other particular sort of manners, but
having the same manner for all human souls: in short,

behaving as if you were in Heaven, where there are no
third-class carriages.
George Bernard Shaw 1856–1950: *Pygmalion* (1916)

8 He is the very pineapple of politeness!
Richard Brinsley Sheridan 1751–1816: *The Rivals* (1775)

Constance Markievicz (1868–1927)

1 She was like an extinct volcano, her former violent self
reduced to something burnt out.
of Constance Markievicz in old age
Mary Colum 1880?–1957: *Life and the Dream* (1947)

2 Hers is not the image of Irish womanhood we want to
present to the outside world. The crude, charmless, virago-
picture almost imposes itself—and then one meets one of
her comrades in arms . . . and it is like coming out of a dark
tunnel into the strong, sweet air of her own west coast.
commenting on ambivalent views of Constance Markievicz
Elizabeth Coxhead 1909– : *The Daughters of Erin* (1979)

3 And when the Treaty emptied the British jails,
A haggard woman returned and Dublin went wild to greet
  her.
But still it was not enough: an iota
Of compromise, she cried, and the Cause fails.
C. Day-Lewis 1904–72: 'Remembering Con Markievicz' (1970)

4 Whoever misunderstood Madame, the poor did not.
Eamon de Valera 1882–1975: Diana Norman *Terrible Beauty* (1987)

5 It was as though joyous martial music had been suddenly
silenced.
on the death of Constance Markievicz
Dorothy Macardle 1889–1958: Diana Norman *Terrible Beauty* (1987)

6 No part of her melted into the cause of Ireland, nor did she
ever set a foot on the threshold of Socialism. She looked at
the names over the door, and then thought she was one of

the family. But the movements were no more to her than
the hedges over which her horses jumped.
Sean O'Casey 1880–1964: *Drums Under the Window* (1945)

7 One thing she had in abundance—physical courage: with
that she was clothed as with a garment.
Sean O'Casey 1880–1964: *Drums Under the Window* (1945)

8 Age dropped from her completely . . . she had found within
herself in her last prime summer, more of the pure vigour
of nature, than at any time in the height of her youth and
beauty.
of Constance Markievicz in 1919
Sean O'Faolain 1900–91: Diana Norman *Terrible Beauty* (1987)

Marriage

1 WLTM/RC/GSOH/WVTA.
= *Would Like To Meet Roman Catholic, With Good Sense of
Humour, With View To Above*
Anonymous: standard abbreviations in personal columns

2 A husband's first praise is a Friend and Protector:
Then change not these titles for Tyrant and Hector.
Mary Barber c.1690–1757: 'Conclusion of a Letter to the Revd Mr C—'
(1734)

3 The people were saying no two were e'er wed
But one had a sorrow that never was said.
Padraic Colum 1881–1972: 'She Moved Through the Fair'

4 Married in haste, we may repent at leisure.
William Congreve 1670–1729: *The Old Bachelor* (1693)

5 To be sure a love match was the only thing for happiness,
where the parties could any way afford it.
Maria Edgeworth 1767–1849: *Castle Rackrent* (1800) 'Continuation of
Memoirs'

6 I . . . chose my wife, as she did her wedding gown, not for a fine glossy surface, but such qualities as would wear well.
Oliver Goldsmith 1728–74: *The Vicar of Wakefield* (1766)

7 To be married in Rome is the traditional recourse of those who want to avoid fuss and expense but who have all the same a sense of style to keep up.
Anne Haverty: *One Day as a Tiger* (1997)

8 I'm the happiest I have ever been.
the star of Boyzone after his wedding to Yvonne Connolly
Ronan Keating: in *Irish Times* 9 May 1998 'This Week They Said'

9 Call me pathetic . . . but I'm being honest here. I want a bloke, a partner, a long-term commitment. I want the M word.
Marian Keyes: 'Late Opening at the Last Chance Saloon' (1997)

10 We do not squabble, fight or have rows. We collect grudges. We're in an arms race, storing up warheads for the domestic Armageddon.
Hugh Leonard 1926– : *Time Was* (1980)

11 Took her to the altar because he was afraid to ask anyone else. Twenty years his senior for the love of God. Half-blind and hates him from the day she married him!
Patrick McCabe 1955– : *The Butcher Boy* (1992)

12 Nowadays nothing is sacred; men marry men, children divorce their parents, a mixed marriage hardly merits a yawn. But fifty years ago the world was a different place, particularly our world, on this small island.
Liz McManus 1947– : 'Dwelling Below the Skies' (1997)

13 So they were married—to be the more together—
And found they were never again so much together
Divided by the morning tea,
By the evening paper,
By children and tradesmen's bills.
Louis MacNeice 1907–63: 'Les Sylphides' (1941)

14 She would have liked to be a nun, it was better than marrying. Anything was, she thought.
Edna O'Brien 1932– : *The Country Girls* (1960)

15 Marriage is popular because it combines the maximum of temptation with the maximum of opportunity.
George Bernard Shaw 1856–1950: *Man and Superman* (1903)

16 To leave my wife and children for love's sake
and marry you would be a failure of nerve.
I remember love and all that goes to make
the marriage, the affairs, that I deserve.
James Simmons 1933– : 'The End of the Affair'

17 No one can accuse Philippa and me of having married in haste . . . It was but little under five years from that autumn evening on the river when I had said what is called in Ireland 'the hard word', to the day in August when I was led to the altar by my best man, and was subsequently led away from it by Mrs Sinclair Yeates.
Edith Œ. Somerville 1858–1949 and **Martin Ross** 1862–1915: *Some Experiences of an Irish R.M.* (1899)

18 My brother Toby, quoth she, is going to be married to Mrs Wadman.
Then he will never, quoth my father, lie *diagonally* in his bed again as long as he lives.
Laurence Sterne 1713–68: *Tristram Shandy* (1759–67)

19 Marriage was bound to bring awkwardness; you could not expect otherwise, especially when one of the parties was set in his ways.
William Trevor 1928– : *The Silence in the Garden* (1988)

20 'Marriage is a folly,' he said sympathetically, 'but it's a respectable one.'
Mervyn Wall 1908– : *The Return of Fursey* (1948)

21 In married life three is company and two none.
Oscar Wilde 1854–1900: *The Importance of Being Earnest* (1895)

22 They flaunt their conjugal felicity in one's face, as if it were the most fascinating of sins.
Oscar Wilde 1854–1900: *The Picture of Dorian Gray* (1891)

Mayo

1 Mayo—God help us!
Anonymous: traditional saying; Heinrich Böll *Irish Journal* (1957, translated Leila Vennewitz)

2 *Anois teacht an Earraigh beidh an lá 'dul chun sineadh,*
's tar éis na Féil' Brighde árdóidh mé mo sheol;
ó chuir mé im' cheann é ní stopfaidh mé choiche
go seasa mé síos i lár Chontae Mhuigheo.

Now springtime is coming, the days will get longer
And after St Bridget's day, I will set off.
Now it has come into my head, I won't stop once
Until I am standing down in mid-County Mayo.
Antoine Raiftearaí 1779–1835: 'Cill Aodáin'

The Media

1 I sometimes admit that when I think of television and radio and their immense power, I feel somewhat afraid.
Eamon de Valera 1882–1975: at the inauguration of Telefís Éireann in 1961

2 When I started out, people were afraid of parish priests. Now they're afraid of newspaper editors.
Michael D. Higgins 1941– : in 1997, attributed

3 I do not know where the British and American papers get their scare headlines about me. I have never given an interview in my life and do not receive journalists. Nor do I understand why they should consider an unread writer as good copy.
James Joyce 1882–1941: letter, 10 November 1932

4 It is impossible to read the daily press without being
diverted from reality.
Patrick Kavanagh 1904–67: 'Signposts' (1967)

5 What the 'Nation' was when Gavan Duffy edited it, when
Davis, McCarthy, and their brilliant associates contributed
to it, and when its columns maintained with unqualified
zeal the cause of liberty and nationality in every land,
Irishmen can never forget. Seldom has any journal of the
kind exhibited a more splendid combination of eloquence,
of poetry, and of reasoning.
William Lecky 1838–1903: in *Dictionary of National Biography* (1917–)

6 The British Press is always looking for stuff to fill the space
between their cartoons.
Bernadette Devlin McAliskey 1947– : comment, 1970

7 The power of the press is very great, but not so great as the
power of suppress.
office message to the Daily Mail, *1918*
Lord Northcliffe 1865–1922: Reginald Rose and Geoffrey Harmsworth
Northcliffe (1959)

8 The newspapers! Sir, they are the most villainous—
licentious—abominable—infernal—Not that I ever read
them—No—I make it a rule never to look into a
newspaper.
Richard Brinsley Sheridan 1751–1816: *The Critic* (1779)

9 In the old days men had the rack. Now they have the Press.
Oscar Wilde 1854–1900: in *Fortnightly Review* February 1891

10 Television contracts the imagination and radio expands it.
Terry Wogan 1938– : in *Observer* 30 December 1984 'Sayings of the Year'

11 I hate journalists. There is nothing in them but tittering,
jeering emptiness. They have all made what Dante calls the
Great Refusal. That is, they have ceased to be self-centred,
have given up their individuality.
W. B. Yeats 1865–1939: letter to Katharine Tynan, 1888

Men see also Women

1 Since ever the curse of Adam fell on us, a man's no more
   use than a bull calf. What he does he has til be driven to,
   and when that's done, a woman must needs run after him,
   reddin' up.
   Margaret Barrington 1896–1982: *My Cousin Justin* (1939)

2 Boys are born knowing (and girls soon find out) that
   possession of a penis is all the label you need for life.
   Clare Boylan 1948– : in *Irish Times* 20 September 1997 'Quotes of the
   Week'

3 Man is to be held only by the *slightest* chains, with the idea
   that he can break them at pleasure, he submits to them in
   sport.
   Maria Edgeworth 1767–1849: *Letters for Literary Ladies* (1795) 'Letters of
   Julia and Caroline' no. 1

4 The problem with a concept like the New Man is that it
   implied that the problem with men is their personalities.
   The problem with men is their power.
   Maureen Gaffney: *Glass Slippers and Tough Bargains* (1991)

5 Male feminists weren't tuppence ha'penny. Those that
   existed should be cherished, or at least encouraged.
   Katy Hayes: *Forecourt* (1995)

6 I am not interested in men, for I have had the pick of too
   many men.
   to the young Mary Colum
   Constance Markievicz 1868–1927: Mary Colum *Life and the Dream* (1947)

7 You can't help feeling that if the Éamon de Valera
   generation had stayed home and changed the occasional
   nappy, Ireland might well have been better off.
   Joseph O'Connor 1963– : in *Sunday Tribune* April 1994

8 Of all human struggles there is none so treacherous and remorseless as the struggle between the artist man and the mother woman.
George Bernard Shaw 1856–1950: *Man and Superman* (1903)

9 All women become like their mothers. That is their tragedy. No man does. That's his.
Oscar Wilde 1854–1900: *The Importance of Being Earnest* (1895)

Metaphysics

1 The sun shone, having no alternative, on the nothing new.
Samuel Beckett 1906–89: *Murphy* (1938)

2 They are neither finite quantities, or quantities infinitely small, nor yet nothing. May we not call them the ghosts of departed quantities?
on Isaac Newton's infinitesimals
George Berkeley 1685–1753: *The Analyst* (1734)

The Mind

1 Murphy's mind pictured itself as a large hollow sphere, hermetically closed to the world without.
Samuel Beckett 1906–89: *Murphy* (1938)

2 All the choir of heaven and furniture of earth—in a word, all those bodies which compose the mighty frame of the world—have not any subsistence without a mind.
George Berkeley 1685–1753: *A Treatise Concerning the Principles of Human Knowledge* (1710)

3 The march of the human mind is slow.
Edmund Burke 1729–97: *On American Taxation* (1775)

4 What is mind but motion in the intellectual sphere?
Oscar Wilde 1854–1900: *Intentions* (1891)

5 God guard me from those thoughts men think
In the mind alone;
He that sings a lasting song
Thinks in a marrow-bone.
W. B. Yeats 1865–1939: 'A Prayer for Old Age' (1934)

Money

1 In every half-case, people see compensation. Compensatitis
must be the worst disease that we have in the country at
the moment.
Bertie Ahern 1951– : in *Irish Times* 13 December 1997 'This Week They
Said'

2 We could have saved sixpence. We have saved fivepence.
(*Pause*) But at what cost?
Samuel Beckett 1906–89: *All That Fall* (1957)

3 Mrs Ryan had always thought that if the whole wealth of
the world was taken back and divided out equally, giving
the same amount to each person, you'd find in five years
that the same people would end up having money and
power and the same people would end up shiftless and
hopeless. In a changing world, she found this view very
comforting.
Maeve Binchy 1940– : *The Copper Beech* (1992)

4 In general the worst thing you can do for anybody is to
give them money, because in the first place it's easy-come,
and in the second place instead of being grateful they think
it mean of you not to give them more than you did.
Lynn C. Doyle 1873–1961: *Green Oranges* (1947)

5 'Everybody who comes from Ireland *will* have a fine estate
when somebody dies,' said her grace. 'But what have they
at present?'
Maria Edgeworth 1767–1849: *The Absentee* (1800)

6 If my lady had the bank of Ireland to spend, it would go all in one winter.
Maria Edgeworth 1767–1849: *Castle Rackrent* (1800)

7 Money is the sinews of love, as of war.
George Farquhar 1678–1707: *Love and a Bottle* (1698)

8 She had a powerful regard for money—I suppose because we never had any.
Brian Friel 1929– : *The Diviner* (1982)

9 Money couldn't buy friends but you got a better class of enemy.
Spike Milligan 1918– : *Puckoon* (1963)

10 There's only one thing to do with loose change of course. Tighten it.
Flann O'Brien 1911–66: *The Best of Myles* (1968)

11 The universal regard for money is the one hopeful fact in our civilization.
George Bernard Shaw 1856–1950: preface to *Major Barbara* (1905)

Music see also Song

1 Where clerics sing like birds.
of Ireland
St Adamnan 627–704: *Life of St Columba*

2 Oh Danny Boy, the pipes, the pipes are calling,
From glen to glen and down the mountain-side.
Anonymous: 'Londonderry Air', 19th century song

3 Of all the antiquities in the world Ireland possesses the most varied and beautiful music.
Arnold Bax 1883–1953: attributed

4 They didn't have Kalashnikovs but U2 tickets in their
   hands.
   *of the audience at the U2 concert in Sarajevo, 24 September
   1997*
   Bono 1960– : in *Daily Telegraph* 25 September 1997

5 My father and mother were Irish, and I am Irish too;
   I bought a wee fidil for ninepence, and it is Irish too.
   Joseph Campbell 1879–1944: 'The Ninepenny Fidil'

6 Music has charms to sooth a savage breast,
   To soften rocks, or bend a knotted oak.
   William Congreve 1670–1729: *The Mourning Bride* (1697)

7 Hang the harpers wherever found.
   Elizabeth I 1533–1603: proclamation of 1603; in Seán O'Boyle *The Irish
   Song Tradition* (1976)

8 It is next to impossible, I believe, to toss a brick in the air
   anywhere in County Galway without it landing on the
   head of some musician.
   James Galway 1939– : *An Autobiography* (1978)

9 Most people get into bands for three very simple rock and
   roll reasons: to get laid, to get fame, and to get rich.
   Bob Geldof 1954– : in *Melody Maker* 27 August 1977

10 It is in the cultivation of instrumental music I consider the
   proficiency of this people to be worthy of commendation;
   and in this their skill is, beyond all comparison, beyond
   that of any nation I have ever seen.
   Giraldus Cambrensis c.1146–1223: *The History and Topography of Ireland*

11 Carthalawn! Your best! Your Almighty best!
   John B. Keane 1928– : *Sive* (1959)

12 O the bells of Shandon
   Sound far more grand on
   The pleasant waters
   Of the River Lee.
   Francis Sylvester Mahony 1804–66: 'The Bells of Shandon'

13 Music is spiritual. The music business is not.
Van Morrison 1945– : in *The Times* 6 July 1990

14 We are the music makers,
We are the dreamers of dreams.
Arthur O'Shaughnessy 1844–81: 'Ode' (1874)

15 Hell is full of musical amateurs: music is the brandy of the
damned.
George Bernard Shaw 1856–1950: *Man and Superman* (1903)

Names

1 General De Wet's father was from Laune, West of Killarney.
He had no English, but only the Irish, and to each man he
met he said, 'Dia Dhuit'. That was his salute. They called
him De Wet, which was as near as they could get to the
Irish, thinking it was his name.
Eric Cross 1905–80: *The Tailor and Ansty* (1942)

2 Now the Ratschilds were the richest people in the whole
world, and the head of them lived in Tipperary.
Eric Cross 1905–80: *The Tailor and Ansty* (1942)

3 MANUS: What's 'incorrect' about the place-names we have
here?
OWEN: Nothing at all. They're just going to be standardised.
MANUS: You mean changed into English?
OWEN: Where there's ambiguity, they'll be Anglicised.
Brian Friel 1929– : *Translations* (1980)

4 The names of a land show the heart of the race;
They move on the tongue like the lilt of a song.
You say the name and I see the place—

Drumbo, Dungannon, or Annalong.
Barony, townland, we cannot go wrong.
John Hewitt 1907–87: 'Ulster Names'

5　John Millicent Synge.
James Joyce 1882–1941: *Ulysses* (1922)

6　Lawn Tennyson, gentleman poet.
James Joyce 1882–1941: *Ulysses* (1922)

7　Although I was very fond of Meredia, I had to agree that
her name had a certain makeshift, ramshackle, cobbled-
out-of-old-egg-cartons feel to it.
Marian Keyes: *Lucy Sullivan is Getting Married* (1997)

8　We have this London word in our name since 1613—and
really we have never got used to it.
proposing to amend the name Londonderry
Edward McAteer 1914– : in *Irish Times* 26 May 1971 'This Week They Said'

9　Sarsfield is the watchword—Sarsfield is the man.
Patrick Sarsfield *c.*1655–93: at Ballyneety, 11 August 1690

Nationality see also Irishness

1　INTERVIEWER: You are English, Mr Beckett?
BECKETT: *Au contraire.*
Samuel Beckett 1906–89: Fintan O'Toole *The Ex-Isle of Erin* (1997)

2　Other people have a nationality. The Irish and the Jews
have a psychosis.
Brendan Behan 1923–64: *Richard's Cork Leg* (1961)

3　Nor one feeling of vengeance presume to defile
The cause, or the men, of the Emerald Isle.
William Drennan 1754–1820: *Erin* (1795)

4 'Twas for the good of my country that I should be
abroad.—Anything for the good of one's country—I'm a
Roman for that.
George Farquhar 1678–1707: *The Beaux' Stratagem* (1707)

5 Don't be surprised
If I demur, for, be advised
My passport's green.
No glass of ours was ever raised
To toast *The Queen*.
rebuking the editors of The Penguin Book of Contemporary
British Poetry *for including him among its authors*
Seamus Heaney 1939– : *Open Letter* (Field Day pamphlet no. 2, 1983)

6 I'm an Ulsterman, of planter stock. I was born in the island
of Ireland, so secondarily I'm an Irishman. I was born in
the British archipelago and English is my native tongue, so
I am British. The British archipelago consists of offshore
islands to the continent of Europe, so I'm European. This is
my hierarchy of values and so far as I am concerned,
anyone who omits one step in that sequence of values is
falsifying the situation.
John Hewitt 1907–87: in *The Irish Times* 4 July 1974

7 When the soul of a man is born in this country, there are
nets flung at it to hold it back from flight. You talk to me of
nationality, language, religion. I shall try to fly by those
nets.
James Joyce 1882–1941: *A Portrait of the Artist as a Young Man* (1916)

8 Nations may respect one another; they cannot love.
John O'Leary 1830–1907: Nicholas Mansergh *The Irish Question* (ed. 3,
1975)

9 No man has a right to fix the boundary of the march of a
nation; no man has a right to say to his country—thus far
shalt thou go and no further.
Charles Stewart Parnell 1846–91: speech at Cork, 21 January 1885, in *The
Times* 22 January 1885

10 To unite the whole people of Ireland, to abolish the
memory of all past dissension and to substitute the
common name of Irishman in place of the denominations of
Protestant, Catholic and Dissenter.
Wolfe Tone 1763–98: in August 1796; Marianne Elliott *Wolfe Tone* (1989)

11 Because a man is born in a stable, that does not make him
a horse.
*rejecting the view that his Irish birthplace determined his
nationality*
Duke of Wellington 1769–1852: attributed

12 My country is Kiltartan Cross;
My countrymen Kiltartan's poor!
W. B. Yeats 1865–1939: 'An Irish Airman Foresees his Death' (1919)

Negotiation

1 Sinn Féin has one advantage over other parties—we've
brought a camp bed. We don't share it, of course.
Gerry Adams 1948– : in *Irish Times* 11 April 1998 'This Week They Said'

2 If we are talking about setting up north-south bodies that
are not executive and are really ad-hoc 'chat shows', then I
am not in the business of negotiating.
Bertie Ahern 1951– : in *Daily Telegraph* 2 April 1998

3 This is about negotiations, but the answer to that question
is 'No'.
*asked if the Irish Government would compromise on
North–South bodies*
David Andrews 1936– : in *Irish Times* 11 April 1998 'This Week They Said'

4 The people have spoken and the politicians have had to
listen.
on the outcome of the referendum on the Good Friday agreement
Gerry Fitt 1926– : in *Sunday Telegraph* 24 May 1998

5　I am for doing business and making peace.
Timothy Michael Healy 1855–1931: letter to Beaverbrook, 1920; Frank
Callanan *T. M. Healy* (1996)

6　I am tired, sore and exhausted, but I am feeling quite proud
about the work that has been achieved . . . It's a beautiful
day so far today.
during the final stages of the Northern Irish talks
Mitchell McLaughlin: in *Daily Telegraph* 11 April 1998

7　Sunningdale for slow learners.
assessing the earlier stages of the Northern Irish talks
Seamus Mallon 1936– : in *Daily Telegraph* 6 April 1998

8　I am pleased to announce that the two governments and
the political parties in Northern Ireland have reached
agreement.
George Mitchell 1933– : in *Times* 11 April 1998

9　People at home say to me, 'What have you agreed since the
talks began? I say to them: 'Well, nothing.'
David Trimble 1944– : in *Irish Times* 28 March 1998 'This Week They Said'

10　This agreement is as good and as fair as it gets.
David Trimble 1944– : in *Irish Times* 18 April 1998 'This Week They Said'

1916 see **Easter 1916**

The North see also **Loyalism, The Union**

1　God made us Catholics but the armalite made us equal.
Anonymous: graffiti, Belfast, 1970s

2　*L'Ulster est l'Écosse de l'Irlande.*
Ulster is Scotland in Ireland.
Gustave de Beaumont 1802–66: *L'Irlande sociale, politique et religieuse*
(1839)

3 I feel a greater kinship with a Protestant from Antrim than
I do with a Catholic from Cork.
Neil Blaney 1922– : view of a Nationalist TD, 1970

4 A difficulty arises, as to defining Ulster. My own view is
that the whole of Ulster should be excluded [from Home
Rule] but the minimum would be the six plantation
counties.
Edward Carson 1854–1935: letter to Bonar Law, June 1913

5 The whole map of Europe has been changed . . . but as the
deluge subsides and the waters fall short we see the dreary
steeples of Fermanagh and Tyrone emerging once again.
The integrity of their quarrel is one of the few institutions
that has been unaltered in the cataclysm which has swept
the world.
Winston Churchill 1874–1965: speech, House of Commons, 16 February
1922

6 The senseless line which separates our two countries.
*as Chancellor of Queen's University Belfast to students of
Belfast and Dublin*
Tyrone Guthrie 1900–71: James Forsyth *Tyrone Guthrie* (1976)

7 My heart besieged by anger, my mind a gap of danger,
I walked among their old haunts, the home ground where
    they bled;
And in the dirt lay justice like an acorn in the winter
Till its oak would sprout in Derry where the thirteen men
    lay dead.
of Bloody Sunday, Londonderry, 30 January 1972
Seamus Heaney 1939– : 'The Road to Derry'

8   The famous
Northern reticence, the tight gag of place
And times: yes, yes. Of the 'wee six' I sing
Where to be saved you only must save face
And whatever you say, you say nothing.
Seamus Heaney 1939– : 'Whatever You Say Say Nothing' (1975)

North

9 Kelt, Briton, Roman, Saxon, Dane, and Scot,
time and this island tied a crazy knot.
John Hewitt 1907–87: 'Ulsterman' (*Collected Poems*, 1991)

10 The tragedy of Northern Ireland is that it is now a society
in which the dead console the living.
Jack Holland 1947– : in *New York Times Magazine* 15 July 1979

11 I feel like an exile at heart—the call of the North is always
there.
in June 1984, while living in the South
Mary McAleese 1951– : in *Irish Times* 20 September 1997

12 A culture built upon profit;
Free speech nipped in the bud,
The minority always guilty.
Why should I want to go back
To you, Ireland, my Ireland?
Louis MacNeice 1907–63: *Autumn Journal* (1939)

13 A generation of Highland thieves and red-shanks who,
being neighbourly admitted . . . by the courtesy of England,
to hold possessions in our province, a country better than
their own, have with worse faith than those heathen,
proved ungrateful and treacherous guests to their best
friends and entertainers.
*of Scottish planters in Ulster, who supported the Scots against
the Long Parliament*
John Milton 1608–74: *Observations* (1648)

14 'A mind not too deeply fascinated by the florid virtues, the
warm overflowing of generous and ardent qualities, will
find in the Northerns of this island much to admire and
esteem; but on the heart they make little claim, and from
its affections they receive but little tribute.'
  'Then in the name of all that is warm and cordial,' said I,
'let us hasten back to the province of Connaught.'
Lady Morgan ?1776–1859: *The Wild Irish Girl* (1807)

15 Ulster the fifth part of Ireland is a large province, woody, fenny, in some parts fertile, in other parts barren, but in all parts green and pleasant to behold, and exceedingly stored with cattle.
Fynes Moryson 1566–1630: *An Itinerary Containing the Ten Years' Travel* (1617)

16 I think it fair to say that most people in the Republic do not actually want Northern Ireland. They are simply in the habit of hearing, and of repeating, that Northern Ireland has no right to exist.
Conor Cruise O'Brien 1917– : attributed

17 How could Southern Ireland keep a bridal North in the manner to which she is accustomed.
Terence O'Neill 1914–90: in *Irish Times* 16 January 1971

18 The Catholics have been intervening in Ulster affairs since 1641.
Ian Paisley 1926– : comment, 1970s

19 My country's future will be decided over a bottle of liquor with you and the Dublin ministry.
Ian Paisley 1926– : to Patrick Mayhew, December 1992

20 A disorderly set of people whom no king can govern and no God can please.
Boyle Roche 1743–1807: attributed

21 They say the situation in Northern Ireland is not as bad as they say it is.
Dennis Taylor 1949– : attributed

22 We in Northern Ireland are not Irish, and it is an insult for Dublin to refer to us as being so. We do not speak Gaelic, play GAA nor jig at crossroads.
John Taylor: comment, 1993

of the troubles in Northern Ireland:
23 A disease in the family that is never mentioned.
William Trevor 1928– : in *Observer* 18 November 1990

O

Openness see Secrecy and Openness

Optimism see also Hope

1 Have the good word!
Anonymous: traditional expression of positive policy

2 Sure what harm!
Anonymous: traditional response to bad news

3 But they might as well go chasin' after moonbeams
Or light a penny candle from a star.
Anonymous: 'Galway Bay', 19th century song

4 There is hope for all of us. Well, anyway, if you don't die
you live through it, day in, day out.
Mary Beckett 1926– : *A Belfast Woman* (1980)

5 One of the thieves was saved. (*Pause*) It's a reasonable
percentage.
Samuel Beckett 1906–89: *Waiting for Godot* (1955)

6 I had expected disrespect and instead got devotion, I had
expected infidelity and instead got commitment, I had
expected upheaval and instead got predictability and (most
disappointing of all) I had expected a wolf and been fobbed
off with a sheep.
Marian Keyes: *Lucy Sullivan is Getting Married* (1997)

7 I am gloriously, magnificently, totally wrong.
on the outcome of the Northern Ireland talks
Kevin Myers 1947– : in *Irish Times* 18 April 1998 'This Week They Said'

8 A lament in one ear, maybe; but always a song in the
other. And to me life is simply an invitation to live.
Sean O'Casey 1880–1964: Eileen O'Casey *Eileen* (1976)

9 We are all in the gutter, but some of us are looking at the stars.
Oscar Wilde 1854–1900: *Lady Windermere's Fan* (1892)

Order and Chaos

1 To find a form that accommodates the mess, that is the task of the artist nowadays.
Samuel Beckett 1906–89: in conversation, 1961

2 Ministers are behaving like sheep scattered in a fog on a mountainside.
John Bruton 1947– : in 1994, criticizing the Fianna Fáil administration

3 Good order is the foundation of all good things.
Edmund Burke 1729–97: *Reflections on the Revolution in France* (1790)

4 For my part I hate coercion. I hate the name. I hate the thing . . . But we hate disorder more.
in 1881, signalling his opposition to Irish independence
Joseph Chamberlain 1836–1914: *A Political Memoir 1880–92* (1953)

5 Harry—it has come to this! Of all things it has come to this.
at the outbreak of the Civil War in 1922; Harry Boland was killed by Free State troops three days later
Michael Collins 1890–1922: letter to Harry Boland, 28 July 1922

6 It was a bizarre happening, an unprecedented situation, a grotesque situation, an almost unbelievable mischance.
on the series of events leading to the resignation of the Attorney General; the acronym GUBU was subsequently coined by Conor Cruise O'Brien to describe Haughey's style of government
Charles Haughey 1925– : at a press conference in 1982

7 God, it's like a big rabbit rock festival!
Graham Linehan and **Arthur Mathews**: 'The Plague' (1996), episode from *Father Ted* (Channel 4 TV, 1994–)

8 The whole worl's in a state o' chassis!
Sean O'Casey 1880–1964: *Juno and the Paycock* (1925)

9   This is a recipe for disaster, and there will be serious
    problems for the economy as a result, unless things change
    quickly.
    on the millennium bug
    Pat Rabbitte: in *Irish Times* 7 June 1997

10 Flurry's participation in events of this kind seldom failed to
    be of an inflaming character.
    Edith Œ. Somerville 1858–1949 and **Martin Ross** 1862–1915: *Some
    Experiences of an Irish R.M.* (1899)

11 Now days are dragon-ridden, the nightmare
    Rides upon sleep.
    W. B. Yeats 1865–1939: 'Nineteen Hundred and Nineteen'

12 Things fall apart; the centre cannot hold;
    Mere anarchy is loosed upon the world,
    The blood-dimmed tide is loosed, and everywhere
    The ceremony of innocence is drowned.
    W. B. Yeats 1865–1939: 'The Second Coming' (1921)

Parents

1   A mother's love is a blessing.
    Anonymous: title of 19th century song

2   Let me go to hell, that's all I ask, and go on cursing them
    there, and them look down and hear me, that might take
    some of the shine off their bliss.
    Samuel Beckett 1906–89: *From an Abandoned Work* (1958)

3   I am what her savage loving has made me.
    of his mother
    Samuel Beckett 1906–89: James Knowlson *Damned to Fame* (1996)

4 The authoritarian, didactic, primitive Irish parent is world famous—as is his frequently neurotic, deceitful and anxious child.
Noel Browne 1915–97: in 1973, attributed

5 My parents and his mother ganged up and had pan-parent meetings.
Katy Hayes: *Forecourt* (1995)

6 O, father forsaken,
Forgive your son!
James Joyce 1882–1941: 'Ecce Puer'

7 'All that praying you made us do,' complained Maggie. 'And making us go to Mass. And starving us on Good Friday . . . And making us feel ashamed of our bodies and guilty about absolutely everything. No, Ma, you were the pits.'
  Nuala glowed with pride. Truly, she had been the best of Catholic mothers.
Marian Keyes: 'Late Opening at the Last Chance Saloon' (1997)

8 My father, the least happy
man I have known.
John Montague 1929– : 'The Cage'

9 It is not that I half knew my mother. I knew half of her: the lower half—her lap, legs, feet, her hands and wrists as she bent forward.
Flann O'Brien 1911–66: *The Hard Life* (1961)

10 The natural term of the affection of the human animal for its offspring is six years.
George Bernard Shaw 1856–1950: *Heartbreak House* (1919)

11 I am their wall against all danger,
Their door against the wind and snow,
Thou Whom a woman laid in manger
Take me not till the children grow!
Katharine Tynan 1861–1931: 'Any Woman'

Parents

12 To lose one parent, Mr Worthing, may be regarded as a misfortune; to lose both looks like carelessness.
Oscar Wilde 1854–1900: *The Importance of Being Earnest* (1895)

13 Children begin by loving their parents; after a time they judge them; rarely, if ever, do they forgive them.
Oscar Wilde 1854–1900: *A Woman of No Importance* (1893)

Charles Stewart Parnell (1846–91)

1 The uncrowned king of Ireland.
Anonymous: popular nickname for Parnell

2 It was the tyrant Gladstone and he said unto himself,
'I never will be aisy till Parnell is on the shelf;
So make the warrant out in haste and take it by the mail,
And we'll clap the pride of Erin's isle in cold Kilmainham
    Jail.'
Anonymous: street ballad, 1881

3 I am not responsible for the member for Meath and cannot control him. I have, however, a duty to discharge to the great nation of Ireland and I think I should discharge it best when I say I disapprove entirely of the conduct of the honourable member for Meath.
of the parliamentary delaying tactics instigated by Parnell
Isaac Butt 1813–79: in the House of Commons, 12 April 1877

4 An Englishman of the strongest type moulded for an Irish purpose.
Michael Davitt 1846–1905: *The Fall of Feudalism in Ireland* (1906)

5 A marvellous man, a terrible fall.
W. E. Gladstone 1809–98: in December 1895; Robert Kee *The Laurel and the Ivy* (1993)

6 REDMOND: Gladstone is now master of the Party!
   HEALY: Who is to be mistress of the Party?
   *at the meeting of the Irish Parliamentary Party on 6 December
   1890, when the Party split over Parnell's involvement in the
   O'Shea divorce; Healy's reference to Katherine O'Shea was
   particularly damaging*
   Timothy Michael Healy 1855–1931: Robert Kee *The Laurel and the Ivy*
   (1993)

7 Poor Parnell! he cried loudly. My dead king!
   James Joyce 1882–1941: *A Portrait of the Artist as a Young Man* (1916)

8 He would walk the streets of Dublin with a follower far into
   the night, rather than sit in his hotel by himself.
   R. Barry O'Brien 1847–1918: *Life of Parnell* (1898)

9 I should no more have voted Parnell's displacement on the
   Divorce Court proceedings alone than England would have
   thought of changing the command on the eve of the Battle
   of Trafalgar in a holy horror of the frailties of Lady
   Hamilton and her lover.
   William O'Brien 1852–1928: attributed; Mary Kenny *Goodbye to Catholic
   Ireland* (1997)

10 Two ghosts brooded over my boyhood in Munster and the
   cottages there. One was the ghost of Gladstone, the last
   statesman anywhere with moral courage, and the other
   the ghost of the Chief, a pale, indomitable, fighting ghost.
   P. S. O'Hegarty 1879–1955: Ulick O'Connor *The Troubles* (rev. ed., 1996)

11 For Parnell was a proud man,
   No prouder trod the ground.
   W. B. Yeats 1865–1939: 'Come Gather Round Me, Parnellites' (1937)

Parting

1 Let him go, let him tarry,
   Let him sink or let him swim,
   He doesn't care for me nor I don't care for him,

He can go and get another, that I hope he will enjoy,
For I'm going to marry a far nicer boy.
Anonymous: traditional song

2 Oh! hast thou forgotten this day we must part?
It may be for years and it may be for ever.
Julia Crawford ?1800–?1855: 'Kathleen Mavourneen'

3 I felt, if we were ever to part, it would be easier for us both,
especially for me, to do it soon, because later it would be
bitter for me. But I'd love you just the same.
Kitty Kiernan d. 1945: letter to Michael Collins, 1921

4 I have that bittersweet feeling that comes in life. I am dying
to leave but I hate to go.
after the signing of the Good Friday agreement
George Mitchell 1933– : in *Independent* 11 April 1998

5 Now this is the last day of our acquaintance
I will meet you later in somebody's office
I'll talk but you won't listen to me
I know your answer already.
Sinéad O'Connor 1966– : 'The Last Day of Our Acquaintance' (1990)

6 I abandoned my comrades; regret, if it were felt, was not
expressed by Flurry.
Edith Œ. Somerville 1858–1949 and **Martin Ross** 1862–1915: *Further Experiences of an Irish R.M.* (1908)

Past and Present

1 It is an exciting time to be Irish.
view of the Irish Ambassador to Britain of Ireland's economic and cultural renaissance
Ted Barrington: in *Irish Post* 4 July 1998

2 One of the first things I remember in my life was wakening
up with my mother screaming downstairs when we were
burnt out in 1921.
Mary Beckett 1926– : *A Belfast Woman* (1980)

3 It's not perfect, but to me on balance Right Now is a lot
better than the Good Old Days.
Maeve Binchy 1940– : in *Irish Times* 15 November 1997

4 If we live influenced by wind, and sun, and tree, and not by
the passions and deeds of the past, we are a thriftless and
hopeless people.
Thomas Davis 1814–45: *Literary and Historical Essays* (1846)

5 Ireland never was contented . . .
Say you so? You are demented.
Ireland was contented when
All could use the sword and pen,
And when Tara rose so high
That her turrets split the sky,
And about her courts were seen
Liveried angels robed in green.
Walter Savage Landor 1775–1864: 'The Last Fruit Off an Old Tree' (1853)

6 Men have been dying for Ireland since the beginning of
time and look at the state of the country.
Frank McCourt 1930– : *Angela's Ashes* (1996)

7 So the years hang like old clothes, forgotten in the
wardrobe of our minds. Did I wear that? Who was I then?
Brian Moore 1921– : *No Other Life* (1993)

8 The harp that once through Tara's halls
The soul of music shed,
Now hangs as mute on Tara's walls
As if that soul were fled.—
So sleeps the pride of former days,
So glory's thrill is o'er;
And hearts, that once beat high for praise,
Now feel that pulse no more.
Thomas Moore 1779–1852: *Irish Melodies* (1807) 'The harp that once
through Tara's halls'

9 We Irish are always being accused of looking backwards
too much. Sometimes, however, we don't look back far
enough—or carefully enough, or honestly enough.
Dervla Murphy 1931- : *A Place Apart* (1978)

10 Here be ghosts that I have raised this Christmastide, ghosts
of dead men that have bequeathed a trust to us living men.
Ghosts are troublesome things in a house or in a family, as
we knew even before Ibsen taught us. There is only one
way to appease a ghost. You must do the thing it asks you.
The ghosts of a nation sometimes ask very big things and
they must be appeased, whatever the cost.
Patrick Pearse 1879–1916: on Christmas Day, 1915; Conor Cruise O'Brien
Ancestral Voices (1994)

11 In ancient shadows and twilights
Where childhood had strayed,
The world's great sorrows were born
And its heroes were made.
In the lost boyhood of Judas
Christ was betrayed.
George William Russell (Æ) 1867–1935: 'Germinal' (1931)

12 We have never said that because someone has a past, they
can't have a future.
*on the involvement of Sinn Fein and others in the new Northern
Ireland Assembly*
David Trimble 1944- : in *Guardian* 3 July 1998

13 Romantic Ireland's dead and gone,
It's with O'Leary in the grave.
W. B. Yeats 1865–1939: 'September, 1913' (1914)

14 The ghost of Roger Casement
Is beating on the door.
W. B. Yeats 1865–1939: 'The Ghost of Roger Casement' (1939)

Peace

1 Peace cannot be built on exclusion. That has been the price
of the past 30 years.
Gerry Adams 1948– : in *Daily Telegraph* 11 April 1998

2 It is a day we should treasure. Today is about the promise
of a bright future, a day when we hope a line will be drawn
under the bloody past.
Bertie Ahern 1951– : in *Guardian* 11 April 1998

3 Peace is no longer a dream. It is a reality.
on the outcome of the referendum on the Good Friday agreement
William Jefferson Clinton 1946– : in *Sunday Times* 24 May 1998

4 I pray that my coming to Ireland today may prove to be the
first step towards an end of strife among her people,
whatever their race or creed. In that hope I appeal to all
Irishmen to pause, to stretch out the hand of forbearance
and conciliation, to forgive and forget, and to join with me
in making for the land they love a new era of peace,
contentment and goodwill.
*speech to the new Ulster Parliament at Stormont, 22 June
1921*
George V 1865–1936: Kenneth Rose *King George V* (1983)

5 My mission is to pacify Ireland.
*on receiving news that he was to form his first cabinet, 1st
December 1868*
W. E. Gladstone 1809–98: H. C. G. Matthew *Gladstone 1809–1874* (1986)

6 What I have signed I will stand by, in the belief that the
end of the conflict of centuries is at hand.
Arthur Griffith 1871–1922: statement to Dáil Eireann before the debate on
the Treaty, December 1921

7 Unity has got to be thought of as a spiritual development
which will be brought about by peaceful, persuasive
means.
Sean Lemass 1899–1971: in *Irish Press* 28 January 1969

8 We cannot as the largest organization in this country shirk
our responsibility or role in achieving and contributing to
peace.
*the president of the Gaelic Athletic Association on the proposal
to abolish Rule 21, which prohibits members of the British and
Northern Ireland security forces from joining the association*
Joe McDonagh: in *Irish Times* 20 April 1998

9 Nobody ever said it would be easy—and that was an
understatement.
on the peace talks
George Mitchell 1933– : in *Times* 19 February 1998

10 Peace, political stability and reconciliation are not too
much to ask for. They are the minimum that a decent
society provides.
George Mitchell 1933– : in *Irish Post* 18 April 1998

11 I will walk on no grave of Ulster's honoured dead to do a
deal with the IRA or the British government.
*speech at the annual conference of the Democratic Unionist
Party*
Ian Paisley 1926– : in *Irish Times* 6 December 1997 'This Week They Said'

12 The mother of all treachery.
the Democratic Unionist Party's view of the peace agreement
Ian Paisley 1926– : in *Times* 16 April 1998

13 I believe these talks are a farce. There are those prepared to
compromise, and that is totally wrong, totally
unacceptable.
*a criticism of the Sinn Féin leadership by the sister of Bobby
Sands*
Bernadette Sands-McKevitt 1958– : in *Irish Times* 14 March 1998 'This
Week They Said'

14 The settlement shows that the will of the people for peace
and co-operation is stronger than the divide.
Jacques Santer 1937– : in *Times* 11 April 1998

15 We are not here to negotiate with them, but to confront
    them.
    *on entering the Mitchell talks on Northern Ireland with Sinn
    Féin*
    David Trimble 1944– : in *Guardian* 18 September 1997

People see also de Valera, Markievicz, Parnell,
Poets and Poetry, Politicians, Yeats

1 Neck and throat bound in the coils of a white muffler, a
   Jacobin of Jacobins, as his small red-rimmed eyes stab all
   the beauty and sorrow of the world in bursts of anti-English
   rhetoric.
   of Sean O'Casey at a debate in Drumcondra, c.1900
   Anonymous: Ulick O'Connor *The Troubles* (rev. ed., 1996)

2 Few of his critics have noticed that he displayed all the
   careful qualities of a Protestant from Lower Ulster.
   of Henry James
   Elizabeth Bowen 1899–1973: Benedict Kiely *Drink to the Bird* (1991)

3 Yet I would forgive him anything. Because of his sincerity I
   would forgive him anything.
   after the death of Cathal Brugha
   Michael Collins 1890–1922: Diana Norman *Terrible Beauty* (1987)

4 I am unable to think of a time before I had heard of Oscar
   Wilde. It is as if he had been with me always, like Christ
   and the queen.
   after the film Wilde *opened in Dublin*
   Stephen Fry 1957– : in *Irish Times* 1 November 1997 'Quotes of the Week'

5 Stately, plump Buck Mulligan came from the stairhead,
   bearing a bowl of lather on which a mirror and a razor lay
   crossed. A yellow dressinggown, ungirdled, was sustained

gently behind him on the mild morning air. He held the
bowl aloft and intoned:
   —*Introibo ad altare Dei.*
'*Buck Mulligan*' *is based on Oliver St John Gogarty*
James Joyce 1882–1941: *Ulysses* (1922)

6 She wasn't just a brilliant writer. She was a proper
   countrywoman. She rode beautifully and gave great,
   ordinary hunting lunches.
   of Elizabeth Bowen
   Molly Keane 1904–96: in *Independent* 1 June 1996

7 Bold Robert Emmet, the darling of Erin.
   Tom Maguire b. 1870: 'Bold Robert Emmet'

8 Lots of good people have become lost in the wilderness of
   Irish politics. But I believed that if anybody could pull it off,
   it was my husband. He is all that has been written about
   him.
   of George Mitchell
   Heather Mitchell: in *Irish Times* 18 April 1998 'This Week They Said'

9 Her interest in native things and people was not healthy
   when demented Black and Tans were at large and unused
   to making fine distinctions.
   of Lady Gregory
   Flann O'Brien 1911–66: *Myles Away from Dublin* (1990)

10 In the early nineteenth century secret societies
   flourished . . . Ribbonmen, Blackfeet, and Whitefeet. JKL
   fought them like a tiger; a very lean tiger, for he was a lean
   man, all lath and plaster: an ascetic who thought the
   Jesuits at Clongowes were all too fat.
   of James Warren Doyle ('JKL'), *Catholic Bishop of Kildare and
   Leighlin*
   Sean O'Faolain 1900–91: *An Irish Journey* (1940)

11 He was like a man who takes a machine-gun to a shooting
    gallery. Everybody falls flat on his face, the proprietor at
    once takes to the hills, and when you cautiously peep up,
    you find he has wrecked the place but got three perfect
    bull's-eyes.
    of Frank O'Connor
    Sean O'Faolain 1900–91: attributed

12 In my definition they were good men—men, that is, who
    willed no evil. No person living is the worse off for having
    known Thomas MacDonagh.
    James Stephens 1882–1950: *The Insurrection in Dublin* (1916)

13 Two girls in silk kimonos, both
    Beautiful, one a gazelle.
    W. B. Yeats 1865–1939: 'In Memory of Eva Gore Booth and Con Markiewicz'
    (1933)

14 Swift has sailed into his rest;
    Savage indignation there
    Cannot lacerate his breast.
    Imitate him if you dare,
    World-besotted traveller; he
    Served human liberty.
    W. B. Yeats 1865–1939: 'Swift's Epitaph' (1933)

Perfection

1 Finality is death. Perfection is finality.
   Nothing is perfect. There are lumps in it.
   James Stephens 1882–1950: *The Crock of Gold* (1912)

2 The condition of perfection is idleness: the aim of perfection
   is youth.
   Oscar Wilde 1854–1900: in *Chameleon* December 1894

Places see also Belfast, Clare, Coleraine, Cork, Donegal, Dublin, Galway, Garryowen, Kerry, Kildare, Lough Derg, The North, Tipperary, The West, Wicklow

1 Grey, grey is Abbey Assaroe, near Belashanny town.
William Allingham 1824–89: 'Abbey Assaroe'

2 Abbeyfeale for flour and meal,
And Cahiramee for horses.
Anonymous: traditional

3 And what is more glorious—there's naught more
     uproarious—
Huzza for the humours of Donnybrook Fair!
Anonymous: 19th century song

4 Mallow, Tallow, Cappoquin,
Doneraile and Charlesville.
Broken windows, upside down;
Hi! for the rakes of Mallow town.
Anonymous: song, 19th century

5 Now in Kilkenny it is reported
They've marble stones there, as black as ink.
Anonymous: 'Carrickfergus', traditional song

6 O Naas it is an awful place,
Athy is just as bad.
But of all the places in the world,
Jaysus, Kinnegad!
Anonymous: traditional jingle

7 And the Thirty-two Counties of the Four Provinces of
     Ireland
Are thus divided: the Four Counties are in the Four Camps
Munster South in Reuben's Gate, Connaut West in Joseph's
     Gate,

Ulster North in Dan's Gate, Leinster East in Judah's Gate.
William Blake 1757–1827: *Jerusalem* (1815) 'The Emanation of Giant
Albion'

8 And the names of the Thirty-two Counties of Ireland are
　　these,
Under Judah and Issachar are Lowth, Longford,
Eastmeath, Westmeath, Dublin, Kildare, King's County,
Queen's County, Wicklow, Catherloh, Wexford, Kilkenny,
And those under Reuben and Simeon and Levi are these
Waterford, Tipperary, Cork, Limerick, Kerry, Clare,
And those under Ephraim, Manasseh, and Benjamin are
　　these,
Galway, Roscommon, Mayo, Sligo, Leitrim,
And those under Dan, Asher, and Naphthali are these,
Donegal, Antrim, Tyrone, Fermanagh, Armagh,
　　Londonderry,
Down, Managhan, Cavan. These are the land of Erin.
William Blake 1757–1827: *Jerusalem* (1815) 'The Emanation of Giant
Albion'

9 There grows the wild ash; and a time-stricken willow
Looks chidingly down on the mirth of the billow,
As, like some gay child that sad monitor scorning,
It lightly laughs back to the laugh of the morning.
Jeremiah John Callanan 1795–1829: 'Gougane Barra' (1826)

10 The vast marshes of Ireland, its immense thickets
stretching towards the west, in Connaught especially, for
centuries offered a sure refuge to the indomitable Celts, and
allowed them to maintain a savage independence at the
cost of poverty and suffering of every kind.
Count Cavour 1810–61: *Thoughts on Ireland* (1868)

11 These things were long before my day,
I only speak with borrowed words.
But that is how the story goes
In Iveragh of the singing birds.
Sigerson Clifford 1913– : 'The Ballad of the Tinker's Daughter'

12 I have appeared in Knock more often than the Virgin Mary.
Sean Doherty 1944– : comment of a TD in the 1980s

13 Come back, Paddy Reilly, to Ballyjamesduff;
Come home, Paddy Reilly, to me.
Percy French 1854–1920: 'Come Back, Paddy Reilly'

14 Oh Mary, this London's a wonderful sight,
With the people all working by day and by night . . .
But for all that I found there, I might as well be
Where the Mountains of Mourne sweep down to the sea.
Percy French 1854–1920: 'The Mountains of Mourne'

15 My place of clear water.
Seamus Heaney 1939– : 'Anahorish' (1972)

16 The savage rock sides are painted of a hundred colours.
Does the sun ever shine there? When the world was
moulded and fashioned out of formless chaos, this must
have been *the bit over*—a remnant of chaos.
on visiting the Giant's Causeway
William Makepeace Thackeray 1811–63: *The Irish Sketch-book* (1847)

17 Meath and Louth are what you might get if you brought
Norfolk to the boil . . . a country of bubbles.
T. H. White 1906–64: Sylvia Townsend Warner *T. H. White* (1967)

Poets and Poetry see also Yeats

1 Poetry's a mere drug, Sir.
George Farquhar 1678–1707: *Love and a Bottle* (1698)

2 Generations of gifted northern poets have let the linguistic
cat out of the sectarian bag, setting it free in the great street
carnival of 'protholics and catestants'.
Seamus Heaney 1939– : in *Observer* 12 April 1998

3 It was an unearthly and ghostly figure, in a brown
garment: the same garment, to all appearance, which
lasted to the day of his death; the blanched hair was totally
unkempt, the corpse-like features still as marble; a large
book was in his arms, and all his soul was in the book.
James Clarence Mangan seen in Trinity College Library
John Mitchel 1815–75: introduction to *Poems by James Clarence Mangan*
(1859)

4 Oh! blame not the bard, if he fly to the bowers,
Where Pleasure lies, carelessly smiling at Fame.
Thomas Moore 1779–1852: *Irish Melodies* (1807) 'Oh! blame not the bard'

5 *Mise Raifteirí an file,*
lán dóchais is grá
le súile gan solas,
le ciúineas gan crá

I am Raftery the poet,
full of hope and love.
My eyes without light;
Peaceful, uncomplaining.
Antoine Raifteará 1779–1835: 'Mise Raifteará'

6 In our neighbour country Ireland, where truly learning
goeth very bare, yet are their poets held in a devout
reverence.
Philip Sidney 1554–86: *Apologie for Poetrie* (1595)

7 I think it better that in times like these
A poet's mouth be silent, for in truth
We have no gift to set a statesman right;
He has had enough of meddling who can please
A young girl in the indolence of her youth,
Or an old man upon a winter's night.
W. B. Yeats 1865–1939: 'On being asked for a War Poem' (1919)

8 Irish poets, learn your trade,
  Sing whatever is well made.
  W. B. Yeats 1865–1939: 'Under Ben Bulben' (1939)

Political Parties

1 The Labour Party is like the Widow Macree's dog who will
  go a piece of the road with anyone.
  of the Labour Party's readiness to enter into coalitions
  Gerry Collins 1938– : comment, 1979; cf. **Animals 5**

2 The Provisional IRA is no more a left-wing movement than
  Hitler's National Socialist Party was.
  Garret Fitzgerald 1926– : comment, 1973

3 There's one thing we have that Fine Gael can never have,
  and that's a love for the four green fields of Ireland.
  Padraig Flynn 1939– : in June 1982 as Minister for the Gaeltacht,
  attributed

4 We intend to decry the work of no Irish party . . . but we
  feel certain that if the eyes of the Irish nation are
  continually focussed on England, they will inevitably
  acquire a squint. For in our experience, we have known
  some good Irishmen who by too constant gazing on the
  Union Jack have acquired a degree of colour blindness,
  which caused them to perceive in it an emerald green
  tinge.
  Arthur Griffith 1871–1922: in *United Irishman* 1900

5 Every party in Ireland was founded on the gun.
  John Hume 1937– : in 1995, attributed

6 The Massachusetts ticket is all Irish; its members have the
  cold eyes and slack faces of IRA members who have gone
  into another line of work.
  Murray Kempton 1917– : *America Comes of Middle Age* (1963)

7 When in office, the Liberals forget their principles and the
Tories remember their friends.
Thomas Kettle 1880–1916: Nicholas Mansergh *The Irish Question* (ed. 3,
1975)

8 The main difference is that we're in and they're out.
*on being asked what was the principal difference between Fianna
Fáil and Fine Gael*
Sean Lemass 1899–1971: attributed

9 The divide of Irish politics, Fine Gael versus Fianna Fáil,
has its roots in the civil war, but it is the divide itself, rather
than the war, that is the significant element.
John Waters 1955– : *Jiving at the Crossroads* (1991)

Political Sayings and Slogans

1 England's difficulty is Ireland's opportunity.
Anonymous: recorded from the mid-nineteenth century

2 *Érin go brágh.*
Ireland for ever.
Anonymous: title of song (19th century)

3 *Gan teanga, gan tír.*
No language, no nation!
Patrick Pearse 1879–1916: attributed

4 Hell or Connaught.
*traditional summary of the plan to transport the Catholic
population to a few western counties, leaving the land free for
settlers*
Oliver Cromwell 1599–1658: attributed

5 He that will England win,
Must with Ireland first begin.
Anonymous: proverbial saying recorded from the 16th century

6 No surrender!
   motto of the siege of Derry
   Anonymous: Jonathan Bardon *A History of Ulster* (1992)

7 Remember Orr!
   *rallying cry of the United Irishmen, c.1798; William Orr
   (1766–97), a prosperous County Antrim farmer, was hanged
   at Carrickfergus in 1797 for allegedly adminstering the United
   Irish Oath to two soldiers*
   Anonymous: Oliver Knox *Rebels and Informers* (1997)

8 *Sinn féin.*
   Ourselves.
   *coined in 1904 for Arthur Griffith's new policy, and echoing
   the title and refrain of Thomas Davis's ballad 'Ourselves Alone'*
   Máire Butler: Robert Welch (ed.) *The Oxford Companion to Irish Literature*
   (1997)

9 Together with the Union.
   *the Ulster Unionist Party's official slogan for the Assembly
   elections, 1998*
   Anonymous: in *Irish Times* 4 June 1998

10 Ulster says no.
   *slogan coined in response to the Anglo-Irish Agreement of 15
   November 1985*
   Anonymous: in *Irish Times* 25 November 1985

11 What have you got in your hand?
   A green bough.
   Where did it first grow?
   In America.
   Where did it bud?
   In France.
   Where are you going to plant it?
   In the crown of Great Britain.
   oath of the United Irishmen, c.1797
   Anonymous: R. F. Foster *Modern Ireland* (1988)

Politicians see also Parnell, de Valera, People

1 We want him to be the last British Prime Minister with
jurisdiction in Ireland.
of Tony Blair
Gerry Adams 1948– : in *Irish Times* 18 October 1997

2 Most of the people here are sheep. If David got up and said
'ba ba ba' they would clap.
*an unidentified delegate on the response to David Trimble at the
Ulster Unionist Party conference*
Anonymous: in *Irish Times* 28 March 1998 'This Week They Said'

3 What's the difference between David Trimble and Wolfe
Tone? 200 years.
poster denouncing Unionist support for the Belfast Agreement
Anonymous: in *Irish Times* 16 May 1998 'This Week They Said'

4 That rare phenomenon, a silent Irishman.
of Arthur Griffith
Winston Churchill 1874–1965: Ulick O'Connor *The Troubles* (rev. ed., 1996)

5 Like the silver plate on a coffin.
of Robert Peel's smile
John Philpot Curran 1750–1817: quoted by Daniel O'Connell in the House
of Commons, 26 February 1835

6 A thundering disgrace.
of President Cearbhaill Ó Dálaigh
Patrick Donegan: comment, 1976

7 His indifference to politics bewrayed him for a Unionist, his
indifference to religion bewrayed him for a Protestant.
of Horace Plunkett (1884–1932)
John Eglinton 1868–1961: *Irish Literary Portraits* (1935)

8 People in his own party and others have attributed to Deputy Haughey an overweening ambition, a wish to dominate—even to own the State.
on Charles Haughey's succession to the leadership of Fianna Fáil
Garret Fitzgerald 1926– : comment, 1979

9 There is the noble Marquis. Like a pike at the bottom of a pool.
of Lord Hartington, apparently asleep on the Opposition bench
Timothy Michael Healy 1855–1931: Herbert Gladstone *After Thirty Years* (1928)

10 He knew Ireland too little, and the English House of Commons too well.
of John Redmond
Dorothy Macardle 1889–1958: Diana Norman *Terrible Beauty* (1987)

11 A man of giant proportions in body and in mind; with no profound learning, indeed, even in his own profession of the law, but with a vast and varied knowledge of human nature, in all its strength, and especially all its weakness, with a voice like thunder and earthquake, yet musical and soft at will, as the song of birds.
of Daniel O'Connell
John Mitchel 1815–75: *Jail Journal* (1854)

12 If I saw Mr Haughey buried at midnight at a crossroads, with a stake driven through his heart—politically speaking—I should continue to wear a clove of garlic round my neck, just in case.
Conor Cruise O'Brien 1917– : in *Observer* 10 October 1982

13 The strength of these men was that each of them could look a Pearsean ghost in the eye . . . Each of them, in their youth, had done the thing the ghost asked them to do, in 1916 or 1919—21 or both. That was it; from now on they would do what seemed reasonable to themselves in the interests of the actual people inhabiting the island of

Ireland and not of a personified abstraction, or of a disembodied voice, or of a ghost.
of Sean Lemass (1899–1971) and other senior Irish politicians in the 1960s
Conor Cruise O'Brien 1917– : *Ancestral Voices* (1994)

14 The majority of the members of the Irish parliament are professional politicians, in the sense that otherwise they would not be given jobs minding mice at crossroads.
Flann O'Brien 1911–66: *The Hair of the Dogma* (1977)

15 Gladstone, the last statesman anywhere with moral courage.
P. S. O'Hegarty 1879–1955: Ulick O'Connor *The Troubles* (rev. ed., 1996)

16 The mules of politics: without pride of ancestry, or hope of posterity.
of the Liberal Unionists
John O'Connor Power 1848–1919: H. H. Asquith *Memories and Reflections* (1928)

17 I met Michael for the first and last time on Saturday last, and am very glad I did. I rejoice in his memory, and will not be so disloyal to it as to snivel over his valiant death.
So tear up your mourning and hang up your brightest colours in his honour; and let us all praise God that he had not to die in a snuffy bed of a trumpery cough, weakened by age.
of Michael Collins
George Bernard Shaw 1856–1950: letter to Johanna Collins, 24 August 1922

18 He flung a sturdy brood of ideas upon the world without a rag to cover them.
of Daniel O'Connell
Richard Lalor Sheil 1791–1851: Charles Chevenix Trench *The Great Dan* (1984)

19 It's not for nothing Mr Ahern is known as the Flurry Knox
of Fianna Fáil.
Dick Walsh: in *Irish Times* 28 March 1998 'This Week They Said'

20 Had Cosgrave eaten Parnell's heart, the land's
Imagination had been satisfied,
Or lacking that, government in such hands,
O'Higgins its sole statesman had not died.
W. B. Yeats 1865–1939: 'Parnell's Funeral'

Politics see also **Political Parties, Political Sayings and Slogans, Politicians**

1 That's one less rip we'll have to deal with.
*an unidentified Fianna Fáil colleague on the resignation from
political life of Máire Geoghegan-Quinn*
Anonymous: in *Irish Times* 1 February 1997

2 It is a general popular error to suppose the loudest
complainers for the public to be the most anxious for its
welfare.
Edmund Burke 1729–97: *Observations on the Present State of the Nation*
(1769)

3 Magnanimity in politics is not seldom the truest wisdom;
and a great empire and little minds go ill together.
Edmund Burke 1729–97: *On Conciliation with America* (1775)

4 You're killed working, running and racing to every
dogfight.
of life as a member of the Dáil
Mary Coughlin: in *Irish Times* 26 May 1997

5 All politics is local politics.
earlier used by the American politician Tip O'Neill
Padraig Flynn 1939– : comment, 1990s

6 We can cope with ordinary emergencies.
Padraig Flynn 1939– : on the firemen's strike, 1988

7 Politics is the chloroform of the Irish people, or, rather, the hashish.
Oliver St John Gogarty 1878–1957: *As I Was Going Down Sackville Street* (1937)

8 Every TD, from the youngest or newest in the House, dreams of being Taoiseach.
Charles Haughey 1925– : in *Irish Times* 23 May 1970 'This Week They Said'

9 Politics can only be a small part of what we are. It's a *way* of seeing, it's not all-seeing in itself.
Brian Keenan 1950– : *An Evil Cradling* (1992)

10 The mainstream male politics of Northern Ireland have been not only macho in style but macho in agenda.
Monica McWilliams: in *Irish Times* 25 October 1997 'This Week They Said'

11 Our ancestors believed in magic, prayers, trickery, browbeating and bullying: I think it would be fair to sum that list up as 'Irish politics'.
Flann O'Brien 1911–66: *The Hair of the Dogma* (1977)

12 DAVITT: They have kept the ball rolling.
PARNELL: I don't want them to keep the ball rolling any longer. The League must be suppressed or I will leave public life.
of the Ladies' Land League (founded by Anna Parnell)
Charles Stewart Parnell 1846–91: Nicholas Mansergh *The Irish Question* (ed. 3, 1975)

13 Mr Parnell deceives himself . . . when he tells us he wants Grattan's Parliament. Does Mr Parnell want a parliament in Dublin controlled by a few nominees of the British Cabinet who, under the Viceroy, constitute an Irish government in no way responsible to the Irish House of

Commons? If not, then it is not Grattan's Parliament he
wants, and it is not Grattan's Parliament he should ask for.
John O'Connor Power 1848–1919: *The Anglo-Irish Quarrel* (1880)

14 We're all running around the Titanic arguing about the
placing of the deck chairs.
Ruairi Quinn 1946– : on the abortion amendment, 1983

15 You get the big things right, the small things trip you up.
Albert Reynolds 1933– : in 1994, attributed

16 What more can I do in politics? I started at the bottom and
I went to the top and there is nowhere else to go.
announcing his retirement
Albert Reynolds 1933– : in *Irish Independent* 13 March 1998

17 Don't learn the rules. Then they can't accuse you of
breaking them.
Mary Robinson 1944– : in 1985, attributed

18 An Irishman . . . can't be intelligently political . . . If you
want to interest him in Ireland you've got to call the
unfortunate island Kathleen ni Hoolihan and pretend she's
a little old woman.
George Bernard Shaw 1856–1950: *John Bull's Other Island* (1904)

19 God help the woman politician who has yet to meet the
man in her life and has to worry whether he'll love the
world he finds himself in.
of the pressure of life in the Dáil
Mary Wallace: in *Irish Times* 1 February 1997

20 The modern literature of Ireland, and indeed all that stir of
thought which prepared for the Anglo-Irish war, began
when Parnell fell from power in 1891. A disillusioned and
embittered Ireland turned from parliamentary politics; an
event was conceived; and the race began, as I think, to be
troubled by that event's long gestation.
W. B. Yeats 1865–1939: *Autobiographies* (1955)

Poverty

1 We were so poor, we used to sell clothes-pegs to the tinkers.
Anonymous: traditional saying

2 I have seen the Indian in his forests and the negro in his
irons, and I believed, in pitying their plight, that I saw the
lowest ebb of human misery; but I did not then know the
degree of poverty to be found in Ireland.
Gustave de Beaumont 1802–66: *L'Irlande sociale, politique et religieuse*
(1839)

3 Whose fault is it if poor Ireland still continues poor?
George Berkeley 1685–1753: *The Querist* (1737)

4 When she died in a pauper bed, in love
All the poor of Dublin rose to lament her.
C. Day-Lewis 1904–72: 'Remembering Con Markievicz' (1970)

5 To marry the Irish is to look for poverty.
J. P. Donleavy 1926– : *The Ginger Man* (1955)

6 I'm very lonely now, Mary,
For the poor make no new friends.
Helen, Lady Dufferin 1807–67: 'The Lament of the Irish Emigrant'

7 There is a wealth of poverty in Northern Ireland which
must be overcome.
Lord Enniskillen: speech in the House of Lords, 3 December 1968

8 I have fed purely upon ale; I have eat my ale, drank my
ale, and I always sleep upon ale.
George Farquhar 1678–1707: *The Beaux' Stratagem* (1707)

9 People with a culture of poverty suffer much less repression
than we of the middle-class suffer and indeed, if I may
make the suggestion with due qualification, they often
have a lot more fun than we have.
Brian Friel 1929– : *The Freedom of the City* (1973)

10 Laws grind the poor, and rich men rule the law.
Oliver Goldsmith 1728–74: *The Traveller* (1764)

11 To be out of work
to be out of money
to be out of fashion
to be out of friends
to be in for the Vincent De Paul man.
Rita Ann Higgins 1955– : 'Some People Know What It Is Like'

12 I was deeply moved by the tragic shabbiness of this sinister
country.
Henry James 1843–1916: on visiting Dublin, March 1895

13 Everyone was poor and proud. My parents didn't know
anything to be proud of, so they just carried on.
Patrick Kavanagh 1904–67: *The Green Fool* (1938)

14 Hell has no terror for me. I have lived there. Thirty six
years of hunger and poverty have been my portion. They
cannot terrify me with hell. Better to be in hell with Dante
and Davitt than to be in heaven with Carson and Murphy.
in 1913, during the 'Dublin lockout' labour dispute
James Larkin 1876–1947: Ulick O'Connor *The Troubles* (rev. ed., 1996)

15 This is my own mother, begging . . . It's the worst kind of
shame, almost as bad as begging on the streets where the
tinkers hold up their scabby children.
Frank McCourt 1930– : *Angela's Ashes* (1996)

16 The Scotch Quarter was a line of residential houses
But the Irish Quarter was a slum for the blind and halt.
Louis MacNeice 1907–63: 'Carrickfergus' (1937)

17 Mother realised, to her great astonishment, that Betty was
a Protestant as well. Nobody had ever explained to her that
Protestants could also be poor.
Frank O'Connor 1903–66: *An Only Child* (1961)

18 A rich land and a poor country. I ask you a question. Why
is this?
Humphrey O'Sullivan 1780–1837: *The Diary of an Irish Countryman*
1827–35 (translated Tomás de Bháldraithe, 1979)

19 That foreign devils have made our land a tomb,
That the sun that was Munster's glory has gone down
Has made me a beggar before you, Valentine Brown.
Aodhagán Ó Rathaille *c.*1670–1729: 'A Grey Eye Weeping' (translated by
Frank O'Connor)

20 Like dear St Francis of Assisi I am wedded to Poverty: but
in my case the marriage is not a success.
Oscar Wilde 1854–1900: letter June 1899

Practicality

1 Put your trust in God, my boys, and keep your powder dry.
often attributed to Oliver Cromwell himself
Valentine Blacker 1728–1823: 'Oliver's Advice' in E. Hayes *Ballads of
Ireland* (1856) vol. 1

2 The age of chivalry is gone.—That of sophisters,
economists, and calculators, has succeeded; and the glory
of Europe is extinguished for ever.
Edmund Burke 1729–97: *Reflections on the Revolution in France* (1790)

3 Whenever our neighbour's house is on fire, it cannot be
amiss for the engines to play a little on our own.
Edmund Burke 1729–97: *Reflections on the Revolution in France* (1790)

4 I found out that those fellows we put on the spot were
going to put a lot of us on the spot, so we got in first.
of the elimination of the 'Cairo Gang' in 1920
Michael Collins 1890–1922: Diana Norman *Terrible Beauty* (1987)

5 'They took my sleeve to strain the soup!' repeated Philippa,
in a crystal clarity of wrath.
Edith Œ. Somerville 1858–1949 and **Martin Ross** 1862–1915: *Further
Experiences of an Irish R.M.* (1908)

6 And he gave it for his opinion, that whoever could make
two ears of corn or two blades of grass to grow upon a spot
of ground where only one grew before, would deserve
better of mankind, and do more essential service to his
country than the whole race of politicians put together.
Jonathan Swift 1667–1745: *A Critical Essay upon the Faculties of the Mind*
(1709)

7 'The party' . . . required that the candidate should be a safe
man, one who would support 'the party',—not a
cantankerous, red-hot semi-Fenian running about to
meetings at the Rotunda, and suchlike, with views of his
own about tenant-right and the Irish Church.
Anthony Trollope 1815–82: *Phineas Finn* (1869)

Praise

1 Of praise a mere glutton, he swallowed what came,
And the puff of a dunce he mistook it for fame.
Oliver Goldsmith 1728–74: *Retaliation* (1774)

2 When a young man came up to him in Zurich and said,
'May I kiss the hand that wrote *Ulysses*?' Joyce replied,
somewhat like King Lear, 'No, it did lots of other things
too.'
James Joyce 1882–1941: Richard Ellmann *James Joyce* (1959)

3 Won't you come into the garden? I would like my roses to
see you.
to a young lady
Richard Brinsley Sheridan 1751–1816: attributed

Prejudice

1 I love Ireland: were she only not Catholic! but would she be
Ireland otherwise?
William Allingham 1824–89: *Diary* (rev. ed. 1967)

2 There is, however, a limit at which forbearance ceases to be
a virtue.
Edmund Burke 1729–97: *Observations on a late Publication on the Present
State of the Nation* (2nd ed., 1769)

3 I'm glad he made that remark. It helps establish the
balance because I'm afraid I'm a bit inclined to think the
other way.
*c.1940, on hearing that a member of the Cabinet had made a
pro-German, anti-British comment*
Eamon de Valera 1882–1975: Tony Gray *The Lost Years: the Emergency in
Ireland 1939–45* (1997)

4 I always suspected she had Scotch blood in her veins,
anything else I could have looked over in her from a regard
to the family.
Maria Edgeworth 1767–1849: *Castle Rackrent* (1800)

5 Hard-mouthed Ribbonmen and Orange bigots.
Seamus Heaney 1939– : 'Station Island'

6 One master will hit you if you don't know that Eamon de
Valera is the greatest man that ever lived. Another master
will hit you if you don't know that Michael Collins was the
greatest man that ever lived . . .
   If you ever say anything good about Oliver Cromwell
they'll all hit you.
Frank McCourt 1930– : *Angela's Ashes* (1996)

7 And one read black where the other read white, his hope
The other man's damnation:
Up the Rebels, To Hell with the Pope,
And God Save—as you prefer—the King or Ireland.
Louis MacNeice 1907–63: *Autumn Journal* (1938)

8 You must always look for the *Ulsterior* motive.
of C. S. Lewis as an Ulsterman
J. R. R. Tolkien 1892–1973: A. N. Wilson *Life of C. S. Lewis* (1986)

(P)

Present see Past and Present

The Presidency

1 Personally I would probably vote for Mary McAleese if I had a vote.
Gerry Adams 1948– : in *Irish Times* 18 October 1997

2 There's nothing in the Constitution to say I can't sing as President.
the singer announcing her candidacy for the Presidency
Dana: in *Irish Times* 7 August 1997

3 I would vote for Donald Duck if they opposed Mary McAleese. I think she will make a very dangerous and tribal president.
Eoghan Harris 1943– : in *Irish Times* 18 October 1997

4 I sense a mood among the people that they want a president who can speak to them from above politics. It will look at an Ireland where people are not pigeon-holed any more.
after being selected as Fianna Fáil candidate
Mary McAleese 1951– : in *Irish Times* 20 September 1997

5 This is a republic and I was elected first citizen of the Republic, but a first citizen among equals.
reviewing her first 100 days in office
Mary McAleese 1951– : in *Irish Times* 28 February 1998

6 Much has been made of the way the women's vote went to her. I suspect that what was so evident as to draw comment was the proud jubilance of women voters at having a splendid candidate to vote for who also happened, icing-on-a-cake fashion, to be a woman. That was one in the eye for the ah-ya-boy-ya crowd, all right. But what's truly significant is that she got the men's vote . . . The men

of Ireland went unhesitatingly out and voted for a woman
President because she represented their views.
on the election of Mary Robinson
Mary Maher: in *Irish Times* 12 November 1990

7 Presidents, under the Irish Constitution, don't have
policies. But . . . a President can have a theme.
Cearbhall Ó Dálaigh: attributed

8 May it be a presidency where I the President can sing to
you, citizens of Ireland, the joyous refrain of the 14th
century Irish poet as recalled by W. B. Yeats: 'I am of
Ireland . . . come dance with me in Ireland.'
Mary Robinson 1944– : inaugural speech as President, 1990; cf. **Ireland 1**

Property

1 The land of Ireland belongs to the people of Ireland.
John Devoy 1842–1928: comment, 1878

2 Well! some people talk of morality, and some of religion,
but give me a little snug property.
Maria Edgeworth 1767–1849: *The Absentee* (1812)

3 Spare all I have, and take my life.
George Farquhar 1678–1707: *The Beaux' Stratagem* (1707)

4 It is with ideas as with umbrellas, if left lying about they
are peculiarly liable to change of ownership.
Thomas Kettle 1880–1916: attributed

5 O Woman of Three Cows, *agra*, don't let your tongue thus
rattle!
Oh, don't be saucy, don't be stiff, because you may have
cattle.
I have seen—and here's my hand to you, I only say what's
true—

A many a one with twice your stock not half so proud as
you.
James Clarence Mangan 1803–49: 'The Woman of Three Cows' (from a 17th
century Irish poem)

6 Land is the only thing in the world worth working for,
worth fighting for, worth dying for, because it's the only
thing that lasts. It will come to you, this love of the land.
Margaret Mitchell 1900–49: *Gone With The Wind* (1939)

7 Property is organized robbery.
George Bernard Shaw 1856–1950: preface to *Major Barbara* (1907)

8 A leprechaun without a pot of gold is like a rose without
perfume, a bird without a wing, or an inside without an
outside.
James Stephens 1882–1950: *The Crock of Gold* (1912)

9 There's a proud array of soldiers—
What do they round your door?
They guard our master's granaries
From the thin hands of the poor.
Jane Francesca Wilde ('Speranza') 1821–96: 'The Famine Years'

10 If property had simply pleasures, we could stand it; but its
duties make it unbearable. In the interest of the rich we
must get rid of it.
Oscar Wilde 1854–1900: in *Fortnightly Review* February 1891

Proverbs and Sayings

1 *Aithníonn ciaróg ciaróg eile.*
One beetle will recognize another.
Anonymous: traditional saying

2 *Briseann an dúchas tré súilibh an chait.*
A cat's nature breaks out through its eyes.
i.e., nature cannot be concealed
Anonymous: traditional saying

3 *Cad a dhéanfaidh mach an chait ac luch do mharú?*
What will the cat's son do but kill a mouse?
Anonymous: traditional saying

4 *Céad Míle Fáilte.*
A hundred thousand welcomes.
Anonymous: traditional greeting

5 *Ceo ar Muisire is Clára lom,*
Rian an soinnine is fearr sa domhan!

Mist on Mushera and Clara clear is the best sign of fine
weather in the world.
referring to two adjacent Cork–Kerry mountains
Anonymous: traditional saying

6 *Dia idir sinn is an tolc.*
The Lord between us and all harm.
Anonymous: traditional saying

7 *Do bhata féin is each do chomharsan.*
Your own stick and your neighbour's horse.
meaning, 'rights without responsibility'
Anonymous: traditional saying

8 *Fiche bliain id' leinbh;*
Fiche bliain ar mire;
Fiche bliain id' dhuine
Agus ina dhiaidh sin tairiscint do úrnaí.

Twenty years an infant; twenty years speeding; twenty
years a person; and after turn to praying.
Anonymous: traditional saying

9 *Filleann an feall ar an bhfeallaire.*
The ill deed rebounds on the evildoer.
Anonymous: traditional saying

10 *Is buaine port ná glór na n-éan*
    Is buaine focal ná toice an tsaoil.

A tune is more lasting than the song of the birds, and a
word more lasting than the wealth of the world.
Anonymous: traditional saying

11 *Is deise cabhair Dé ná an doras.*
God's help is nearer than the door.
Anonymous: traditional saying

12 *Is maith an tanlann an tocras.*
Hunger is the best sauce.
Anonymous: traditional saying

13 *Is treise dúchas ná oiliúint.*
Nature is stronger than learning.
Anonymous: traditional saying

14 *Marbh le té is marbh gan é.*
Dead from tea and dead without it.
Anonymous: traditional saying

15 *Níl aon tinteán mar do thinteán féin.*
There's no hearth like your own.
i.e., there's no place like home
Anonymous: traditional saying

16 *Níl meas ar an uisce go triomaítear an tobar.*
There's no regard for water until the well runs dry.
Anonymous: traditional saying

17 *Ní mar a síltear a bítear.*
Things don't turn out as they're expected.
Anonymous: traditional saying

18 *Pós bean sléibhe is pósfaidh tú an sliabh.*
Marry a woman from the mountain, and you marry the
mountain.
Anonymous: traditional saying

19 That beats Banagher, and Banagher beats the Devil.
Anonymous: traditional saying

20 You can take the boy out of the country, but you can't take the country out of the boy.
Anonymous: traditional saying

Publishing

1 In a profession where simple accountancy is preferable to a degree in English, illiteracy is not considered to be a great drawback.
Dominic Behan 1928– : *The Public World of Parable Jones* (1989)

2 As repressed sadists are supposed to become policemen or butchers, so those with an irrational fear of life become publishers.
Cyril Connolly 1903–74: *Enemies of Promise* (1938)

3 All her life to labour and labour for Faber and Faber.
Seamus Heaney 1939– : attributed; in *Sunday Telegraph* 24 September 1995

4 Publishers and printers alike seemed to agree among themselves, no matter how divergent their points of view were in other matters, not to publish anything of mine as I wrote it.
James Joyce 1882–1941: letter, 2 April 1932

5 For you know, dear—I may, without vanity, hint—
Though an angel should write, still 'tis *devils* must print.
Thomas Moore 1779–1852: *The Fudges in England* (1835)

6 EDMUND BURKE: You must remember that booksellers deal in commodities they are not supposed to understand.
ARTHUR MURPHY: True, some of 'em do deal in morality.
Arthur Murphy 1727–1805: in *Thraliana* (1942, ed. K. C. Balderston)

7 You shall see them on a beautiful quarto page where a neat
rivulet of text shall meander through a meadow of margin.
Richard Brinsley Sheridan 1751–1816: *The School for Scandal* (1777)

8 I suppose publishers are untrustworthy. They certainly
always look it.
Oscar Wilde 1854–1900: letter, February 1898

Rebellion

1 On the Curragh of Kildare,
The boys they will be there,
With their pikes in good repair,
Says the sean-bhean bhocht.
Anonymous: 'The Sean-Bhean Bhocht' (traditional song, *c.*1798)

2 Kings will be tyrants from policy when subjects are rebels
from principle.
Edmund Burke 1729–97: *Reflections on the Revolution in France* (1790)

3 Where all your rights become only an accumulated wrong;
where men must beg with bated breath for leave to subsist
in their own land, to think their own thoughts, to sing
their own songs, to garner the fruits of their own
labours . . . then surely it is a braver, a saner and truer
thing, to be a rebel in act and deed against such
circumstances as these than tamely to accept it as the
natural lot of men.
Roger Casement 1864–1916: statement from prison, 29 June 1916

4 I am still an Irish rebel to the backbone and the spinal
marrow, a rebel for the same reason that John Hampden
and Algernon Sidney, George Washington and Charles

Carrol of Carroltown, were rebels—because tyranny had
supplanted the law.
arriving in Australia in 1856
Charles Gavan Duffy 1816–1903: Cyril Pearl *The Three Lives of Gavan Duffy*
(1979)

5 The Sinns won in three years what we did not win in forty.
You cannot make revolutions with rosewater, or omelettes
without breaking eggs.
Timothy Michael Healy 1855–1931: letter to his brother; Frank Callanan *T.
M. Healy* (1996)

6 The organization of the north being thus deranged, the
colonels flinched and the chief of the Antrim men Robert
Simms not appearing, the duty fell on Henry J. McCracken.
Jemmy Hope ?1765–1846: attributed

7 He would make a rebel out of me if I weren't one already.
of John Mitchel (1815–75)
Douglas Hyde 1860–1949: diary, 1881

8 They rose in dark and evil days.
John Kells Ingram 1823–1907: 'The Memory of the Dead'

9 Somewhere and somehow and by someone, a beginning
must be made, and the first act of armed resistance is
always premature, imprudent and foolish.
James Finton Lalor 1807–49: Diana Norman *Terrible Beauty* (1987)

10 I wish it then to be clearly understood that under present
conditions I am definitely opposed to any proposal that may
come forward involving insurrection.
Eoin MacNeill 1867–1945: memorandum to Irish Volunteers, February 1916

11 An insurrection, indeed, has been too long deferred; yet, in
the present condition of the island, no rising must *begin* in
the country. Dublin streets for that.
John Mitchel 1815–75: *Jail Journal* (1854)

12 The first great act of intellectual resistance to the first great
experiment in totalitarian innovation.
of Burke's writings on the French Revolution
Conor Cruise O'Brien 1917– : *The Great Melody* (1992)

13 Revolutions have never lightened the burden of tyranny:
they have only shifted it to another shoulder.
George Bernard Shaw 1856–1950: *Man and Superman* (1903) 'The
Revolutionist's Handbook' foreword

Religion

1 Christ with me, Christ before me, Christ behind me,
Christ in me, Christ under me, Christ over me,
Christ to the right of me, Christ to the left of me.
Anonymous: 'St Patrick's Breastplate' (from 8th century Old Irish)

2 Jew, Turk or atheist
May enter here but not a Papist.
written on the walls of Bandon town
Anonymous: 17th century rhyme

3 Whoever wrote this wrote it well
For the same is written on the gates of Hell.
written on the walls of Bandon town
Anonymous: riposte to preceding verse

4 After all her teaching, this is what they thought. They
thought the point of this beautiful prayer to Our Lady was
never to let yourself say one more Hail Mary than was
necessary.
. . . Perhaps the Mother of God would be touched and
pleased by the innocence of children. Mother Francis
would, at this particular lunch time, have liked to take
them out individually and murder them one by one.
Maeve Binchy 1940– : *Circle of Friends* (1990)

5 Man is by his constitution a religious animal; atheism is against not only our reason, but our instincts.
Edmund Burke 1729–97: *Reflections on the Revolution in France* (1790)

6 Old religious factions are volcanoes burnt out.
Edmund Burke 1729–97: speech on the petition of the Unitarians, 11 May 1792

7 In his thirties, he started to read a notorious French writer called Voltaire, who was on the Catholic index of forbidden authors, and soon after he hung a placard on the wall of his living room, with the slogan CRUSH THE INFAMOUS ONE painted in red on a black background; he said that was his and Voltaire's Declaration of Faith. Then he went blind, became ill and caved in by being restored to the bosom of the Church before he died.
Seamus Deane 1940– : *Reading in the Dark* (1996)

8 I said one Hail Mary and four Our Fathers, because I preferred the Our Fathers to the Hail Mary and it was longer and better.
Roddy Doyle 1958– : *Paddy Clarke Ha Ha Ha* (1993)

9 Spread not the beds of Brugh for me
When restless death-bed's use is done;
But bury me at Rosnaree,
And face me to the rising sun.

For all the Kings who lie in Brugh
Put trust in gods of wood and stone;
And 'twas at Ross that first I knew
One, Unseen, who is God alone . . .
according to legend, the 3rd century king Cormac mac Airt refused to be buried with his ancestors in Newgrange by Druid rites
Samuel Ferguson 1810–86: 'The Burial of King Cormac'

10 Lady Conyngham is giving them all lunch at Slane for a visit to Newgrange, which is described as a pre-Christian cemetery, but this would be misleading except to us who

know that the suggestion of subsequent Christianity is
unfounded.
Oliver St John Gogarty 1878–1957: letter to Lady Leslie about the guests
for the Taillteann Games, 1924; Ulick O'Connor *Oliver St John Gogarty*
(1964)

11 I fear their creed as we have always feared
    The lifted hand between the mind and truth.
    John Hewitt 1907–87: 'The Glens' (1948)

12 Strictly speaking she isn't a Protestant. She comes from a
    family of Non-Subscribing Presbyterians, otherwise known
    as Dissenters, Arians, Unitarians, or New Light Thinkers.
    Liz McManus 1947– : 'Dwelling Below the Skies' (1997)

13 Ireland remains a deeply religious country, with the two
    main denominations being 'us' and 'them'.
    Frank McNally: in *Irish Times* 11 March 1998

14 I was the rector's son, born to the anglican order,
    Banned for ever from the candles of the Irish poor;
    The Chichesters knelt in marble at the end of a transept
    With ruffs about their necks, their portion sure.
    Louis MacNeice 1907–63: 'Carrickfergus' (1937)

15 The Catholics have a church without a religion, and the
    Dissenters a religion without a church.
    view of the Protestant Archbishop of Dublin
    William Magee 1766–1831: sermon in St Patrick's Cathedral, Dublin, 24
    October 1822

16 You are not an agnostic . . . You are just a fat slob who is
    too lazy to go to Mass.
    Conor Cruise O'Brien 1917– : attributed

17 There's no reason to bring religion into it. I think we ought
    to have as great a regard for religion as we can, so as to
    keep it out of as many things as possible.
    Sean O'Casey 1880–1964: *The Plough and the Stars* (1926)

18 Fight the real enemy!
Sinéad O'Connor 1966– : tearing up a picture of the Pope on US television in 1992

19 If you treat Roman Catholics with due consideration and kindness, they will live like Protestants, in spite of the authoritative nature of their Church.
Terence O'Neill 1914–90: speech, 1969

20 The Roman Catholic Church is getting nearer to Communism every day.
Ian Paisley 1926– : in *Irish Times* 13 September 1969

21 In Ireland, the people is the Church, and the Church is the people.
George Bernard Shaw 1856–1950: attributed

22 His followers threw a Rosary and a Bible at me, which I felt was at least an ecumenical gesture, and there was a near riot.
of Ian Paisley
Lord Soper 1903– : speech in the House of Lords, 3 December 1968

23 I conceive some scattered notions about a superior power to be of singular use for the common people, as furnishing excellent materials to keep children quiet when they grow peevish, and providing topics of amusement in a tedious winter-night.
Jonathan Swift 1667–1745: *An Argument Against Abolishing Christianity* (1708)

24 He put this engine [a watch] to our ears, which made an incessant noise like that of a water-mill; and we conjecture it is either some unknown animal, or the god that he worships; but we are more inclined to the latter opinion.
Jonathan Swift 1667–1745: *Gulliver's Travels* (1726) 'A Voyage to Lilliput'

25 We have just enough religion to make us hate, but not enough to make us love one another.
Jonathan Swift 1667–1745: *Thoughts on Various Subjects* (1711)

26 But for their religion . . . Irishmen would probably have
forgotten political separation as the Scots have forgotten
Jacobitism.
Arland Ussher 1899–1980: *The Face and Mind of Ireland* (1949)

Revenge

1 *Your Distresses*: . . . How are your wants remedied and your
distress removed by these associations? Is it by the breaking
of canals, by destroying cattle, by the burning of houses,
corn and hay, and establishing a reign of terror throughout
the entire country, that you are to obtain employment?
James Warren Doyle 1786–1834: 'Pastoral Address to the Deluded and
Illegal Association of Ribbonmen' (1822)

2 Who would connive
in civilised outrage
yet understand the exact
and tribal, intimate revenge.
Seamus Heaney 1939– : 'Punishment' (1975)

3 My policy is not a policy of conciliation, but a policy of
retaliation.
*in 1877, on his parliamentary tactics in the House of Commons
as leader of the Irish party*
Charles Stewart Parnell 1846–91: in *Dictionary of National Biography*
(1917–)

4 If I got your hand, it is I would take it
But not to shake it, O Denis Browne,
But to hang you high with a hempen cable
And your feet unable to find the ground.
Antoine Raiftearaí 1779–1835: 'Na Buachaillí Bána' ('The Whiteboys',
*c.*1800)

Rhetoric

1 *Bérla na bhfileadh.*
The language of the poets.
Anonymous: in early Irish literature, a term applied to rhetorical passages in texts.

2 As I was saying to you before I was interrupted . . .
speaking at Ennis, where he had been arrested during a speech seven years before
Eamon de Valera 1882–1975: speech, 1924

3 An' as it blowed an' blowed, I often looked up at the sky
an' asked meself the question—what is the stars, what is the stars?
Oh a darlin' question! A darlin' question!
Sean O'Casey 1880–1964: *Juno and the Paycock* (1925)

Royalty

1 The *rath* in front of the oak wood
belonged to Bruidge, and Cathal,
belonged to Aedh, and Ailill,
belonged to Conaing, and Cuilíne
and to Mael Dúin before them
—all kings in their turn.
The *rath* survives; the kings
are covered in clay.
Anonymous: 6th century Irish poem; Thomas Kinsella (ed.) *The New Oxford Book of Irish Verse* (1986)

2 I feel like the Queen.
on his own annus horribilis *of 1996*
John Bruton 1947– : attributed

3 I thought ten thousand swords must have leapt from their
scabbards to avenge even a look that threatened her with
insult.
of Marie Antoinette
Edmund Burke 1729–97: *Reflections on the Revolution in France* (1790)

4 I signed it the same way as I signed an autograph for a
newspaper.
*on taking the oath of allegiance to the King before entering Dáil
Éireann*
Eamon de Valera 1882–1975: in 1932, attributed

5 We hear from good authority that the King was much
pleased with Castle Rackrent—he rubbed his hands and
said what—what—I know something now of my Irish
subjects.
Richard Lovell Edgeworth 1744–1817: letter to D. A. Beaufort, 26 April
1800

6 She conquers at once by her charms;
And the smile in her eye is sufficient alone
To subdue their warm hearts and make Ireland her own.
Rowland Eyles Egerton-Warburton 1804–91: 'On the Visit of the Empress
of Austria to Kildare' (February, 1879)

7 The Famine Queen.
of Queen Victoria
Maud Gonne 1867–1953: in *L'Irlande Libre* 1900

8 How could I ever meet Paddy Pearse or Jim Connolly in the
hereafter if I took an oath to a British king?
*in 1926, on her refusal to take the oath which would allow her
to enter the Dáil*
Constance Markievicz 1868–1927: Diana Norman *Terrible Beauty* (1987)

9 It used to occur to me when I lived in London . . . that it
can't be easy being a queen. The poor old dear has had one
annus horribilis after another. The kids are splitting up, the
palace is falling down, the mother is on the gin. It is all like
a particularly atrocious episode of *Eastenders*.
Joseph O'Connor 1963– : *The Secret World of the Irish Male* (1995)

Royalty

10 She has become a parrot.
    *expressing the view that the Queen simply repeats the words of
    her Prime Minister*
    Ian Paisley 1926– : in *Daily Telegraph* 27 May 1998

11 As low as we now are, change kings with us, and we will
    fight it over again with you.
    *to English officers during negotiations for the Treaty of
    Limerick, 1690*
    Patrick Sarsfield c.1655–93: in *Dictionary of National Biography* (1917–)

12 Your majesty seems to have won the race.
    *after the Battle of the Boyne, James II complained to Lady
    Tyrconnell that her countrymen had run away*
    Lady Tyrconnell d. 1731: Elizabeth Longford (ed.) *The Oxford Book of Royal
    Anecdotes* (1989)

Sacrifice

1 I want no mercy—I'll have no mercy. I'll die as many
   thousands have died, for the sake of their beloved land and
   in defence of it. I will die proudly and triumphantly in
   defence of republican principles and the liberty of an
   oppressed and enslaved people.
   *speech from the dock during the trial of the Manchester
   Martyrs, 1867*
   William O'Meara Allen d. 1867: Robert Kee *The Bold Fenian Men* (1989)

2 With those who died for this country, on the gallows, in
   battle, or by the bullets of execution squads, must be
   counted those who died of broken hearts—O'Connell,
   Parnell, Redmond.
   Elizabeth Bowen 1899–1973: *The Shelbourne* (1951)

3 I am not for a mere game of bluff, and, unless men are
prepared to make great sacrifices which they clearly
understand, the talk of resistance is no use.
Edward Carson 1854–1935: letter to James Craig, 1911

4 The last thing we need in Ireland is to reinforce the cult of
the blood sacrifice, which was poeticised by Pearse in such
a way that, frankly, makes your flesh crawl.
Proinsias de Rossa: in 1991, attributed

5 Further sacrifice of life would now be in vain ... Military
victory must be allowed to rest for the moment with those
who have destroyed the Republic.
Eamon de Valera 1882–1975: message to the Republican armed forces,
24 May 1923

6 There's a very thin line between dying for Ireland and
killing for Ireland.
John Hume 1937– : in 1994, attributed

7 Our fathers died that we might be free men. Are we going
to allow their sacrifices to be as naught? Or are we going to
follow in their footsteps at the Rising of the Moon?
James Larkin 1876–1947: in *Irish Worker* July 1914

8 She's the sort of woman who lives for others—you can
always tell the others by their hunted expression.
C. S. Lewis 1898–1963: *The Screwtape Letters* (1942)

9 Cathleen-Anorexia encourages women to join a male
death-cult which has a peculiarly masochistic martyrology.
Edna Longley 1940– : 'From Cathleen to Anorexia' (1989)

10 The master says it's a glorious thing to die for the Faith and
Dad says it's a glorious thing to die for Ireland and I
wonder if there's anyone in the world who would like us to
live.
Frank McCourt 1930– : *Angela's Ashes* (1996)

11 O my God, I offer my pain for Ireland. She is on the rack.
Terence MacSwiney 1879–1920: letter from Brixton Prison, 5 October 1920

12 'I am just going outside and may be some time.'
   The others nod, pretending not to know.
   At the heart of the ridiculous, the sublime.
   Derek Mahon 1941– : 'Antarctica' (1985)

13 There are things a man must not do to save a nation.
   John O'Leary 1830–1907: Nicholas Mansergh *The Irish Question* (ed. 3, 1975)

14 Bloodshed is a cleansing and sanctifying thing, and the nation which regards it as the final horror has lost its manhood.
   Patrick Pearse 1879–1916: speech, 1913

15 'God save Ireland!' said the heroes;
   'God save Ireland', say they all:
   Whether on the scaffold high
   Or the battlefield we die,
   Oh, what matter when for Erin dear we fall.
   Timothy Daniel Sullivan 1827–1914: 'God Save Ireland' (1867); cf. **Last Words 1**

16 For this Edward Fitzgerald died,
   And Robert Emmet and Wolfe Tone.
   W. B. Yeats 1865–1939: 'September, 1913' (1914)

Sayings see Political Sayings and Slogans, Proverbs and Sayings

Science

1 Men will not be content to manufacture life: they will want to improve on it.
   J. D. Bernal 1901–71: *The World, the Flesh and the Devil* (1929)

2 Science becomes dangerous only when it imagines that it has reached its goal.
   George Bernard Shaw 1856–1950: preface to *The Doctor's Dilemma* (1911)

3 He had been eight years upon a project for extracting sun-beams out of cucumbers, which were to be put into vials hermetically sealed, and let out to warm the air in raw inclement summers.
Jonathan Swift 1667–1745: *Gulliver's Travels* (1726)

The Sea

1 Tis all about the history of a bold young Irish tar,
Who sailed as man before the mast on board of the *Calabar*.
Anonymous: 'The Cruise of the *Calabar*', 19th century song

2 The wind is fierce tonight
It tosses the sea's white hair
I fear no wild Vikings
Sailing the quiet main.
Anonymous: 9th century scribal manuscript annotation; R. F. Foster *The Oxford Illustrated History of Ireland* (1989)

3 The long arms of the harbour like an entreaty in the blue sea.
of Dun Laoghaire
Samuel Beckett 1906–89: *More Pricks than Kicks* (1934)

4 How happy is the sailor's life,
From coast to coast to roam;
In every port he finds a wife,
In every port a home.
Isaac Bickerstaffe 1733–*c*.1808: 'Thomas and Sally'

5 The little waves of Breffny go stumbling through my soul.
Eva Gore-Booth 1870–1926: 'The Waves of Breffny' (1920)

6 The snotgreen sea. The scrotumtightening sea.
James Joyce 1882–1941: *Ulysses* (1922)

7 'A man who is not afraid of the sea will soon be drownded,' he said 'for he will be going out on a day he shouldn't. But we do be afraid of the sea, and we do only be drownded now and again.'
John Millington Synge 1871–1909: *The Aran Islands* (1907)

8 They're all gone now, and there isn't any more the sea can do to me . . . I'll have no call now to be going down and getting Holy Water in the dark nights after Samhain, and I won't care what way the sea is when the other women will be keening.
John Millington Synge 1871–1909: *Riders to the Sea* (1905)

9 That dolphin-torn, that gong-tormented sea.
W. B. Yeats 1865–1939: 'Byzantium' (1933)

The Seasons

1 Advent. What was there to say about it except that it went on for ever and was nearly as bad as Lent?
Maeve Binchy 1940– : *The Glass Lake* (1994)

2 It is about five o'clock in an evening that the first hour of spring strikes—autumn arrives in the early morning, but spring at the close of a winter day.
Elizabeth Bowen 1899–1973: *The Death of the Heart* (1938)

3 There is something about winter
which pares things down to their essentials
a bare tree
a black hedge
hold their own stark throne in our hearts.
Moya Cannon 1956– : 'Winter Paths' (1997)

4 A hot, hot summer was melting into a parched and sticky fall, like a runny ice cream going down the sleeve of a jumper.
Katy Hayes: *Curtains* (1997)

5 August is a wicked month.
Edna O'Brien 1932– : title of novel (1965)

6 I hope it will be winter when I die
For no one from the North could die in spring.
Helen Waddell 1889–1965: 'I Shall Not Go To Heaven'

Secrecy and Openness

1 She was miserly about her information. She could keep a
secret very well. Secrets never escaped from her hoard.
Katy Hayes: *Curtains* (1997)

2 Why . . . are you accusing me of accusing you of
misleading the House when what I accused you of was
concealing information?
to the Tanaiste, Mary Harney
Pat Rabbitte: in *Irish Times* 28 February 1998 'This week they said'

3 There are no secrets better kept than the secret everybody
guesses.
George Bernard Shaw 1856–1950: *Mrs Warren's Profession* (1898)

4 'I don't pretend to be a judge of horses . . . but I like this
one awfully.'
    As even Philippa said afterwards, she would not have
given herself away like that over buying a reel of cotton.
Edith Œ. Somerville 1858–1949 and **Martin Ross** 1862–1915: *Some
Experiences of an Irish R.M.* (1899)

5 If there's anyone in the parliamentary party who has
anything to say to me, let them put their cards on the table.
The one thing I do not like is this talking into their hands
behind my back.
Dick Spring 1950– : in *Irish Times* 1 November 1997 'Quotes of the Week'

1798

1 He saw the '98, and damned alike
   The yeoman's pitch-cap and the rebel's pike.
   William Allingham 1824–89: *Laurence Bloomfield in Ireland* (1864)

2 Remember '98 says the gay old hag,
   When our Boys you did defeat, says the gay old hag,
   Then our Boys you did defeat, but we'll beat you out
      compleat,
   Now you're nearly out of date, says the fine old hag.
   Anonymous: 'The Gay Old Hag' (traditional ballad)

3 A wet winter, a dry spring,
   A bloody summer, and no king.
   Anonymous: prophecy for 1798

4 Until, on Vinegar Hill, the fatal conclave.
   Terraced thousands died, shaking scythes at cannon.
   Seamus Heaney 1939– : 'Requiem for the Croppies' (1969)

5 Who fears to speak of Ninety-Eight?
   Who blushes at the name?
   John Kells Ingram 1823–1907: 'The Memory of the Dead'

6 And if for want of leaders we lost at Vinegar Hill,
   We're ready for another fight and love our country still.
   We are the Boys of Wexford who fought with heart and
      hand
   To burst in twain the galling chain, and free our native
      land.
   Robert Dwyer Joyce 1830–83: 'The Boys of Wexford' (*Ballads of Irish Chivalry*, 1908)

7 At the siege of Ross did my father fall,
   And at Gorey my loving brothers all.
   I alone am left of my name and race;
   I will go to Wexford and take their place . . .
   At Geneva barrack that young man died,
   And at Passage they have his body laid.

> Good people who live in peace and joy,
> Breathe a prayer and a tear for the Croppy boy.
> **William McBurney:** 'The Croppy Boy', a ballad of '98

8   Let us prove by our lives and our actions that the fight of
    the men of '98 is not over yet.
    William O'Brien 1852–1928: speech in Sligo, 1898

9   In this anniversary year of 1798 it is ironic that we are
    being asked by the Government to dilute yet again the
    degree of sovereignty that we have in the 26 counties.
    on the Amsterdam Treaty
    Caoimhghín Ó Caoláin: in *Irish Times* 7 March 1998 'This Week They Said'

10 He speaks of '98! Their struggle was of blood and defeated
    in blood. The means they adopted weakened Ireland and
    enabled England to carry the Union.
    *in a debate with the Young Irelander, John Mitchel, 13 July
    1846*
    Daniel O'Connell 1775–1847: Charles Chevenix Trench *The Great Dan*
    (1984)

Sex

1   There was never sex in Ireland before television.
    Oliver J. Flanagan 1920–87: *c*.1965, attributed

2   Sex was a competitive event in those days and the only
    thing you could take as a certainty was that everyone else
    was lying, just as you were.
    Bob Geldof 1954– : *Is That It?* (1986)

3   Only the Lion and the Cock;
    As Galen says, withstand Love's shock.
    So, dearest, do not think me rude
    If I yield now to lassitude,
    But sympathize with me. I know
    You would not have me roar or crow.
    Oliver St John Gogarty 1878–1957: 'After Galen' (1957)

4 He kissed me under the Moorish wall and I thought well as well him as another and then I asked him with my eyes to ask again yes and then he asked me would I yes to say yes my mountain flower and first I put my arms around him yes and drew him down to me so he could feel my breasts all perfume yes and his heart was going like mad and yes I said yes I will Yes.
James Joyce 1882–1941: *Ulysses* (1922)

5 Of all the stages in a woman's life, none is so dangerous as the period between her acknowledgment of a passion for a man, and the day set apart for her nuptials.
Hugh Kelly 1739–77: *Memoirs of a Magdalen* (1767, ed. 1782)

6 The people before us didn't rat on their children for the sake of Protestant schooling, land or soup; surely we won't for the sake of easy sex.
Cornelius Lucey 1902–82: in *Irish Times* 1 May 1971 'This Week They Said'

7 Honesty and mate-jettisoning horrified Grainne. Yet she felt prepared to believe the part of the message which said that good sex made you a healthier and better-balanced person.
Julia O'Faolain 1932– : *No Country for Young Men* (1980)

8 When, panting beside her, he recovered enough breath to speak he expressed his surprise that one so cool, so ladylike in public could be so different in private. She grunted peacefully, and said in her muted brogue, 'Ah, shure, dürling, everything changes in the beddaroom.'
Sean O'Faolain 1900–91: 'The Faithless Wife'

9 When the parish priest rebuked him for his celibacy, saying it would lead him into debauchery and sin, he said that a man who had to be muzzled by a wife as a protection against debauchery was not worthy of the joy of innocence. After that people began to treat him with priestly respect.
Liam O'Flaherty 1897–1984: 'The Mermaid'

10 'Pray, my dear,' quoth my mother, 'have you not forgot to
wind up the clock?'—'Good G—!' cried my father, making
an exclamation, but taking care to moderate his voice at
the same time,—'Did ever woman, since the creation of the
world, interrupt a man with such a silly question?'
Laurence Sterne 1713–68: *Tristram Shandy* (1759–67)

Sickness see Health and Sickness

Silence

1 A silent mouth is melodious.
Anonymous: traditional saying

2 I shall state silence more competently than ever a better
man spangled the butterflies of vertigo.
Samuel Beckett 1906–89: *A Dream of Fair to Middling Women* (written
1932)

3 Still-born Silence! thou that art
Floodgate of the deeper heart.
Richard Flecknoe d. *c.*1678: 'Invocation of Silence' (1653)

The Skies

1 Our windy, untidy loft
where old people had flung up old junk
they'd thought might come in handy
ploughs, ladles, bears, lions, a clatter of heroes.
Moya Cannon 1956– : 'The Stars' (1997)

2 My memories are full of enormous skies, as bright as water,
in which clouds sailed bigger than any others; fleets of
monsters moving in one vast school up from the horizon

and over my head, a million miles up, as it seemed to me,
and then down again to the far-off mountains of Derry.
Joyce Cary 1888–1957: *A House of Children* (1941)

3 You'll see O'Ryan any night
  Amid the constellations.
  Charles Halpine 1829–68: 'Constellation of O'Ryan'

4 The heaventree of stars hung with humid nightblue fruit.
  James Joyce 1882–1941: *Ulysses* (1922)

5 AD 1767—in the beginning of the month of May . . . an
  awfully dark night came down on Chapelizod and all the
  country round.
    I believe there was no moon, and the stars had been
  quite put out under the 'wet blanket of the night', which
  impenetrable muffler overspread the sky with a funereal
  darkness.
  J. Sheridan Le Fanu 1814–73: *The House by the Churchyard* (1863)

6 The western hills and the clouds which are their legitimate
  accompaniment are inseparable; the eye is carried upward
  from the hill-tops for thousands of feet into the infinite blue.
  The cloudland is indeed so wonderful a creation that
  Ireland would be a dull place without it: here it is almost
  always with us, as vital to our enjoyment as is the
  landscape itself.
  Robert Lloyd Praeger 1865–1953: *The Way That I Went* (1937)

7 . . . that little tent of blue
  Which prisoners call the sky.
  Oscar Wilde 1854–1900: *The Ballad of Reading Gaol* (1898)

Smoking

1 No more th'unwary youth whom beauty fires,
  Through naseous tube polluted air respires,
  Whose putrid smack his humid lips retain

And makes each maid his loathsome kiss refrain.
James Arbuckle 1700–42: 'Snuff' (1719)

2 She forgot to smoke her cigarette and it burned away in the ash-tray, leaving a long round stick of ash. A cigarette cremated, rather than smoked.
Katy Hayes: *Curtains* (1997)

3 Sucking on a burning scrag of rotting leaf is not the best way to stay young.
Joseph O'Connor 1963– : *The Secret World of the Irish Male* (1994)

4 You'd get a person who'd refuse tobacco, but there's nobody alive would turn the back of his hand to a cup of tea.
Peig Sayers 1873–1958: *An Old Woman's Reflections* (translated by Séamus Ennis, 1962)

5 A cigarette is the perfect type of a perfect pleasure. It is exquisite, and it leaves one unsatisfied. What more can one want?
Oscar Wilde 1854–1900: *The Picture of Dorian Gray* (1891)

Socialism

1 Then raise the scarlet standard high!
Within its shade we'll live or die.
Tho' cowards flinch and traitors sneer,
We'll keep the red flag flying here.
James M. Connell 1852–1929: 'The Red Flag' (1889)

2 The worker is the slave of capitalist society, the female worker is the slave of that slave.
James Connolly 1868–1916: *The Re-conquest of Ireland* (1915)

3 We're fighting for the working class. Call us what you like.
of herself and other Irish socialists
Constance Markievicz 1868–1927: Diana Norman *Terrible Beauty* (1987)

4 'Socialism,' he said, 'is worse than Communism . . .
Socialists are a Protestant variety of Communists.'
view of a putative priest in Dingle
Conor Cruise O'Brien 1917– : 1970s

5 To make men Socialists is nothing, but to make Socialism
human is a great thing.
Oscar Wilde 1854–1900: in *Pall Mall Gazette* 15 February 1889

Solitude

1 She did not object to frequent the haunts of pleasure but
she was as much alone there as in the depths of solitude.
She walked about in a sad reverie, apparently unconscious
of the world about her.
of Sarah Curran in later life
Washington Irving 1783–1859: attributed

2 Are you ever sitting at home and feeling good about
yourself but you're actually feeling that lonely that you
check to see that the telephone's working?
Sean Hughes 1966– : in *Independent* 10 January 1998

3 I hate what every poet hates in spite
Of all the solemn talk of contemplation.
Oh, Alexander Selkirk knew the plight
Of being king and government and nation.
A road, a mile of kingdom, I am king
Of banks and stones and every blooming thing.
Patrick Kavanagh 1904–67: 'Inniskeen Road: July Evening' (1936)

4 'Tis the last rose of summer
Left blooming alone;
All her lovely companions

Are faded and gone.
Thomas Moore 1779–1852: *Irish Melodies* (1807) "'Tis the last rose of summer'

5 So goes the lone of soul amid the world—
   No love upon his breast, with singing, cheers;
   But Sorrow builds her home within his heart,
   And, nesting there, will rear her brood of tears.
   Dora Sigerson 1866–1918: 'The Lone of Soul'

6 I will arise and go now, and go to Innisfree,
   And a small cabin build there, of clay and wattles made;
   Nine bean rows will I have there, a hive for the honey bee,
   And live alone in the bee-loud glade.
   W. B. Yeats 1865–1939: 'The Lake Isle of Innisfree' (1893)

Song

1 The English words and the air are like a quarrelling man
   and wife; *the Irish melts into the tune*, but the English
   doesn't.
   *an Irishwoman who had been asked to sing the English version
   of an Irish song*
   Anonymous: William Carleton introduction to *Traits and Stories of the Irish peasantry* (1830)

2 Meanwhile I'll sing that famous old song, 'The Hound that
   Caught the Pubic Hare'.
   Brendan Behan 1923–64: *Hostage* (1958)

3 The great national monuments of Ireland are dead
   heroes—preferably those who died young, unfulfilled and
   beautiful, leaving legend and inspiration behind, but rarely
   tangible improvements in the lot of those they inspired; and
   if such a hero left a young girl bereft, *intacta* and keening
   behind him, so much the better for a sad song.
   Polly Devlin 1944– : *All of Us There* (1983)

4 They'd been in the folk mass choir when they were in school but that, they knew now, hadn't really been singing. Jimmy said that real music was sex . . . They were starting to agree with him. And there wasn't much sex in Morning Has Broken or The Lord Is My Shepherd.
Roddy Doyle 1958- : *The Commitments* (1987)

5 Remember the old song about the meeting by the river, with pikes on your shoulders by the rising of the moon. I would ask you to meet me at the old spot in O'Connell street and you men come on.
giving notice of a banned meeting
James Larkin 1876-1947: speech, August 1913

6 As it rises, and fades—and swells and falls, it is like a sweet wind sighing across Ireland.
hearing a woman singing 'Slievenamon' in Irish on the radio
Sean O'Faolain 1900-91: *An Irish Journey* (1940)

7 When Satan makes impure verses, Allah sends a divine tune to cleanse them.
George Bernard Shaw 1856-1950: *The Adventures of the Black Girl in her Search for God* (1932)

8 It was absolutely deadly . . . a sort of lyrical geography— the map of Ireland set to music! Bantry Bay, Killarney, the Mountains of Somewhere, the Waters of Somewhere else, all Irish, of course! I get so sick of Ireland and her endearing young charms—and all the entreaties to Erin to remember! As if she ever forgot!
of a concert
Edith Œ. Somerville 1858-1949 and **Martin Ross** 1862-1915: *Mount Music* (1919)

9 I sang a king out of three kingdoms.
said to have been Wharton's boast after 'A New Song' ('Lilliburlero') became a propaganda weapon against James II
Thomas Wharton 1648-1715: in *Dictionary of National Biography* (1917-)

10 I love it for all its magnificent foolishness, its grand illusion
that it brings together the diverse peoples and cultures of
Europe on one great wing of song, when all it makes
manifest is how far apart everybody is.
of the Eurovision Song Contest
Terry Wogan 1938- : in *Irish Times* 9 May 1998 'This Week They Said'

Sorrow

1 The doctor came and gave her pills and medicines. She'd
take them and become calmer, but her grief just collected
under the drugs like a thrombosis.
Seamus Deane 1940- : *Reading in the Dark* (1996)

2 No one ever told me that grief felt so like fear.
C. S. Lewis 1898-1963: *A Grief Observed* (1961)

3 I . . . broke into a raging passion of tears—tears bitter and
salt—tears of wrath, pity, regret, remorse—but not of base
lamentation for my own fate.
John Mitchel 1815-75: *Jail Journal* (1854)

4 The first sense of sorrow I ever knew was upon the death of
my father, at which time I was not quite five years of age;
but was rather amazed at what all the house meant, than
possessed with a real understanding why nobody was
willing to play with me.
Richard Steele 1672-1729: 'On Recollections of Childhood' in *Tatler* no.
181

5 I have put away sorrow like a shoe that is worn out and
muddy, for it is I have had a life that will be envied by great
companies.
John Millington Synge 1871-1909: *Deirdre of the Sorrows* (1909)

Speech and Language

1 Lady Dashfort imitated the Irish brogue in perfection;
  boasted that 'she was mistress of fourteen different brogues,
  and had brogues for all occasions'.
  Maria Edgeworth 1767–1849: *The Absentee* (1812)

2 It can happen that a civilization can be imprisoned in a
  linguistic contour which no longer matches the landscape
  of . . . fact.
  Brian Friel 1929– : *Translations* (1980)

3 The true use of speech is not so much to express our wants
  as to conceal them.
  Oliver Goldsmith 1728–74: in *The Bee* 20 October 1759 'On the Use of
  Language'

4 They spoke in the same Tipperary way, the long sonorous
  Rs, the slow but explosive delivery of some Tipperary-style
  quip.
  Anne Haverty: *One Day as a Tiger* (1997)

5   HERE IS THE NEWS,
  Said the absolute speaker. Between him and us
  A great gulf was fixed where pronunciation
  Reigned tyrannically.
  Seamus Heaney 1939– : 'A Sofa in the Forties' (1996)

6 When we look into the beautiful speech that Lady Gregory
  learnt as she moved among her people, we find that it
  consists of no more than a dozen turns of speech, dropped
  into pages of English so ordinary, that redeemed from these
  phrases it might appear in any newspaper without
  attracting attention.
  George Moore 1852–1933: *Hail and Farewell* (1911–14)

7 A false-brogue, as every Irishman knows, is a sure sign that the speaker is about to say something so true that he wants to blunt the edge of it by presenting it as a kind of family joke.
Sean O'Faolain 1900–91: *The Heat of the Sun* (1966)

Speechmaking

1 *Cúpla focal.*
A couple of words.
Anonymous: traditional phrase for a prepared speech

2 Everybody heard Dan. For Dan raised his hand and told all about the platform to repeat his words. He said 'Silence', and silence came to us as the wind upon barley. Then each man spoke after Dan, and every other man said the words, and out to us all on the edge of the crowd came the speech of Dan O'Connell.
account of a member of O'Connell's audience of how his speeches were heard by all present
Anonymous: Brian MacArthur *The Penguin Book of Historic Speeches* (1995), introduction

3 Harris' words rang like the blow of a hammer on an anvil and made sparks fly which lit the country.
a Mayo shepherd remembering the Fenian orator Matthew Harris
Anonymous: Ulick O'Connor *The Troubles* (rev. ed., 1996)

4 I was not qualified for public speaking. My mind was like Swift's church: the more that was inside the slower the mass came out.
Jemmy Hope ?1765–1846: attributed

5 The most popular speaker is the one who sits down before he stands up.
John Pentland Mahaffy 1839–1919: W. B. Stanford and R. B. McDowell *Mahaffy* (1971)

Sport

1 In all your days roving, you'll find none so jovial
   As that Muskerry sportsman, the Bould Thady Quill.
   Anonymous: 'The Bould Thady Quill', early 20th century song

2 The great fallacy is that the game is first and last about
   winning. It's nothing of the kind. The game is about glory.
   It's about doing things in style.
   of football
   Danny Blanchflower 1926–93: Hunter Davies *The Glory Game* (1972)

3 Rule 21 is Catch 22.
   *commenting that the Gaelic Athletic Association inhibits
   Catholics from joining the 'unacceptable' Royal Ulster
   Constabulary*
   Con Houlihan: letter to the Editor, *Irish Times* 16 June 1998

4 I'll be having my glass of wine while the lads are struggling
   up the Wicklow Gap.
   *on being asked if he would miss taking part in the Tour de
   France*
   Sean Kelly 1956– : in *Irish Times* 16 May 1998 'This Week They Said'

5 It may be that all games are silly. But then, so are humans.
   Robert Lynd 1879–1949: attributed

6 I miss the things like the cameraderie in the gym. I don't
   miss being smacked in the mouth every day.
   on retirement from the ring
   Barry McGuigan 1961– : in *Irish Times* 18 April 1998 'This Week They Said'

7 'The hay is saved and Cork are bate,'
   All round the crowd did sing.
   You speak too soon, my sweet gorsoon,
   For here comes Christy Ring.
   Bryan MacMahon 1909–98: 'The Ballad of Christy Ring'

8 Irfu is the most damning prefix in Irish life.
   of the acronym of the Irish Rugby Football Union
   Kevin Myers 1947– : in *Irish Times* 27 February 1998

9 In those days you were nothing if you weren't a hurler.
Cardinal Logue is a hurler and a native Irish speaker,
revered by Pope and man.
Flann O'Brien 1911–66: *The Hard Life* (1961)

10 I see young thullabawns of fellows got out in baggy
drawers playing this new game of golf out beyond on the
Bull Island. For pity's sake sure that isn't a game at all.
Flann O'Brien 1911–66: *The Hard Life* (1961)

11 The national sport of hurling . . . the blood-and-bandages
game you called it.
Críostóir Ó Floinn 1927– : *Sanctuary Island* (1971)

12 I will miss his mischief, generosity and five-a-side skills.
on the death of his co-star Dermot Morgan ('Father Ted')
Ardal O'Hanlon: in *Irish Times* 7 March 1998 'This Week They Said'

13 The clash of the ash.
Michael O'Hehir 1920–96: catchphrase for hurling

14 Eclipse first, the rest nowhere.
comment at Epsom, 3 May 1769
Dennis O'Kelly c.1720–87: in *Annals of Sporting* vol. 2 (1822); the
Dictionary of National Biography gives the occasion as the Queen's Plate at
Winchester, 1769

15 Horrocks-Taylor came towards me with the ball. Horrocks
went one way, Taylor went the other, and I was left
holding the hyphen.
Tony O'Reilly: attributed

16 When you are two stone overweight and 44 years of age,
winning one as a manager isn't bad either.
*on the victory in the All-Ireland football championship of the
Kerry team trained by him*
Páidí O'Sé: in *Irish Post* 3 October 1997

17 Cheltenham is the Irish Lourdes. It is the racing people's
Lourdes. It is the Mecca of jump racing.
Peter O'Sullevan 1918– : in *Irish Post* 14 March 1998

18 I'd rather stay at home and play golf in Ballybunion.
on not going to the World Cup
Dick Spring 1950– : in 1994, attributed

19 I don't think there's a part of me that's left without a
bruise.
after the Irish rugby team's narrow defeat in France
Keith Wood: in *Irish Post* 14 March 1998

Storytelling

1 . . . shanachies and wise old talk of Erin's days gone by,
Who trenched the rath on such a hill, and where the bones
   may lie
Of saint or king or warrior chief.
William Allingham 1824–89: 'The Winding Banks of Erne'

2 In Ireland long 'go . . .
Anonymous: traditional opening words

3 I haven't really written my plays and books—I've heard
them. The stories are there already, singing in your genes
and in your blood.
Sebastian Barry 1955– : in *Irish Times* 19 February 1998

4 VLADIMIR: That passed the time.
ESTRAGON: It would have passed in any case.
VLADIMIR: Yes, but not so rapidly.
Samuel Beckett 1906–89: *Waiting for Godot* (1955)

5 She told us bedtime stories when we were younger, with
good and bad fairies; or mothers whose children had been
taken by fairies but were always restored; haunted houses;
men who escaped from danger and got back to their
families; stolen gold; unhappy rich people and their lonely
children; houses becoming safe and secure after
overcoming threats from evicting landlords and police . . .
She had so many accents and so many voices that it hardly

mattered to us if we got mixed up in the always
labyrinthine plot.
Seamus Deane 1940– : *Reading in the Dark* (1996)

6 'There was a young man once living in Ventry parish,' she
said, and I knew by the traditional opening that a tale was
coming.
Robin Flower 1881–1946: *The Western Island* (1944)

7 Twenty years ago his mind was alive with antique
memories, and in him, and in men like him, the old stable
world endured as it had endured for centuries. But now the
fatal drip of printer's ink has obliterated the agelong
pattern.
Robin Flower 1881–1946: *The Western Island* (1944)

8 Company keeping under the stars at night has succeeded in
too many places the good old Irish custom of visiting,
chatting and story-telling from one house to another.
view of the Archbishop of Tuam in 1926
Archbishop Gilmartin: Dermot Keogh *Twentieth Century Ireland* (1994)

9 The line was unbroken from the Ireland of heroes and
minstrels to the hour when he chanted over the poem that
some bard in the remote ages had fashioned.
*of his meeting with James Kelly, a storyteller living on Cark
Mountain*
Stephen Gwynn 1864–1950: *Irish Books and Irish People* (1919) 'The
Shanachy'

10 That ideal reader suffering from an ideal insomnia.
James Joyce 1882–1941: *Finnegans Wake* (1939)

11 In my father's time . . .
Éamon Kelly 1914– : customary phrase

12 Shorten the road for me.
Éamon Kelly 1914– : request to be entertained with a story

13 Things rested so.
Éamon Kelly 1914– : customary phrase

14 Three things one should do every year—listen to a
storyteller at a fireside, give a hand in a corn harvest field,
and climb an Irish mountain.
Michael J. Murphy 1913– : *Mountain Year* (1964)

15 *Má faighim-se sláinte, is fada bheas tráchtadh*
Ar an méid do bháitheadh as Anach Chuan.

If my health is spared, I'll be long relating
Of the numbers drowned out from Anach Chuan.
Antoine Raiftearaí 1779–1835: 'Anach Chuan'

16 The stories we tell determine the kind of history we make
and remake.
Mary Robinson 1944– : inaugural speech as President, 1990

17 The story is a true one, and would have killed me but that I
got it out of my system in this way.
of writing the story 'Hunger' about a family slowly starving
James Stephens 1882–1950: P. J. Kavanagh *Voices in Ireland* (1994)

18 Digressions, incontestably, are the sunshine;—they are the
life, the soul of reading;—take them out of this book for
instance,—you might as well take the book along with
them.
Laurence Sterne 1713–68: *Tristram Shandy* (1759–67)

Style

1 For God's sake don't talk politics. I'm not interested in
politics. The only thing that interests me is style.
James Joyce 1882–1941: Richard Ellmann *James Joyce* (1982)

2 Elegance is good taste *plus* a dash of daring.
Carmel Snow 1887–1961: in *The World of Carmel Snow* (1962)

3 Proper words in proper places, make the true definition of a
style.
Jonathan Swift 1667–1745: *Letter to a Young Gentleman lately entered into
Holy Orders* 9 January 1720

4 I don't wish to sign my name, though I am afraid
everybody will know who the writer is: one's style is one's
signature always.
sending a letter for publication
Oscar Wilde 1854–1900: letter to the *Daily Telegraph*, 2 February 1891

Success

1 We have just heard that David Trimble won the vote at the
Ulster Unionist Party meeting . . . Well done, David.
at the Sinn Féin ardfheis, 18 April 1998
Gerry Adams 1948– : in *Independent on Sunday* 19 April 1998

2 It's enormously emotional for me. I've been the bridesmaid
here so many times. It's great to be the bride.
*after being named Ireland's European of 1997, an award for
which she had been unsuccessfully nominated many times*
Mary Banotti: in *Irish Times* 21 February 1998 'This Week They Said'

3 The conduct of a losing party never appears right: at least
it never can possess the only infallible criterion of wisdom
to vulgar judgements—success.
Edmund Burke 1729–97: *Letter to a Member of the National Assembly*
(1791)

4 My first priority is to fix the heater in my car, then to pay
the taxman and the Visa bill I ran up researching the book
in America.
after his first novel Every Dead Thing *was bought by a London
publishing house for a £350,000 sterling advance*
John Connolly: in *Irish Times* 21 February 1998 'This Week They Said'

5 I went back to the study hall where I met my husband at a
   debating competition and where, I am pleased to put it on
   record, I beat him.
   as President, revisiting her old school in Belfast
   Mary McAleese 1951– : in *Irish Times* 6 December 1997 'This Week They
   Said'

6 They never miss an opportunity to miss an opportunity.
   of the Ulster Unionists
   Conor Cruise O'Brien 1917– : in *Daily Express* July 1997

7 I shall be like that tree, I shall die at the top.
   Jonathan Swift 1667–1745: Sir Walter Scott (ed.) *Works of Swift* (1814)

8 Success is a science; if you have the conditions, you get the
   result.
   Oscar Wilde 1854–1900: letter ?March–April 1883

Suffering

1 Michael Collins rose, looking as though he was going to
   shoot someone, preferably himself. In all my life I never
   saw so much passion and suffering in restraint!
   *in the concluding stages of the Treaty negotiation, when Arthur
   Griffith had agreed to sign*
   Winston Churchill 1874–1965: *The Aftermath* (1929)

2 Far as distress the soul can wound
   'Tis pain in each degree;
   Bliss goes but to a certain bound,
   Beyond is agony.
   Frances Greville *c.*1724–89: 'A Prayer for Indifference' (1759)

3 Is there a life before death? That's chalked up
   In Ballymurphy. Competence with pain,
   Coherent miseries, a bite and sup,
   We hug our little destiny again.
   Seamus Heaney 1939– : 'Whatever You Say Say Nothing' (1975)

4 It is not those who can inflict the most, but those that can
   suffer the most who will conquer.
   while on hunger strike in Brixton Prison, 1920
   Terence MacSwiney 1879–1920: Diana Norman *Terrible Beauty* (1987)

5 I hear a sudden cry of pain!
   There is a rabbit in a snare:
   Now I hear the cry again,
   But I cannot tell from where . . .
   Little one! Oh, little one!
   I am searching everywhere.
   James Stephens 1882–1950: 'The Snare' (1915)

6 Too long a sacrifice
   Can make a stone of the heart.
   O when may it suffice?
   W. B. Yeats 1865–1939: 'Easter, 1916' (1921)

The Supernatural

1 Up the airy mountain,
   Down the rushy glen,
   We daren't go a-hunting,
   For fear of little men.
   William Allingham 1824–89: 'The Fairies' (1850)

2 Superstition is the religion of feeble minds.
   Edmund Burke 1729–97: *Reflections on the Revolution in France* (1790)

3 I met the Love-Talker one eve in the glen,
   He was handsomer than any of our handsome young men,
   His eyes were blacker than the sloe, his voice sweeter far
   Than the crooning of old Kevin's pipes beyond in
       Coolnagar.
   Ethna Carbery 1866–1902: 'The Love-Talker'

4 He dug up a fairy-mount against my advice, and had no
   luck afterwards.
   Maria Edgeworth 1767–1849: *Castle Rackrent* (1800)

5 The ghosts at Aragon were only seen and heard by the
Fox's, and the Fox's were usually afraid of them and denied
their presence. When one of the family was near death they
would keep all together and lights burning and drinking,
and fires roaring up the chimneys, and no lonely venturing
round the house after nightfall.
Molly Keane 1904–96: *Two Days in Aragon* (1941)

6 In Ireland long ago every family that had the least
pretension to respectability had a banshee of its own.
Without one its members would be regarded as not Irish at
all, only upstarts, vagabonds and 'sprus'.
Edmund Lenihan: *Aoibheall the Banshee* (1991)

7 . . . enchanted Earl Gerald who
changed himself into a stag, to
a great green-eyed cat of
the mountain.
Marianne Moore 1887–1972: 'Spenser's Ireland' (1941)

8 Rich and rare were the gems she wore,
And a bright gold ring on her wand she bore.
Thomas Moore 1779–1852: *Irish Melodies* (1807) 'Rich and rare were the
gems she wore'

9 The Pooka MacPhillimey, a member of the devil class, sat
in his hut in the middle of a firwood meditating on the
nature of the numerals and segregating in his mind the odd
ones from the even.
Flann O'Brien 1911–66: *At Swim-Two-Birds* (1939)

10 There are many strange things in the world beyond our
knowledge, and maybe there are ghosts too, though I do
not understand why they should come back to this world
when they have gone from it.
Peig Sayers 1873–1958: *The Western Island* (1944)

11 I lectured . . . on Fairy lore to an audience of Orangemen.
W. B. Yeats 1865–1939: letter, 16 December 1894

Supernatural

Taxes

1 To tax and to please, no more than to love and to be wise, is not given to men.
Edmund Burke 1729–97: *On American Taxation* (1775)

2 He thought it was some outrageous tax the government had brought in and he was about to say its time they quit or they have the country destroyed when I said ah no its not the government at all. It was invented by me, and its only the people I say.
Patrick McCabe 1955– : *The Butcher Boy* (1992)

3 A government which robs Peter to pay Paul can always depend on the support of Paul.
George Bernard Shaw 1856–1950: *Everybody's Political What's What?* (1944)

4 There were two major events in Ireland last Saturday night: the Eurovision Song Contest and a dinner for the Association of Inspectors of Taxes. The Taoiseach got the Song Contest and I got the tax dinner.
Dick Spring 1950– : in 1994, attributed

The Theatre

1 There is no disappointment in the rehearsal room.
of his love for the theatre
Sebastian Barry 1955– : in *Irish Times* 19 February 1998

2 My play wasn't written for this box. My play was written for small men locked in a big space.
on the televising of Waiting for Godot
Samuel Beckett 1906–89: James Knowlson *Damned to Fame* (1996)

*on being asked 'What was the message of your play' after a
performance of* The Hostage:

3 Message? Message? What the hell do you think I am, a
bloody postman?
Brendan Behan 1923–64: Dominic Behan *My Brother Brendan* (1965)

4 Acting is . . . the lowest of the arts, if it be an art at all.
George Moore 1852–1933: *Impressions and Opinions* (1991)

5 The drama's altar isn't a stage: it is candlesticked and
flowered in the box office. There is the gold, though there
be no frankincense or myrrh; and the gospel for the day
always The Play will Run for a Year.
Sean O'Casey 1880–1964: *Sunset and Evening Star* (1954)

6 The most famous building in the heart of Dublin is the
architecturally undistinguished Abbey Theatre, once the
city morgue and now entirely restored to its original
purpose.
Frank O'Connor 1903–66: *Leinster, Munster and Connaught* (1950)

7 English audiences cry during the performance. Here people
sit very still and lean forward as though they want to hear
every word. Afterwards, when they talk to you, they often
start to weep.
on performing 'Electra' in Ireland
Fiona Shaw: in *Irish Times* 13 February 1992

8 I open with a clock striking, to beget an awful attention in
the audience—it also marks the time, which is four o'clock
in the morning, and saves a description of the rising sun,
and a great deal about gilding the eastern hemisphere.
Richard Brinsley Sheridan 1751–1816: *The Critic* (1779)

9 In a good play every speech should be as fully flavoured as
a nut or an apple.
John Millington Synge 1871–1909: introduction to *The Playboy of the
Western World* (1907)

10 William Congreve is the only sophisticated playwright
    England has produced; and like Shaw, Sheridan and Wilde,
    his nearest rivals, he was brought up in Ireland.
    Kenneth Tynan 1927–80: *Curtains* (1961) 'The Way of the World'

11 Did that play of mine send out
    Certain men the English shot?
    W. B. Yeats 1865–1939: 'The Man and the Echo' (1939)

12 We Cromwellian Directors laid down this principle twenty-
    five years ago, and have not departed from it: never accept
    or reject a play because of its opinions.
    W. B. Yeats 1865–1939: in *Dublin Magazine* 1926

13 You have disgraced yourselves again.
    to the rioting audience at the production of O'Casey's The
    Plough and the Stars, *1926*
    W. B. Yeats 1865–1939: P. J. Kavanagh *Voices in Ireland* (1994)

Time

1 Time like a last oozing, so precious and worthless together.
   Samuel Beckett 1906–89: letter to Kay Boyle, 23 August 1973

2 Men talk of killing time, while time quietly kills them.
   Dion Boucicault 1820–90: *London Assurance* (1841)

   *on arriving at Dublin Castle for the handover by British forces
   on 16 January 1922, and being told that he was seven minutes
   late:*
3 We've been waiting 700 years, you can have the seven
   minutes.
   Michael Collins 1890–1922: Tim Pat Coogan *Michael Collins* (1990)

4 Time was away and somewhere else.
   Louis MacNeice 1907–63: 'Meeting Point' (1939)

5 Greenwich Mean Time, indeed. Just imagine if we had tried
that caper in Ireland. Dublin Mean Time. BallyJamesDuff
Mean Time. The County Cork Meridian.
Joseph O'Connor 1963– : *The Secret World of the Irish Male* (1995)

6 Which beginning of time according to our Chronology, fell
upon the entrance of the night preceding the twenty third
day of *Octob.* in the year of the Julian Calendar, 710 [i.e.
4004 BC].
James Ussher 1581–1656: *The Annals of the World* (1658)

7 Time is waste of money.
Oscar Wilde 1854–1900: in *Chameleon* December 1894

8 The years like great black oxen tread the world,
And God the herdsman goads them on behind,
And I am broken by their passing feet.
W. B. Yeats 1865–1939: *The Countess Cathleen* (1895)

9 The innocent and the beautiful
Have no enemy but time.
W. B. Yeats 1865–1939: 'In Memory of Eva Gore Booth and Con Markiewicz'
(1933)

Tipperary

1 But never more we'll lift a hand—
We swear by God and Virgin Mary!
Except in war for Native Land,
And *that's* the Vow of Tipperary!
Thomas Davis 1814–45: 'The Vow of Tipperary' (1845)

2 We had now entered the notorious county of Tipperary, in
which more murders and assaults are committed in one
year than in the whole Kingdom of Saxony in five.
J. G. Kohl 1808–78: *Ireland, Scotland and England* (1844)

3 'It's in Tipperary—not at all a desirable country to live in.'
   'Oh, dear, no! Don't they murder the people?'
   Anthony Trollope 1815–82: *The Eustace Diamonds* (1872)

4 It's a long, long way to Tipperary,
   It's a long way to go;
   It's a long way to Tipperary,
   To the sweetest girl I know!
   Jack Judge 1878–1938 and **Harry Williams** 1874–1924: 'It's a Long Way to
   Tipperary' (1912 song)

Tír Na nÓg

1 As to Oisín, some say it was hundreds of years he was in
   the Country of the Young, and some say it was thousands
   of years he was in it; but whatever time it was, it seemed
   short to him.
   Anonymous: 'The Fenian Cycle', translated by Lady Gregory as *Gods and
   Fighting Men* (1904)

2 Men thought it a region of sunshine and rest,
   And they called it Hy-Brasail, the isle of the blest.
   Gerald Griffin 1803–40: 'Hy-Brasail'

3 She suddenly felt ancient. She felt like Oisín, that she had
   for the first time put her feet on terra firma, after a lifetime
   spent in Tír na n-Óg, the land of the forever young.
   Katy Hayes: *Curtains* (1997)

4 Don't talk to me about the Isles of Youth. These are the
   Isles of Senescence, of Inactivity . . . I do not want to sleep
   or dream of Tir n'an Og.
   Louis MacNeice 1907–63: *I Crossed the Minch* (1938)

5 *Tá tír na nÓg chúl an tí,*
   Tír álainn trína chéile.

   The Land of Youth's at the back of the house,
   A beautiful upside-down land.
   Seán O Ríordáin 1916–77: 'Cúl an Tí'

Toasts

1 'A health to King James,' and they bent as they quaffed,
'Here's to George the *Elector*,' and fiercely they laughed.
Thomas Davis 1814–45: 'The Battle-Eve of the Brigade' (1845)

2 No glass of ours was ever raised
To toast *The Queen*.
rebuking the editors of The Penguin Book of Contemporary
British Poetry *for including him among its authors*
Seamus Heaney 1939– : *Open Letter* (Field Day pamphlet no. 2, 1983)

3 He's all a knave or half a slave
Who slights his country thus:
But a *true* man, like you, man,
Will fill your glass with us.
John Kells Ingram 1823–1907: 'The Memory of the Dead' (1845)

4 Fat, fair and forty were all the toasts of the young men.
John O'Keeffe 1747–1833: *The Irish Mimic* (1795)

5 Let the toast pass,
Drink to the lass,
I'll warrant she'll prove an excuse for the glass.
Richard Brinsley Sheridan 1751–1816: *The School for Scandal* (1777)

6 Drink a health to all the wonders of the western world, the
pirates, preachers, poteen-makers, with the jobbing jockeys;
parching peelers, and the juries fill their stomachs selling
judgements of the English law.
John Millington Synge 1871–1909: *The Playboy of the Western World*
(1907)

Translation

1 I don't know why the Swedes or the Dutch need to
translate books into their own languages because they can
all speak and read English so well. But this isn't the kind of

thing you'd say to nice Swedish publishers, especially when they invite you over to celebrate the launch of a book.
Maeve Binchy 1940– : in *Irish Times* 8 November 1997

2 I do not profess to give a merely literal version of my originals . . . Besides the spirit which they breathe, and which lifts the imagination far above the tameness, let me say, the *injustice*, of such a task—there are many complex words, which could not be translated literally.
Charlotte Brooke ?1740–93: preface to *Reliques of Irish Poetry* (1789)

3 Choose an author as you choose a friend.
Wentworth Dillon, Lord Roscommon c.1633–1685: *Essay on Translated Verse* (1684)

4 I understand that you are to translate *Ulysses*, and I have come from Paris to tell you not to alter a single word.
James Joyce 1882–1941: Richard Ellmann *James Joyce* (1982)

5 Egad I think the interpreter is the hardest to be understood of the two!
Richard Brinsley Sheridan 1751–1816: *The Critic* (1779)

6 'A translation is no translation,' he said, 'unless it will give you the music of a poem along with the words of it.'
John Millington Synge 1871–1909: *The Aran Islands* (1907)

Transport

1 Trottin' to the fair,
Me and Moll Maloney,
Seated, I declare
On a single pony.
Arthur Percival Graves 1846–1931: 'Riding Double'

2 Take up car maintenance and find the class is full of other thirty-something women like me, looking for a fella.
Marian Keyes: 'Late Opening at the Last Chance Saloon' (1997)

3 Men might as well project a voyage to the moon as attempt to employ steam navigation against the stormy North Atlantic Ocean.
Dionysius Lardner 1793–1859: speech to the British Association for the Advancement of Science, 1838

4 FATHER STACK: While you were out, I got the keys to your car. And drove it into a big wall. And if you don't like it, tough. I've had my fun, and that's all that matters.
Graham Linehan and **Arthur Mathews:** 'New Jack City' (1996), episode from *Father Ted* (Channel 4 TV, 1994–8)

5 I fly round town on my bike for exercise . . . There are very few women on bikes in the winter, so a hunted beast on a bike is very remarkable.
while on the run in 1919
Constance Markievicz 1868–1927: letter to her sister, Eva Gore-Booth, 1919

6 People who spend most of their natural lives riding iron bicycles over the rocky roadsteads of this parish get their personalities mixed up with the personalities of their bicycles as a result of the interchanging of the atoms of each of them and you would be surprised at the number of people in these parts who nearly are half people and half bicycles.
Flann O'Brien 1911–66: *The Third Policeman* (1967)

7 Afterwards we walked and trotted home; it seemed to take hours. Back in the house, I felt someone had put planks in my legs and turned my buttocks into wooden boxes.
his first experience of riding
V. S. Pritchett 1900–97: *Midnight Oil* (1971)

Travel and Exploration

1 Oh it's six miles from Bangor to Donaghadee.
Anonymous: 'The Widow of Donaghadee', 19th century song

2 Westward the course of empire takes its way;
The first four acts already past,
A fifth shall close the drama with the day:
Time's noblest offspring is the last.
George Berkeley 1685–1753: 'On the Prospect of Planting Arts and
Learning in America' (1752)

3 Through the midlands of Ireland I journeyed by diesel
And bright in the sun shone the emerald plain.
John Betjeman 1906–84: 'A Lament for Moira McCavendish'

4 A man who leaves home to mend himself and others is a
philosopher; but he who goes from country to country,
guided by a blind impulse of curiosity, is a vagabond.
Oliver Goldsmith 1728–74: *The Citizen of the World* (1762)

5 Worth seeing, yes; but not worth going to see.
of the Giant's Causeway
Samuel Johnson 1709–84: James Boswell *Life of Samuel Johnson* (1791)
12 October 1779

6 I pedalled on towards Athlone through slashing rain across
brown miles of harvested bog—looking like a child's dream
of a world made of chocolate.
Dervla Murphy 1931– : *A Place Apart* (1978)

7 So geographers, in Afric-maps,
With savage-pictures fill their gaps;
And o'er unhabitable downs
Place elephants for want of towns.
Jonathan Swift 1667–1745: 'On Poetry' (1733)

8 To Ireland, I.
William Shakespeare 1564–1616: *Macbeth* (1606)

9 Life on board a pleasure steamer violates every moral and physical condition of healthy life except fresh air . . . It is a guzzling, lounging, gambling, dog's life. The only alternative to excitement is irritability.
George Bernard Shaw 1856–1950: letter, 17 October 1899

10 I pity the man who can travel from Dan to Beersheba and cry, "Tis all barren!'
Laurence Sterne 1713–68: *A Sentimental Journey* (1768)

11 I always love to begin a journey on Sundays, because I shall have the prayers of the church, to preserve all that travel by land, or by water.
Jonathan Swift 1667–1745: *Polite Conversation* (1738)

12 And therefore I have sailed the seas and come
To the holy city of Byzantium.
W. B. Yeats 1865–1939: 'Sailing to Byzantium' (1928)

13 Michelangelo left a proof
On the Sistine Chapel roof,
Where but half-awakened Adam
Can disturb globe-trotting Madam.
W. B. Yeats 1865–1939: 'Under Ben Bulben' (1939)

The Treaty

1 Don't you realize that, if you sign this thing, you will split Ireland from top to bottom?
to de Valera, December 1921
Cathal Brugha 1874–1922: Jim Ring *Erskine Childers* (1996)

2 Think—what I have got for Ireland? Something which she has wanted these past seven hundred years. Will anyone be satisfied at the bargain? Will anyone? I tell you this—early this morning I signed my death warrant. I thought at the

time how odd, how ridiculous—a bullet may just as well
have done the job five years ago.
on signing the treaty establishing the Irish Free State; he was
shot from ambush in the following year
Michael Collins 1890–1922: letter, 6 December 1921, in T. R. Dwyer
Michael Collins and the Treaty (1981)

3 The greatest of all the many crimes that English statesmen
have committed against Ireland was committed by Lloyd
George in December 1921 when, under the threat of an
immediate and terrible war, he compelled the signatures of
our delegates to an impossible treaty.
Eamon de Valera 1882–1975: in 1923, attributed

4 We have brought back the flag; we have brought back the
evacuation of Ireland after 700 years by British troops and
the formation of an Irish army. We have brought back to
Ireland her full rights.
moving acceptance of the Treaty in the Dáil, December 1921
Arthur Griffith 1871–1922: Diana Norman *Terrible Beauty* (1987)

5 Mother was in favour of accepting the Treaty. I fell out
with her over that. But she changed as soon as the
executions started.
of Maud Gonne MacBride in 1922
Seán MacBride 1904–88: Diana Norman *Terrible Beauty* (1987)

6 I stand here for the will of the people, and the will of the
people of Ireland is their freedom, which this so-called
Treaty does not give them.
rejecting the Treaty in the Dáil debate
Mary MacSwiney: Diana Norman *Terrible Beauty* (1987)

7 I have seen the stars, and I am not going to follow a
flickering will o' the wisp.
rejecting the Treaty in the Dáil debate
Constance Markievicz 1868–1927: Diana Norman *Terrible Beauty* (1987)

Truth

1 Truth is the cry of all, but the game of the few.
George Berkeley 1685–1753: *Siris* (1744)

2 I will not serve that in which I no longer believe whether it call itself my home, my fatherland or my church: and I will try to express myself in some mode of life or art as freely as I can and as wholly as I can, using for my defence the only arms I allow myself to use, silence, exile, and cunning.
James Joyce 1882–1941: *A Portrait of the Artist as a Young Man* (1916)

3 The Irish Fact, definable as anything they will tell you in Ireland, where you get told a great deal and had best assume a demeanour of wary appreciation.
Hugh Kenner 1923– : *A Colder Eye* (1983)

4 Oh, no, 'twas the truth in her eyes ever dawning
That made me love Mary, the Rose of Tralee.
William Mulchineck 1820–64: 'The Rose of Tralee'

5 All great truths begin as blasphemies.
George Bernard Shaw 1856–1950: *Annajanska* (1919)

6 The truth is rarely pure, and never simple.
Oscar Wilde 1854–1900: *The Importance of Being Earnest* (1895)

The Union

1 From the day I first entered parliament up to the present, devotion to the union has been the guiding star of my political life.
Edward Carson 1854–1935: in *Dictionary of National Biography* (1917–)

2 England has not any right to do Ireland *good against her
   will.*
   Maria Edgeworth 1767–1849: letter to Sophy Muxton, 29 January 1800

3 The God of nature never intended that Ireland should be a
   province, and by God she never will.
   Thomas Goold 1766–1846: speaking against the Act of Union at a meeting
   of the Irish Bar, 9 December 1799

4 He . . . quoted as I have heard him do before, a saying of
   Grattan about 'the Channel forbidding Union, the Ocean
   forbidding separation'.
   Lord Derby recalling Gladstone
   Henry Grattan 1746–1820: R. F. Foster *Paddy and Mr Punch* (1993)

5 I shall be as brief as I can upon this subject, for it is quite
   clear, that no man ever yet rose to address a more
   unwilling audience.
   introducing a motion for the Repeal of the Union
   Daniel O'Connell 1775–1847: speech in the House of Commons, 22 April
   1834

6 They have graduated from the devil's school. They have
   destroyed the Act of Union and given the title deeds of
   Ulster to Dublin on a plate.
   on those Unionists who support the Belfast Agreement
   Ian Paisley 1926– : in *Irish Times* 16 May 1998 'This Week They Said'

7 For us, the Act of Union has no binding moral or legal
   force. We regard it as our fathers regarded it before us, as a
   great criminal act of usurpation carried by violence and
   fraud.
   John Redmond 1856–1918: in 1905; Nicholas Mansergh *The Irish Question*
   (ed. 3, 1975)

8 I will drive a coach and six horses through the Act of
   Settlement.
   Stephen Rice 1637–1715: W. King *State of the Protestants of Ireland*
   (1672)

9 There is no Levitical degrees between nations, and on this
occasion I can see neither sin nor shame in marrying our
own sister.
debate in the Irish Parliament on the Act of Union between
Great Britain and Ireland, c.1800
Boyle Roche 1743–1807: Jonah Barrington *Personal Sketches and*
Recollections of his own Times (1827)

10 Those that walk out leave the Union undefended. The
Ulster Unionist Party will ensure that the Union is
defended.
David Trimble 1944– : in *Irish Times* 20 September 1997

11 We will not agree anything that undermines the rights of
the people of Northern Ireland, still less any Trojan horse
that would be, in the fateful words of Hugh Logue in 1974,
a vehicle that will trundle us into a united Ireland.
David Trimble 1944– : in *Irish Times* 1 November 1997

12 The fundamental Act of Union is there, intact.
of the Northern Ireland settlement
David Trimble 1944– : in *Daily Telegraph* 11 April 1998

13 Even politicians liberal as was Mr Monk—liberal as was Mr
Turnbull—could not trust themselves to think that
disunion could be good for the Irish.
Anthony Trollope 1815–82: *Phineas Finn* (1869)

Violence

1 The strategy of the ballot box in one hand and the gun in
the other was . . . originated by the Nazis.
John Bruton 1947– : in *Irish Times* 10 October 1996

2 It has pleased God to bless our endeavours at
   Drogheda . . . I believe we put to the sword the whole
   number of the defendants.
   Oliver Cromwell 1599–1658: letter to Bradshaw, September 1649

3 Now as news comes in
   of each neighbourly murder
   we pine for ceremony,
   customary rhythms.
   Seamus Heaney 1939– : 'Funeral Rites' (1975)

4 On my knees, I beg you to turn away from the paths of
   violence and to return to the ways of peace.
   John Paul II 1920– : address by the Pope at Drogheda, 29 September 1979

5 Unless I am mistaken, by the steps we have taken [in
   Ireland] we have murder by the throat.
   David Lloyd George 1863–1945: speech at the Mansion House, 9 November
   1920

6 We don't have guns and we have no bombs. What we have
   seen is that violence does pay. We have seen concession
   after concession.
   David McNarry: on BBC Radio 4 *Today* programme, 9 July 1998

7 Be it in the defence, or be it in the assertion of a people's
   liberty, I hail the sword as a sacred weapon.
   Thomas Francis Meagher 1823–1867: speech in Dublin, 28 July 1846

8 But will anyone here object if with a ballot box in this hand
   and an Armalite in this hand we take power in Ireland.
   Danny Morrison 1950– : in November 1981; Patrick Bishop and Eamonn
   Mallie *The Provisional IRA* (1987)

9 All I did was throw the silver fork
   he'd left stuck for a week
   in the mud at the base
   of my weeping willow tree
   in the general direction of his chest.
   Julie O'Callaghan 1954– : 'Yuppie Considering Life in her Loft Apartment'

Violence

10 I don't believe the Saxon will ever relax his grip except by
the persuasion of cold lead and steel.
Jeremiah O'Donovan Rossa 1831–1915: Robert Kee *The Bold Fenian Men*
(1989)

11 Captain Moonlight will take my place.
predicting an outbreak of agrarian violence if he were arrested
Charles Stewart Parnell 1846–91: comment, October 1881

12 If this violence continues it will only be a matter of time
before we are following coffins.
David Trimble 1944– : in *Daily Telegraph* 8 July 1998

Virtue

1 Kit wondered . . . whether Mary Paula and Clio, who had
both been pregnant brides in recent months, were actually
in a position to be calling other girls fast.
Maeve Binchy 1940– : *The Glass Lake* (1994)

2 The virtue which requires to be ever guarded is scarce
worth the sentinel.
Oliver Goldsmith 1728–74: *The Vicar of Wakefield* (1766)

3 We have morals in Limerick, you know, morals. We're not
like jackrabbits from Antrim, a place crawling with
Presbyterians.
Frank McCourt 1930– : *Angela's Ashes* (1996)

4 What is virtue but the Trade Unionism of the married?
George Bernard Shaw 1856–1950: *Man and Superman* (1903)

5 Instead of dirt and poison we have rather chosen to fill our
hives with honey and wax; thus furnishing mankind with
the two noblest of things, which are sweetness and light.
Jonathan Swift 1667–1745: *The Battle of the Books* (1704)

6 Duty is what one expects from others, it is not what one
does oneself.
Oscar Wilde 1854–1900: *A Woman of No Importance* (1893)

War see also The Armed Forces

1 When will it all end? When can a man get down to a book
in peace?
Michael Collins 1890–1922: Rex Taylor *Michael Collins* (1958)

2 Eamon de Valera had wanted his country to stay neutral
and neutral it stayed, in one of the greatest diplomatic feats
of the Second World War.
Tim Pat Coogan 1935– : *De Valera: Long Fellow, Long Shadow* (1993)

3 This war is an inconceivable madness which has taken
hold of Europe—It is unlike any other war that has ever
been.
Maud Gonne 1867–1953: letter to W. B. Yeats, 26 August 1914

4 The belief in the possibility of a short decisive war appears
to be one of the most ancient and dangerous of human
illusions.
Robert Lynd 1879–1949: attributed

5 Observe the sons of Ulster marching towards the Somme.
Frank McGuinness 1953– : title of play, 1985

6 The government may tomorrow withdraw every one of
their troops from Ireland. Ireland will be defended by her
armed sons from foreign invasion, and for that purpose the
armed Catholics in the south will be only too glad to join
arms with the armed Protestant Ulsterman. Is it too much
to hope that out of this situation a result may spring that
will be good not merely for the Empire but for the future
welfare and integrity of the Irish nation?
John Redmond 1856–1918: speech in the House of Commons, 3 August
1914

7   You that Mitchel's prayer have heard,
    'Send war in our time, O Lord.'
    W. B. Yeats 1865–1939: 'Under Ben Bulben' (1939)

Wealth

1   Men multiply like mice in a barn if they have unlimited
    means of subsistence.
    Richard Cantillon c.1680–1734: *Essay on the Nature of Trade* (1755)

2   This was the kind of woman who spent vast sums of money
    in lingerie shops. You could tell by looking at her that her
    cashmere sweater was not pulled over a Dunnes Stores bra.
    Katy Hayes: *Curtains* (1997)

3   I have never in my life been in the house of a rich man who
    appeared to care so little for the things of this world as
    Richard Martin.
    of Richard Martin (1754–1834) of Connemara
    Chevalier de Latocnaye: *A Frenchman's Walk Through Ireland, 1796–7*
    (tr. John Stevenson, 1917)

4   Holding that millionaires were necessarily personable folk
    whose friendship could be very beautiful.
    Flann O'Brien 1911–66: *The Best of Myles* (1968)

5   I am a Millionaire. That is my religion.
    George Bernard Shaw 1856–1950: *Major Barbara* (1907)

Weather

1   The rain fell in a uniform untroubled manner. It fell upon
    the bay, the littoral, the mountains and the plains, and
    notably upon the Central Bog it fell with a rather desolate
    uniformity.
    Samuel Beckett 1906–89: 'A Wet Night' (1934)

2 Ireland is broader than Britain, is healthier and has a much
milder climate, so that snow rarely lasts there for more
than three days.
Bede AD 673–735: *Ecclesiastical History of the English People*

3 You can call this rain bad weather, but it is not. It is simply
weather, and weather means rough weather. It reminds us
forcibly that its element is water, falling water. And water
is hard.
Heinrich Böll 1917–85: *Irish Journal* (1957, translated Leila Vennewitz)

4 A fierce rain, where we changed horses . . . wretched
people cowering about to look at us, or beg, nevertheless:
and this ended our rain for that evening.
Thomas Carlyle 1795–1881: *Reminiscences of My Irish Journey* (1849)

5 Sometimes a trailing shower, of mingled mist and rain,
would sweep across the intervening chasm, like the sheeted
spectre of a giant, and present to the spectator that
appearance which supplied the imagination of Ossian with
its romantic images.
Gerald Griffin 1803–40: *The Collegians* (1829)

6 When you can see the Mountains of Mourne, that's a sure
sign it'll rain. Yis, the angels'll be having a pee.
Hugh Leonard 1926– : *Da* (1973)

7 I liked rain. The hiss of the water and the earth so soft
bright green plants would nearly sprout beside you.
Patrick McCabe 1955– : *The Butcher Boy* (1992)

8 The rain drove us into the church—our refuge, our
strength, our only dry place . . . Limerick gained a
reputation for piety, but we knew it was only the rain.
Frank McCourt 1930– : *Angela's Ashes* (1996)

9 I shall never forget the wind
On this God-forsaken coast.
It works itself into the mind
Like the high keen of a lost

Lear-spirit in agony
Condemned for eternity.
Derek Mahon 1941– : 'North Wind' (1979)

10 The divine harbinger of summer—warm rain.
Kevin Myers 1947– : in *Irish Times* 3 April 1985

11 The Irish air is Atlantic air, but quite unlike, for instance,
that of Maine; it is air empowered by the west wind, moist
and rain-smelling, the lethargic air of heathery islands that
are surrounded even more by air than by sea. One is
excited and half asleep by turns.
V. S. Pritchett 1900–97: *At Home and Abroad* (1990)

12 'More rain coming,' said Mr Knox, rising composedly;
'you'll have to put a goose down those chimneys some day
soon; it's the only way in the world to clean them.'
Edith Œ. Somerville 1858–1949 and **Martin Ross** 1862–1915: *Some
Experiences of an Irish R.M.* (1899)

13 Ara! but why does King James stay behind?
Lilli burlero bullen a la
Ho! by my shoul 'tis a Protestant wind
Lilli burlero bullen a la.
*a Williamite song in mockery of Richard Talbot, newly created
Earl of Tyrconnell by the Catholic James II in Dublin in
1688; the refrain parodies the Irish language*
Thomas Wharton 1648–1715: 'A New Song' (written 1687); attribution to
Wharton has been disputed

14 Don't talk to me about the weather . . . Whenever people
talk to me about the weather, I always feel quite certain
that they mean something else.
Oscar Wilde 1854–1900: *The Importance of Being Earnest* (1895)

15 I have never seen snow. I was never on a winter day in the
land when snow was on the ground. Snow doesn't like me.
It melts before I come.
Jack B. Yeats 1871–1957: *The Charmed Life* (1938)

Weather

The West

1 But—hark!—some voice like thunder spake:
The West's awake! the West's awake!
Thomas Davis 1814–45: 'The West's Asleep'

2 As a native of Ballina, one of the most western towns in the
most western province of the most western nation in
Europe, I want to say—'the West's awake.'
Mary Robinson 1944– : inaugural speech as President, 1990

Wicklow

1 Wicklow, rightly termed the garden of Ireland, an ideal
neighbourhood for elderly wheelmen, so long as it didn't
come down.
James Joyce 1882–1941: *Ulysses* (1922)

Wit and Wordplay

1 It was no more than going through the motions.
on swimming through the sewage-laden Liffey
Oliver St John Gogarty 1878–1957: Ulick O'Connor *Oliver St John Gogarty*
(1964)

2 No mouth has the might to set a mearbound to the march
of a landsmaul.
James Joyce 1882–1941: *Finnegans Wake* (1939)

3 An Irish Bull is always pregnant.
John Pentland Mahaffy 1839–1919: W. B. Stanford and R. B. McDowell
Mahaffy (1971)

4 The dusk was performing its customary intransitive
operation of 'gathering'.
Flann O'Brien 1911–66: *The Best of Myles* (1968)

5 Metaphors, said Bobby, are popularly considered to be
   things that flash across the night sky in November.
   Críostóir Ó Floinn 1927– : *Sanctuary Island* (1971)

6 There's no possibility of being witty without a little ill-
   nature; the malice of a good thing is the barb that makes it
   stick.
   Richard Brinsley Sheridan 1751–1816: *The School for Scandal* (1777)

7 If I reprehend any thing in this world, it is the use of my
   oracular tongue, and a nice derangement of epitaphs!
   Richard Brinsley Sheridan 1751–1816: *The Rivals* (1775)

8 Satire is a sort of glass, wherein beholders do generally
   discover everybody's face but their own.
   Jonathan Swift 1667–1745: *The Battle of the Books* (1704) preface

9 I summed up all systems in a phrase, and all existence in
   an epigram.
   Oscar Wilde 1854–1900: letter, from Reading Prison, to Lord Alfred
   Douglas, January–March 1897

Woman's Role see also Women

1 1. In particular, the State recognises that by her life within
   the home, woman gives to the State a support without
   which the common good cannot be achieved.
   2. The State shall, therefore, endeavour to ensure that
   mothers shall not be obliged by economic necessity to
   engage in labour to the neglect of their duties in the home.
   Bunreacht na hÉireann: Article 41.2 of the Irish Constitution, 1937

2 I feel sorry for you. I feel sorrier for the men that have to
   meet you. I feel even sorrier for the young men coming in
   ten or twenty years' time if the girls are going to get even
   worse with all this lib stuff. And they are going to get
   worse. Mark my words. Unless there's a stop put to it.
   Evelyn Conlon 1952– : 'I Deserve a Brandy and Port' (1987)

3 Women are at once the boldest and most unmanageable
revolutionaries.
Eamon de Valera 1882–1975: in conversation, *c.*1975

4 Women's suffrage will, I believe, be the ruin of our Western
civilisation. It will destroy the home, challenging the
headship of men laid down by God. It may come in your
time—I hope not in mine.
c.1912, to a deputation led by Hanna Sheehy Skeffington
John Dillon 1851–1927: Diana Norman *Terrible Beauty* (1987)

5 What a misfortune it is to be born a woman! . . . Why seek
for knowledge, which can prove only that our
wretchedness is irremediable? If a ray of light break in upon
us, it is but to make darkness more visible; to show us the
new limits, the Gothic structure, the impenetrable barriers
of our prison.
Maria Edgeworth 1767–1849: *Leonora* (1806)

6 My mother . . . says there should be more women in male-
dominated jobs. I thought she would be pleased I had got a
job as a petrol pump attendant, but I think she was
thinking more in terms of brain surgery.
Katy Hayes: *Forecourt* (1995)

7 'How is it?' I asked Jesus, 'You haven't even
A single woman among your twelve apostles?'
Brendan Kennelly 1936– : 'The Twelve Apostlettes'

8 During the Irish revolution Nationalist women
discovered—though not all acknowledged or cared— that
their oppression as women did not end with the Dawning
of the Day. The briefly eulogised 'Dáil Girl . . . wielding a
cudgel in one hand and a revolver in the other' soon gave
way to Dev's ideal of 'life within the home'.
Edna Longley 1940– : 'From Cathleen to Anorexia' (1989)

9 I would work for it anywhere, as one of the crying wrongs
of the world, that women because of their sex, should be
debarred from any position or any right that their brains

entitle them to hold . . . Today I would appeal . . . to see
that justice is done to those young women and young girls
who took a man's part in the Terror.
Constance Markievicz 1868–1927: speech in the Dáil; Anne Haverty
Constance Markievicz (1988)

10 I think being a woman is like being Irish. Everyone says
you're important and nice but you take second place all the
same.
Iris Murdoch 1920– : *The Red and the Green* (1965)

11 Instead of rocking the cradle, they rocked the system.
*in her victory speech as President, paying tribute to the women
of Ireland*
Mary Robinson 1944– : in *The Times* 10 November 1990

Women see also Men, Woman's Role

1 I am the hag of Beara; I used to wear a shift that was
always new. Today I am so thin I wouldn't wear out even
an old shift.
Anonymous: 'The Hag of Beara', 11th century poem translated from Old
Irish

2 There were so many of those old crones, stumbling down
the lanes, in the ditches, beside the hedgerows. Ireland is
full of them.
of the central character in the play Not I
Samuel Beckett 1906–89: Deirdre Bair *Samuel Beckett* (1978)

3 Possessed, as are all the fair daughters of Eve, of an
hereditary propensity, transmitted to them undiminished
through succeeding generations, to be 'soon moved with
the slightest touch of blame'; very little precept and
practice will confirm them in the habit, and instruct them
in all the maxims, of self-justification.
Maria Edgeworth 1767–1849: *Letters for Literary Ladies* (1795) 'An Essay
on the Noble Science of Self-Justification'

4 How a little love and good company improves a woman!
George Farquhar 1678–1707: *The Beaux' Stratagem* (1707)

5 If you want to push something in politics, you're accused of being aggressive, and that's not supposed to be a good thing for a woman. If you get upset and show it, you're accused of being emotional.
Mary Harney 1953– : 1990s, attributed

6 Women see things that men don't: dirt, relatives, bargains.
Dylan Moran: in *The Week* 8 February 1997

7 I know women find it hard to hold their tongues.
when a female reporter interrupted him at a press conference
Ian Paisley 1926– : in *Irish Times* 11 April 1998 'This Week They Said'

8 Here's to the maiden of bashful fifteen
Here's to the widow of fifty
Here's to the flaunting, extravagant quean;
And here's to the housewife that's thrifty.
Richard Brinsley Sheridan 1751–1816: *The School for Scandal* (1777)

9 I am separate still,
I am I and not you;
And my mind and my will,
As in secret they grew
Still are secret, unreached and untouched
and not subject to you.
James Stephens 1882–1950: 'The Red-Haired Man's Wife'

10 The women were hunted like rats in the city.
of the treatment of suffragettes in Dublin, June 1912
Katharine Tynan 1861–1931: *Twenty-five Years* (1913)

11 The Bishop gave vent to a long-drawn sigh. 'Did it ever occur to you to wonder why God created women?' he asked. 'It's the one thing that tempts me at times to doubt His infinite goodness and wisdom.'
Mervyn Wall 1908– : *The Unfortunate Fursey* (1946)

12 One should never trust a woman who tells one her real age. A woman who would tell one that, would tell one anything.
Oscar Wilde 1854–1900: *A Woman of No Importance* (1893)

Words

1 There is no use indicting words, they are no shoddier than what they peddle.
Samuel Beckett 1906–89: *Malone Dies* (1958)

2 Those little phrases that seem so innocuous and, once you let them in, pollute the whole of speech.
Samuel Beckett 1906–89: *Murphy* (1938)

3 Words matter. Details are vital. Drafting is crucial.
speech from the steps of Stormont, after George Mitchell's announcement that an agreement had been reached
Tony Blair 1953– : in *Times* 11 April 1998

4 But words once spoke can never be recalled.
Wentworth Dillon, Lord Roscommon c.1633–1685: *Art of Poetry* (1680)

5 Grant me some wild expressions, Heavens, or I shall burst— . . . Words, words or I shall burst.
George Farquhar 1678–1707: *The Constant Couple* (1699)

6 Two such wonderful phrases—'I understand perfectly' and 'That is a lie'—a précis of life, aren't they?
Brian Friel 1929– : *The Communication Cord* (1983)

7 All agog at the plasterer on his ladder
Skimming our gable and writing our name there
With his trowel point, letter by strange letter.
Seamus Heaney 1939– : 'Alphabets' (1987)

8 I fear those big words, Stephen said, which make us so unhappy.
James Joyce 1882–1941: *Ulysses* (1922)

9 An Irishman will always soften bad news, so that a major
   coronary is no more than a 'bad turn' and a near-
   hurricane that leaves thousands homeless is 'good drying
   weather'.
   Hugh Leonard 1926– : *Rover and Other Cats* (1992)

10 Words are men's daughters, but God's sons are things.
   Samuel Madden 1686–1765: *Boulter's Monument* (1745)

11 Phrases make history here.
   as British Ambassador in Dublin
   John Maffey 1877–1969: letter, 21 May 1945

12 He bathes daily in a running tap of words.
   Brian Moore 1921– : *The Colour of Blood* (1987)

13 The present age shrinks from precision and 'understands'
   only soft woolly words which really have no particular
   meaning, like 'cultural heritage' or 'the exigent dictates of
   modern traffic needs'.
   Flann O'Brien 1911–66: *The Hair of the Dogma* (1977)

14 MIKE: There's no word in the Irish language for what you
   were doing.
   WILSON: In Lapland they have no word for snow.
   Joe Orton 1933–67: *The Ruffian on the Stair* (rev. ed. 1967)

Work

1 God is good and Jack is working.
   Anonymous: traditional saying

2 The crafts which require the most time in training or most
   ingenuity and industry must necessarily be the best paid.
   Richard Cantillon *c.*1680–1734: *Essay on the Nature of Trade* (1755)

3 They lie out sunning themselves like pedigree dogs while
  they should be on FÁS employment schemes like everybody
  else.
  a Fine Gael councillor's view of travellers
  John Flannery: in *Irish Times* 16 May 1998 'This Week They Said'

4 'Under it all,' Oliver said, 'The problem was simple.
  How could I make Ireland work?
  The Irish hate work, not knowing what it means.
  I do. Work exists. It is inevitable and stark,
  A dull, fierce necessity.'
  Brendan Kennelly 1936– : *Cromwell* (1983) 'Therefore, I Smile'

5 Term, holidays, term, holidays, till we leave school, and
  then work, work, work till we die.
  C. S. Lewis 1898–1963: *Surprised by Joy* (1955)

6 I killin' meself workin', an' he sthruttin' about from
  mornin' till night like a paycock!
  Sean O'Casey 1880–1964: *Juno and the Paycock* (1925)

7 Work is the curse of the drinking classes.
  Oscar Wilde 1854–1900: H. Pearson *Life of Oscar Wilde* (1946)

Writing

1 Joyce believed in words. All you had to do was rearrange
  them and they would express what you wanted.
  of James Joyce
  Samuel Beckett 1906–89: James Knowlson *Damned to Fame* (1996)

2 I wrote it because I wanted to write something that I would
  want to read.
  of his first novel Every Dead Thing
  John Connolly: in *Irish Times* 7 March 1998 'This Week They Said'

3 Writing is turning one's worst moments into money.
  J. P. Donleavy 1926– : in *Playboy* May 1979

4 Between my finger and my thumb
The squat pen rests.
I'll dig with it.
Seamus Heaney 1939– : 'Digging' (1966)

5 No pen, no ink, no table, no room, no time, no quiet, no
inclination.
James Joyce 1882–1941: letter to his brother, 7 December 1906

6 The task I set myself technically in writing a book from
eighteen different points of view and in as many styles, all
apparently unknown or undiscovered by my fellow
tradesmen, that and the nature of the legend chosen would
be enough to upset anyone's mental balance.
on writing Ulysses
James Joyce 1882–1941: letter, 24 June 1921

7 When once the itch of literature comes over a man,
nothing can cure it but the scratching of a pen.
Samuel Lover 1797–1868: *Handy Andy* (1842)

8 I couldn't get to sleep at night with the lines coming in my
head.
on songwriting
Johnny McCauley 1925– : interview in *Irish Post* 25 April 1998

9 My real motive is to describe how my brain-damaged life is
as normal for me as my friends' able-bodied life is to them.
My mind is just like a spin-dryer at full speed; my thoughts
fly around my skull while millions of beautiful words
cascade down into my lap. Images gunfire across my
consciousness and while trying to discipline them I jump in
awe at the soulfilled bounty of my mind's expanse. Try
then to imagine how frustrating it is to give expression to
that avalanche in efforts of one great nod after the other.
of his reasons for writing The Eye of the Clock
Christopher Nolan 1965– : in *Observer* 8 November 1987

10 THE EDITOR: We can't have much more of this, space must also be found for my stuff.
MYSELF: All right, never hesitate to say so. I can turn off the tap at will.
Flann O'Brien 1911–66: *The Best of Myles* (1968)

11 Do for God's sake write a book about Ireland.
Sean O'Faolain 1900–91: letter to Elizabeth Bowen, 22 April 1937

12 You write with ease, to show your breeding,
But easy writing's vile hard reading.
Richard Brinsley Sheridan 1751–1816: 'Clio's Protest' (written 1771, published 1819)

13 Writing, when properly managed (as you may be sure I think mine is) is but a different name for conversation.
Laurence Sterne 1713–68: *Tristram Shandy* (1759–67)

14 In Ireland, for a few years more, we have a popular imagination that is fiery and magnificent and tender, so that those of us who wish to write start with a chance that is not given to writers in places where the springtime of the local life has been forgotten and the harvest is a memory only, and the straw has been turned into bricks.
John Millington Synge 1871–1909: introduction to *The Playboy of the Western World* (1907)

15 Neither Christ nor Buddha nor Socrates wrote a book, for to do that is to exchange life for a logical process.
W. B. Yeats 1865–1939: *Estrangement* (1909)

16 The friends that have it I do wrong
When ever I remake a song,
Should know what issue is at stake:
It is myself that I remake.
W. B. Yeats 1865–1939: 'The friends that have it I do wrong' (1908)

17 Think like a wise man but express yourself like the common people.
W. B. Yeats 1865–1939: *Letters on Poetry from W. B. Yeats to Dorothy Wellesley* (1940) 21 December 1935

Writing

William Butler Yeats (1865–1939)

1 Scoffed at fairies, but they made his living.
Anonymous: obituary of Yeats in *Daily Express* 30 January 1939

2 You were silly like us; your gift survived it all:
The parish of rich women, physical decay,
Yourself. Mad Ireland hurt you into poetry.
W. H. Auden 1907–73: 'In Memory of W. B. Yeats' (1940)

3 O pity the case of this mystical wit:
In England a Gael and in Ireland a Brit.
Terry Eagleton 1943– : 'The Ballad of Willie Yeats'

4 'An' I think there's a slate,' sez she
'Off Willie Yeats,' sez she.
'He should be at home,' sez she,
'French-polishin' a pome,' sez she,
'An not writin' letters,' sez she,
'About his betters,' sez she,
'Paradin' me crimes,' sez she,
'In the *Irish Times*,' sez she.
Percy French 1854–1920: 'The Queen's After-Dinner Speech'

5 If you asked Yeats for bread, he didn't exactly give you a stone; he gave you a finely polished pebble.
Monk Gibbon 1896–1987: *c.*1960, attributed

6 Poets should never marry. The world should thank me for not marrying you.
Maud Gonne 1867–1953: Nancy Cardozo *Maud Gonne* (1978)

7 Chef Yeats, that master of the use of herbs
could raise a mere stew to a glorious height,
pinch of saga, soupçon of philosophy
carefully stirred in to get the flavour right,

and cook a poem around the basic verbs.
Michael Hartnett 1941– : 'A Farewell to English' (1978)

8   Every time I leave the old man I feel like a thousand dollars.
Frank O'Connor 1903–66: Richard Ellmann *Yeats: the Man and the Masks* (1948)

9   Wherever one cut him, with a little question, he poured, spurted fountains of ideas.
Virginia Woolf 1882–1941: diary, 8 November 1930

10 ACQUAINTANCE: How are you?
    YEATS: Not very well. I can only write prose today.
W. B. Yeats 1865–1939: attributed

Youth see also Children

1   The arrogance of age must submit to be taught by youth.
Edmund Burke 1729–97: letter, 29 July 1782

2   Youth, what man's age is like to be doth show;
    We may our ends by our beginnings know.
John Denham 1615–59: 'Of Prudence' (1668)

3   In my childhood trees were green
    And there was plenty to be seen.
Louis MacNeice 1907–63: 'Autobiography' (1941)

4   Surely, it is in youth man is most thoroughly depraved. Hell lies about us in our infancy. The youthful innocency sung by aged poets (who forget their first childhood) is nothing but ignorance of evil. As the child comes to know evil, he loves it.
John Mitchel 1815–75: *Jail Journal* (1854)

5   You may be young, but you're already pining for the time you can stay in of a summer afternoon and lie on the couch with a large gin and tonic and watch the bloody television, instead of going to rock concerts.
Joseph O'Connor 1963– : *The Secret World of the Irish Male* (1994)

6 No blazoned banner we unfold—
One charge alone we give to youth,
Against the sceptred myth to hold,
The golden heresy of truth.
George William Russell (Æ) 1867–1935: 'On Behalf of Some Irishmen not Followers of Tradition'

7 Youth . . . slips away as the water slips from the sand of the shore.
Peig Sayers 1873–1958: *An Old Woman's Reflections* (translated by Séamus Ennis, 1962)

8 I formerly used to envy my own happiness when I was a schoolboy, the delicious holidays, the Saturday afternoon, and the charming custards in a blind alley; I never considered the confinement ten hours a day, to nouns and verbs, the terror of the rod, the bloody noses, and broken shins.
Jonathan Swift 1667–1745: letter to Charles Ford, 12 November 1708

9 No wise man ever wished to be younger.
Jonathan Swift 1667–1745: *Thoughts on Various Subjects* (1727 ed.)

10 Those whom the gods love grow young.
Oscar Wilde 1854–1900: 'A Few Maxims for the Instruction of the Over-Educated' (1894)

11 Youth! Youth! There is nothing in the world but youth!
Oscar Wilde 1854–1900: *The Picture of Dorian Gray* (1891)

12 Youth is the Lord of Life. Youth has a kingdom waiting for it. Everyone is born a king, and most people die in exile.
Oscar Wilde 1854–1900: *A Woman of No Importance* (1893)

13 But O that I were young again
And held her in my arms.
W. B. Yeats 1865–1939: 'Politics' (1928)

14 That is no country for old men. The young
In one another's arms.
W. B. Yeats 1865–1939: 'Sailing to Byzantium' (1928)

Index of Authors

Bacon, Francis (1902–92)
  Friendship 1
Balfour, Arthur James
(1848–1930)
  Home Rule 1
  Loyalism 6
Banotti, Mary
  Success 2
Barber, Mary
(c. 1690–1757)
  Children 1
  Marriage 2
Barrington, Jonah
(1760–1834)
  Hospitality 3
  Houses 1
Barrington, Margaret
(1896–1982)
  Languages 1
  Men 1
Barrington, Ted
  Past 1
Barry, Michael Joseph
(1817–89)
  Armed Forces 1
Barry, Sebastian (1955–)
  Ireland 4
  Storytelling 3
  Theatre 1
Bax, Arnold (1883–1953)
  Music 3
Beaumont, Gustave de
(1802–66)
  North 2
  Poverty 2
Beckett, Mary (1926–)
  Optimism 4
  Past 2
Beckett, Samuel
(1906–89)
  Age 1
  Body 2
  Celebrations 1
  Censorship 2
  Change 1
  Death 1
  Dress 2
  Elegy 3
  Endurance 1
  Excess 1
  Failure 3, 4

Beckett, Samuel (cont.)
  Fame 1
  Flags and Emblems 4
  God 1, 2
  Graveyards 1
  Health 1
  Justice 2
  Life 2
  Literature 1
  Loss 2
  Love of Country 2
  Metaphysics 1
  Mind 1
  Money 2
  Nationality 1
  Optimism 5
  Order 1
  Parents 2, 3
  Sea 3
  Silence 2
  Storytelling 4
  Theatre 2
  Time 1
  Weather 1
  Women 2
  Words 1, 2
  Writing 1
Bede (AD 673–735)
  Weather 2
Behan, Beatrice
(1921–93)
  Life 3
Behan, Brendan
(1923–64)
  Alcohol 5
  Anglo-Irish 1
  Danger 1
  Dublin 2
  England 1, 2
  Fame 2
  Graveyards 2
  Law 1
  Love of Country 3
  Loyalism 7
  Manners 1
  Nationality 2
  Song 2
  Theatre 3
Behan, Dominic (1928–)
  Ireland/England 1
  Love of Country 4
  Publishing 1

Bell, Sam Hanna
(1909–90)
  Armagh 1
Bentham, Jeremy
(1748–1832)
  Independence 1
Berkeley, George
(1685–1753)
  Food 1
  Ireland 5
  Irish People 2
  Knowledge 2
  Languages 2
  Metaphysics 2
  Mind 2
  Poverty 3
  Travel 2
  Truth 1
Bernal, J. D. (1901–71)
  Science 1
Berryman, John
(1914–72)
  Dublin 3
  Irish People 3
Betjeman, John
(1906–84)
  Clare 2
  Graveyards 3
  Ireland 6
  Travel 3
Bickerstaffe, Isaac
(1733–c. 1808)
  Endurance 2
  Sea 4
Binchy, Maeve (1940–)
  Age 2
  Anglo-Irish 2
  Body 3
  Celebrations 2
  Children 2
  Christmas 2
  Conversation 1
  Dress 3
  Education 1
  Food 2
  God 3
  Happiness 1
  Hope 1
  Hospitality 4
  Humour 2
  Life 4
  Money 3
  Past 3

Binchy, Maeve (cont.)
  Religion 4
  Seasons 1
  Translation 1
  Virtue 1
Birmingham, George A.
(1865–1950)
  Irish People 4
Birrell, Augustine
(1850–1933)
  Easter 1916 2
Bishops' Pastoral Letter
  Dance 2
Blacker, Valentine
(1728–1823)
  Practicality 1
Blair, Tony (1953–)
  Change 2
  Courage 1
  Famine 1
  Good 1
  History 1
  Words 3
Blake, William
(1757–1827)
  Places 7, 8
Blanchflower, Danny
(1926–93)
  Sport 2
Blaney, Neil (1922–)
  North 3
Blessington, Lady
(1789–1849)
  Age 3
  Happiness 2
Boland, Eavan (1944–)
  Art 1
  Emigration 7
  Kildare 3
Böll, Heinrich (1917–85)
  Graveyards 4
  Ireland 7
  Weather 3
Bonar Law, Andrew
(1858–1923)
  Loyalism 8
Bono (1960–)
  Music 4
Boucicault, Dion
(1820–90)
  Garryowen 2
  Time 2

Bowen, Elizabeth
(1899–1973)
  Anglo-Irish 3
  Books 1
  Dublin 4
  Easter 1916 3
  Fate 2
  History 2
  Houses 2
  Ireland 8
  People 2
  Sacrifice 2
  Seasons 2
Boylan, Clare (1948–)
  Men 2
Boyle, William
(1853–1922)
  Animals 5
Bradley, Pat
  Democracy 2
Bright, John (1811–89)
  Ireland/America 1
Brigid of Kildare (d.
c.525)
  Alcohol 6
British Broadcasting
Corporation
  Ireland/England 2
Brontë, Patrick
(1777–1861)
  Biography 1
  Books 2
Brooke, Charlotte
(?1740–93)
  Irish Lang 2
  Translation 2
Brooke, Henry (1703–83)
  Government 3
Brophy, Brigid (1929–95)
  Irishness 1
Brown, Christy (1932–81)
  Art 2
Browne, Noel (1915–97)
  Change 3
  Parents 4
Brugha, Cathal
(1874–1922)
  Determination 1
  Treaty 1

Bruton, John (1947–)
  Order 2
  Royalty 2
  Violence 1
Bunreacht na hÉireann
  Woman's Role 1
Burgh, Walter Hussey
(1742–83)
  Business 1
Burke, Edmund (1729–97)
  Beauty 1
  Business 2
  Change 4
  Danger 2
  Education 2
  Enemies 1
  Excess 2, 3
  Family 1
  Fear 1
  Future 1
  Good 2
  Government 4
  Hope 2
  Ireland/England 3
  Law 2, 3
  Liberty 1
  Lies 1
  Manners 2
  Mind 3
  Order 3
  Politics 2, 3
  Practicality 2, 3
  Prejudice 2
  Rebellion 2
  Religion 5, 6
  Royalty 3
  Success 1
  Supernatural 2
  Taxes 1
  Youth 1
Butler, Máire
  Political Say 8
Butt, Isaac (1813–79)
  Irish People 5
  Parnell 3
Byrne, Gay (1934–)
  Holidays 1
Byron, Lord (1788–1824)
  Famine 2